Hunger and Poverty in South Africa

T0330882

Hunger and Poverty in South Africa: The Hidden Faces of Food Insecurity explores food insecurity as an issue of socioeconomic, political, cultural and environmental inequity and inequality. Based on extensive original research in Free State Province, South Africa, the book explores how people living in poverty make meaning of their food circumstances within the sociocultural, political and economic contexts of post-apartheid South Africa, how they view the government's food security policies and programs and their perceived agency to affect change.

The personal narratives contained in the book show that food insecurity is shaped by many issues, among which are structural poverty, racism, attempts or non-attempts at reconciliation during and after apartheid, public health issues, such as HIV/AIDS, and environmental circumstances. At a time when most discourse around food insecurity focuses on how to provide more food to people facing hunger, this book's multidimensional approach is a valuable contribution to the contemporary dialogue on poverty, food security/insecurity, sustainability and democratic agency both within South Africa and around the world.

This book will be of interest to researchers in the areas of food security, multidimensional poverty, democratic agency and sustainable development, both in South Africa and internationally.

Jacqueline Hanoman is a sociologist, qualitative researcher and educator with a PhD in Cultural Foundations from Purdue University, USA. Her areas of interest include narrative inquiry, multidimensional poverty and social justice, food insecurity and public health issues, critical community education and development for sustainability.

Routledge Studies in African Development

Hunger and Poverty in South Africa

The Hidden Faces of Food Insecurity

Jacqueline Hanoman

LONDON AND NEW YORK

First published 2018
by Routledge

2 Park Square, Milton Park, Abingdon, Oxfordshire OX14 4RN

52 Vanderbilt Avenue, New York, NY 10017

Routledge is an imprint of the Taylor & Francis Group, an informa business

First issued in paperback 2019

British Library Cataloguing-in-Publication Data
A catalogue record for this book is available from the British Library

Library of Congress Cataloging-in-Publication Data
A catalog record for this book has been requested

ISBN: 978-1-138-22308-0 (hbk)
ISBN: 978-0-367-33308-9 (pbk)

Typeset in Times New Roman
by Apex CoVantage, LLC

To the people of the Free State Province, South Africa. May your kindness and generosity toward me extend toward each other, to live together and help each other make this province that is your home blossom into its human greatness.

To John, my husband, without whom this dream of doing meaningful work in South Africa would never have become possible. Thank you for South Africa and for all your support every step of the way. To my mother, Matilde, for always believing in me and for sharing this adventure, and to my father, Eon, I wish you were here to see this dream come true. To our son, Isaac, for being the wonderful young man he is and for sharing the last part of this adventure with me with great patience.

Contents

Tables

Acknowledgements

This book would have never come into being if it had not been for the numerous people in South Africa who helped me out of the kindness of their hearts. I was very fortunate to do my study in the Free State, where I met the most marvelous people who helped me in every way they could. Where can I begin to thank you all? To all the co-creators of this book, thank you for sharing your lives, dreams and hopes with me. I will never forget you, and I hope that my work will help you. I am particularly grateful to Rindi Gordon, who took me under her wing, then, in a whirlwind, took me around Bloemfontein to meet a number of people, see different places and always kept an eye on me while she was there. I would never have been able to carry out much of my research without her help. Thank you so much, Rindi. To Julia and Pulani, who opened their hearts to me and let me into their lives. *Ke a leboha Motswalle*! To all the wonderful friends at the Christian organization who always made me feel welcome with their smiles and gentleness. To my friends at the Faculty of Education of the University of the Free State who welcomed me so wonderfully and always made me feel at home, *Thank you! Baie Dankie! Ke a leboha!* To Molebatsi for his encouragement, and my deepest appreciation to Dipane, who took time out of his busy schedule to work with me. To my Vriendin Adré for our times of 'koek en tee' in which we chatted endlessly and for motivating me on my path to learning Afrikaans, and to Phia, my companion and friend in the painstaking labor of doing research and talking about life. You are all more than my friends; you are my South African family and I will never forget your kindness. To Busi, Sister Electa and Nohlanhla for their patience and generosity in taking the time to share their work in the communities with me. To Professor Corinna Walsh and Dr. Louise van den Berg, who generously shared their research with me, and Dr. Lucia Meko for helping me to carry out my research in Phase 9. Thank you all for your kindness.

Introduction

What defines us is not our hunger. Hunger, food insecurity does not define you;
it's what we do with it that does. In the past, hunger did not define us; it was our
struggle for freedom. Hunger today is a symbol of non-achievement, of poverty, to
be frowned upon and that's not who we were.

—B. Rudi Buys,
Former Dean of Student Affairs of the University of the Free State[1]

Hunger not defining us, but what we do with it that does, and what defines us is
our struggle for freedom, is at the very core of what it means to be a South African
today who has lived through apartheid. It is a powerful statement that goes to the
heart of the relationship between national identity, the struggle for freedom, and
struggle within the context of poverty and hunger in South Africa.

Hunger defining one's existence is a sad and harsh truth for too many around
the world, but it should not define one's being. People who face hunger, in its most
well-known form of starvation, tend to be defined as 'the hungry' or 'the starving', rather than by their individual, community, local, regional or national identities. Many of the narratives and images portrayed by the media have shaped our
views of what hunger is. For example, when many people think about the Ethio-
pians, the Sudanese, the Somali, the first images that come to their minds tend to
be images of starving children with matchstick limbs and protruding bellies, too
weak to move, flies landing on their eyes and nostrils, emaciated mothers holding
their fragile children to their withered breasts, attempting to keep them alive with
whatever drops of milk they can barely bring forth. Stripped of their humanity, in
the eyes of those observing them, these people are defined by their hunger, not by
their exquisite millennial cultures, proud legacies and important contributions to
our human history. This is an enduring problem, despite the commendable, and to
a certain extent successful, worldwide efforts over decades to combat hunger and
poverty. Notwithstanding these efforts, March 2017, the United Nations reported
that there are more than 20 million people in Somalia, South Sudan, Kenya and
Yemen alone who are at risk of starvation in the world's largest humanitarian
crisis since 1945, when the United Nations was created after World War II (UN
News Centre, 2017; Henderson, 2017; Karimi, 2017).

There are many questions that need to be asked in the face of situations such as these, and of these, two I would like ask here are: Who are the hungry? And what does their hunger mean to them? This question does not have only one answer, for 'the hungry' are not the same the world over. The circumstances of their hunger are not necessarily the same, nor are their responses to this hunger. How do we compare the starvation of someone in the South Sudan or Somalia, facing famine, hunger and living through war, and the hunger of a person who is the victim of war in Afghanistan, whose town has been encircled by ISIS/ISIL and is starving to death, to the hunger of someone in the U.S.A., living in structural socioeconomic inequality and inequity within a defined political democratic system? How do we compare the scarcity and high cost of food in Venezuela, whose former president Hugo Chávez declared in 2007 that the country was going to achieve food sovereignty within a few years, with the abundant quantities of food, but the inability of many to pay for this food in South Africa today?

Consequently, the fundamental question is: Is all hunger the same? The short answer is no; the longer, more in-depth answer is that hunger has many faces and varying degrees, for it manifests itself in a number of ways, only one of them being grave or extreme deprivation of food. Moreover, it is a human situation that cannot be examined by itself, for it does not exist in isolation; it is one consequence of a confluence of economic, political, social, cultural, religious and environmental factors that force people to face varying degrees of hunger. There are many books that focus on the forms of hunger as the grave or extreme deprivation of food, but this book is not one of them. This book examines narratives of food insecurity as related to multidimensional poverty. In it, people from different walks of life in one province of South Africa, the Free State Province, narrate their experiences and perceptions of poverty and food insecurity. Each person has their own story.

The Free State Province is a fascinating place socially, culturally and politically, even though many in the country consider it a backwater. In many ways, it is a remnant of the past that Blacks want to forget and Afrikaners who reminisce about that past want to hold on to. It was one of the two former Afrikaner Republics and its capital, Bloemfontein, also the judicial capital of the country, is the birthplace of the two opposing political forces that have shaped the history of South Africa since the beginning of the twentieth century: the South African Native National Congress (SANNC) in 1912, renamed the African National Congress (ANC) in 1923, and the National Party (Nasionale Party in Afrikaans) in 1915 (South African History Online: National Party, 2014). The ANC is the liberation movement that fought against the rule of the White minority, and the National Party is the political party that in 1948 became the architect of apartheid and ruled the country until the ANC came into power in 1994 after 80 years of fighting for freedom (Cameron and Spies, 1992). It is a place of heightened racial tensions and a cradle for racial reconciliation. It is one of the poorest provinces, yet still a food basket of the country. It is a place of contrasts that have woven a most interesting tapestry of contemporary South African life.

In this book, I portray scenarios of poverty and food insecurity in this province. The stories told here are of the people in this one province and are unique in their human essence, yet some of the themes are universal. People around the world also experience the constraints in the lives of the people in this province, some of the challenges they face and the opportunities they have. What makes these people's stories unique is the fact that they are living in what is formally a post-apartheid society, yet we can see in their narratives how very present the structures of apartheid are in their lives and how these structures shape their lives.

People's stories are powerful means of explaining their realities, for their narratives reveal what meanings they make of the situations they are living, how they face these situations and what strategies they formulate to overcome them. Their meaning making is one of the most powerful tools of their agency, and this is what this book reveals. In it, people in the Free State Province, South Africa, who face food insecurity within abundance of food, tell their stories, which reveal their critical consciousness and agency as they struggle to survive in their democracy.

Poverty is a rawness . . . Poverty is struggle . . . Poverty is shame . . . these are some of the strands running through people's narratives in South Africa, as they explained their lives. Many analyses of food insecurity focus on what resources are needed to produce more food. Notwithstanding, even in our contemporary world of knowledge where food insecurity, structural poverty and famine are examined through the capabilities approaches of Amartya Sen and others (see, for example, Sen 2004; Sen, 2002; Dréze and Sen, 1991; Dréze, Sen and Hussain, 1995), as well as through other interesting theorizations, still too few analysts examine the issue of food insecurity through the lenses of social, economic, political and cultural inequality and inequity within spatial context. Neither do they do so sufficiently through the qualitative inquiry lenses of what meanings the people involved in the food system – and particularly the food insecure – make of food insecurity within their particular cultural and historical geography. More focus on people's meaning making of their circumstances is greatly needed. This is the focus of this book.

This book is based on the premise that the food insecure are theorists of their own reality and are in many ways agents in confronting the challenges of multidimensional poverty that they face. Here, I portray the stories of people in the Free State Province, South Africa, and through them, we will be able to see that these stories are unique in some ways, within their historical and geographical context, while at the same time, they have elements that are shared by people who live within multidimensional poverty the world over. This multidimensional poverty includes exhibiting several factors that constitute deprivation, including lack of education, poor health, inadequate living standards, lack of income, poor quality of work and disempowerment (UNDP, 2015; UNDP, 2014) Unfortunately, the voices of the food insecure with regard to how they conceptualize their situations of poverty and food insecurity are not generally heard as they should be, or much less taken into account for policy making. It is important that their voices be heard and, furthermore, be included in the formulation of poverty alleviation and food insecurity. In this case, in South Africa, but the same should be extended to other societies in the world that face similar challenges.

The stories of food insecurity in the Free State have been shaped by many issues, among which are structural poverty, racism, and attempts or non-attempts at reconciliation during and after apartheid, public health issues, such as HIV/AIDS, and environmental circumstances such as increasing drought and off-season rain.

The personal and collective stories in this book contribute to the contemporary dialogue on poverty, food security/insecurity and sustainability in South Africa and around the world.

Theoretically, this book lies at the intersection of the fields of multidimensional poverty and food studies, particularly in the area of food insecurity. Within food studies, the focus is particularly in the emerging field of food democracy, which also intersects with food justice. Hassanein (2012) explains that "food democracy ideally means that all members of an agro-food system have equal and effective opportunities for participation in shaping that system, as well as knowledge about the relevant alternative ways of designing and operating the system" (p. 469). The study this book is based on also contributes to the field of critical adult education. It emphasizes the power of critical adult formal, non-formal and informal education for individuals as part of communities, as well as communities as they identify, understand and strengthen their social resources to foster democratic agency and dismantle power structures that enhance social, economic, political and cultural inequities and inequalities (Merriam, Caffarella and Baumgartner, 2007; Brookfield, 2004; Mayo, 1999). After all, this has been the global objective of the democratic era that began in South Africa in 1994: to right the wrongs of colonization and particularly, the apartheid era, and foster democratic agency among the people to build a new and stronger South Africa.

This work spans six chapters. In Chapter 1, I explain how multidimensional poverty and food insecurity are two of the worst problems a significant proportion of the world's population faces today and delineate the important place that achieving food security has had in the democratic path that South Africa has been carving over the last 20 years since the end of apartheid. Within this context of democracy, I introduce the situations of poverty and insecurity in the Free State Province as I explain the importance of focusing my attention there. In Chapter 2, I delineate the historical, political, socioeconomic and cultural frameworks of South Africa, including the policies of the apartheid era and the social policies after apartheid, with a particular focus on the food programs established from 1994 onwards in South Africa and in the Free State Province.

In Chapters 3, 4 and 5, I share the stories of 12 men and women who live in the Free State Province, life in some communities, food insecurity faced by university students and food initiatives in the province. I narrate how these persons make meaning of the multidimensional poverty they are living and the food insecurity they face, within their social, economic, cultural, political and economic contexts in the democratic South Africa. In Chapters 3 and 4 are the stories of those living in Bloemfontein, which is the capital city of the province, as well as the judicial capital of South Africa. In Chapter 5, I go beyond the city of Bloemfontein and explore the lives of participants in the semi-urban area of Bothsabelo and the towns of Kestell and Harrismith in Thabo Mofutsanyana Municipality in the Eastern Free State. In all these areas, I also describe their agency to confront their challenges and food security initiatives that have been created. These stories are powerful narratives of people's experiences, as told in their own voices, and, through them, I elucidate how poverty and hunger are issues of social and economic injustice. In these chapters, I strive to paint a portrait of urban, semi-urban and rural food insecurity and agency in the province.

In Chapter 6, I bring together the themes from the stories across the province to create a critical dialogue of power, critical consciousness and survival within poverty, through which I explain how food insecurity is never only about food. Within this dialogue, I discuss how food insecurity in the Free State Province is deeply enmeshed in the constructs of race, class, power and culture that shape the multidimensional poverty of the people in the province. Explanations of places and people, as well as the methods used in the research on which this book is based are included in the appendix, titled Notes and Methods. With this, we begin our journey into the world of struggle, hope and agency within poverty in the province at the geographical, historical and political crossroads of South Africa: the Free State Province.

Note

1 Rudi Buys was the Dean of Student Affairs from 2012–2015 at the University of the Free State, a traditionally Afrikaans university, with a history of racially incited violence in the post-apartheid era. He was brought in by Vice Chancellor Jonathan Jansen to embark on transformational change at the university. In this role, he worked tirelessly to improve student relations among the different racial groups at the university. Furthermore, he, Vice Chancellor Jansen and their wives developed the No Student Hungry Programme at the university, for students who face food insecurity, in addition to serving as mentors to the students in this program. I explain the nature of this program in Chapter 4. This is an excerpt from one of our conversations.

References

Cameron, T., and Spies, S. B. (Eds.). (1992). *A new illustrated history of South Africa.* Johannesburg: Southern Book Publishers; Cape Town and Johannesburg: Human & Rousseau.

Dréze, J., and Sen, A. (1991). *Hunger and public action.* Oxford: Oxford University Press.

Dréze, J., Sen, A., and Hussain, A. (Eds.). (1995). *The political economy of hunger. Selected essays.* WIDER studies in development economics. Clarendon Press.

Henderson, B. (2017, March 11). UN says world faces largest humanitarian crisis since 1945 with 20 million at risk of starvation. *The Telegraph,* News. Retrieved from www.telegraph.co.uk/news/2017/03/10/un-says-world-faces-largest-humanitarian crisis since-1945/

Karimi, F. (2017, March 11). 20 million at risk of starvation in world's largest crisis since 1945, UN says. *CNN,* World. Retrieved from www.cnn.com/2017/03/11/africa/un-famine starvation-aid/index.html

Sen, A. (2004). Development as capability expansion. In Fukuda-Parr, S., and Shiva Kumar, A.K. (Eds.), *Readings in human development.* New Delhi and New York: Oxford University Press.

Sen, A. (2002). *Hunger in the contemporary world.* Discussion paper DEDPS/8, November 1997. The Suntory Center. Suntory and Toyota International Centres for Economics and Related Disciplines. London School of Economics and Political Science. Retrieved from http://eprints.lse.ac.uk/6685/1/Hunger_in_the_Contemporary_World.pdf

South African History Online. Towards a People's History. (SAHO). (2014). *National Party (NP)*. Retrieved from www.sahistory.org.za/topic/national-party-np

UN News Centre. (2017, March 10). *UN aid chief urges global action as starvation, famine loom for 20 million across four countries*. Retrieved from www.un.org/apps/news/story.asp?NewsID=56339#.WMRNLRLytsM

United Nations Development Programme (UNDP). (2015). *International human development report 2014. Sustaining human progress: Reducing vulnerabilities and building resilience*. Retrieved from http://hdr.undp.org/en/2014-report

United Nations Development Programme (UNDP). (2014). *Multidimensional poverty index (MPI)*. United Nations development programme human development reports. Retrieved from http://hdr.undp.org/en/statistics/mpi

1 The hidden faces of poverty

> Overcoming poverty is not a task of charity, it is an act of justice. Like slavery and apartheid, poverty is not natural. It is man-made and it can be overcome and eradicated by the actions of human beings . . . Sometimes it falls on a generation to be great. You can be that great generation. Let your greatness blossom.
>
> —Former South African President, Nelson Mandela[1]

Poverty in not natural, but is made by human beings and can be overcome and eradicated by us. We have the power in our hands to do this and should do it. These powerful statements by Nelson Rolihlahla Mandela, the first Black President of South Africa, in his 2005 Campaign to Make Poverty History speech in London (BBC News, 2005), are still very relevant today. The fight to eradicate poverty, injustice and inequality, within their multiple dimensions and dire consequences for human life, is an ongoing one in which we are not making as much progress with as we should, despite the enormous efforts of individuals and organizations around the world, as well as the advances in knowledge, technology, industry and science we have made.

Poverty and hunger have many faces. Across the world, they manifest themselves in a myriad of ways, some more recognizable to the general public than others. The myriad faces of hunger are those of people having substantially varying levels of access to food and, in many cases, with this access not being sustainable. When people have sustainable access to sufficient, safe, nutritious food to maintain a healthy and active life, they are generally considered to be food secure. Poverty and food insecurity are two of the worst problems millions of people around the world face today. The United Nations Development Programme (UNDP) 2014 Human Development Report (HDR) found that nearly 2.2 billion people in the world were living in or near multidimensional poverty, and of these, approximately 842 million people, 12% of the world's population, face chronic hunger (UNDP, 2015b). In 2016, both the UNDP and the World Food Program (WFP) estimated that approximately 795 million today people do not have enough to eat, and one in three people in the world suffer from some form of malnutrition (UNDP, 2017; World Food Program, Zero Hunger, 2017). All of these figures depict grim realities of a significant percentage of our populations, despite the fact that these reports find that from 1990–2015, average human development has improved significantly around the world.

Of all the continents, Africa is often seen as the poster child for the problems of poverty and food insecurity. When many people think about Africa, they think about starving children with bulging bellies, famine and dire poverty, hunger at its very worst. This image may be the reality for some countries, and areas of countries of the continent, including Somalia, South Sudan and Kenya, as we have seen in the March 2017 UN report described in the introduction, but it is not so for all. The World Food Program operates in 42 of the 54 African countries, and South Africa is not one of them. It does, however, operate in the two independent kingdoms that are within the borders of South Africa; Lesotho and Swaziland, where socioeconomic conditions are worse than in South Africa and where there are high levels of food insecurity. Supranational, international and national organizations all project that food production and the import capacity of countries around the world will increase considerably over the next decade, thus increasing the possibility of food security in many countries. Notwithstanding, some of these same organizations, such as the Food and Agriculture Organization and the WFP, estimate that despite these measures, food insecurity will rise in some regions. International assessments such as the International Food Security Assessment 2012–2022 carried out by the United States Department of Agriculture (USDA) estimate that the number of food insecure people in Sub-Saharan Africa will increase by 15.1% in this decade. Even so, the percentage of the food insecure in the region is estimated to decrease from 42% in 2012 to 38% in 2022 (USDA ERS International Food Security Assessment 2012–2022, 2012). These figures express the paradoxical nature of food security/insecurity in our contemporary world.

Africa is a very diverse continent with a very rich tapestry of cultures, languages, religions, nations and ethnicities that exist within it, as well as sociopolitical and economic systems that the 54 countries have had historically. Several of these countries are at present undergoing very interesting processes of transformation politically, economically and socially, of which South Africa is one. Today, South Africa is considered a medium developing country in the United Nations Development Programme Human Development Index (UNDP HDI) index, with great potential for growth (UNDP International Human Development Indicators, 2015a). But despite this status, it is also one of the countries where there are hidden faces of food insecurity; where there is plentiful food, but where a large part of the population is too poor to have economic access to food on a sustainable basis.

South Africa: the road to democracy

South Africa is well known around the world as a country shaped by apartheid for the greater part of the twentieth century. The minority of Whites subjected the non-White population, mainly Blacks, as well as Coloreds and Indians, to acute racial, social, political and economic discrimination and segregation over this period. It formally became a democracy in 1994 with the election of the well-known son of South Africa, Nelson Rolihlahla Mandela, as its first Black president. As head of the government of national unity, he ushered in an era of many promises of racial, social, economic, and political reparation and progress. He was an icon of freedom and struggle greatly admired worldwide. He died in 2013, but his legacy lives on powerfully, both within and beyond South Africa, where he spent the greater part of his life fighting against apartheid and the social injustice and human cruelty of this system. His greater battle, nonetheless, was not only for these reasons. Once he and his comrades in the liberation struggle came into government, dismantling the apartheid system, his greatest concerns were with building up his country and confronting the widespread poverty, deep injustice and gross inequality within. Even after he retired from government and then from public life, he continued to speak out against these, and other, crucial issues of our contemporary world, as illustrated in the excerpt from his 2005 speech at the beginning of this chapter.

With President Mandela's election, his political party, the African National Congress came to power in 1994 and has been in power ever since, even though Mandela himself only served one term. In 2014, South Africa celebrated 20 years of its winding road to democracy, a road that has increasingly been sorely tested, as civil unrest reigns in the country, with mounting protests to government corruption. The ANC has been losing its popularity in the country, and in the August 2016 municipal elections, it only won 53.91% of the total vote, an 8.04% decline as compared to the 2011 elections. This was the lowest percentage of popular support for the party since 1994, and this decline was most markedly in the urban areas. Even though it had marginal gains, and the ANC still holds the largest percentage of national, regional and local offices, it lost control of three metropolitan municipalities to its opposition party, the Democratic Alliance: Nelson Mandela Bay in the Eastern Cape Province; the City of Tshwane; and the City of Johannesburg, both in Gauteng Province (Calland, 2016; Harrison, 2016). Johannesburg is South Africa's chief industrial and financial metropolis and was a major political loss for the ANC.

The new era of democracy in South Africa began with promises of change to the societal dynamics of the country, righting the wrongs of apartheid and a history of Black African oppression by the Whites. One of the first instruments implemented to effectuate the transformation of the society into a more socially, economically and politically equal one was the Reconstruction and Development Programme (RDP). This program had been part of the election platform of the African National Congress in the 1994 elections. The program formulated five major policy programs: (a) Meeting Basic Needs, (b) Developing our Human Resources, (c) Building the Economy, (d) Democratizing the State and Society and (e) Implementing the RDP. Within the first policy program of meeting the basic needs of the people of the nation, achieving national food security was a core objective as the people's right to be free from hunger (ANC, 1994; RDP

White Paper, 1994). In 1996, the new Constitution of the Republic of South Africa, establishing the legal guidelines for the societal transformation, was drawn up. In this constitution, food security became a fundamental right, where every citizen of the nation had the right to have access to sufficient food and water and where the state would ensure the realization of this right (Constitution of the Republic of South Africa, "Statutes", 1996, Provision 27).

The RDP was considered the cornerstone of the government developmental policy, but it was only partially successful. One of its main areas of success was in social security. Through the RDP, the government created an extensive welfare system for the poor, vulnerable and others in need, such as older adults, the disabled, children in need and foster parents who care for children who have been neglected, abandoned or whose parents have died. Through the social welfare system, pregnant women and small children were given free health care and a school food program was implemented for 3.5 to five million schoolchildren in situations of vulnerability (South Africa History Online: South Africa's key economic policies", 2014).

In view of what was considered the poor success of the RDP, the government introduced a macroeconomic policy framework, the Growth, Employment and Redistribution strategy (GEAR), in 1996. It was a switch from a social-democratic model to a neoliberal one. GEAR had the goal of stimulating the more rapid growth of the economy, which was considered necessary to inject financial and human resources into the needs of the country, among which was the social security network. It, too, was only partially successful. Its main area of success was in achieving macroeconomic objectives, but it failed to reach its objectives in confronting the social challenges of the country, especially in the areas of poverty reduction and employment creation, which were sorely needed. It was also highly criticized for its neoliberal approach, especially by the Congress of South Africa's Trade Unions (COSATU), which had been a fundamental actor in the fight against apartheid and in building the new democracy.

Building upon the RDP establishing food as a basic need to be met, the new constitution establishing food security as a fundamental right of all South Africans and following on the guidelines of the 1996 World Food Summit, where South Africa joined other countries in pledging to support the World Summit Plan of Action, under GEAR, a Food Security Policy for South Africa was established. The vision of this policy was that South Africa would become "a country where everyone has access to adequate, safe and nutritious food" (Food Security Working Group, 1997, pt.1.1). The following excerpt explains the rationale underlying this policy. It is important to include here because it explains the context within which the post-1994 path to building food security in South Africa was being carved.

> In common with many countries, South Africa's ability to satisfy essential needs stems from many sources, but poverty and hunger in South Africa are particularly shaped by the impact of apartheid. One aspect of this system was

a process of active disposition of assets such as land and livestock from the black majority, while opportunities to develop, such as access to markets, infrastructure and human development, were denied them. Until 1985 food policies pursued self-sufficiency goals, and thus protected domestic commercial farm production, often at the cost of consumers, and resulting in a total welfare loss to the country as a whole. Despite the dramatic changes in South Africa during the 1990's, many of the distortions and dynamics introduced by apartheid continue to perpetuate conditions that lead to food insecurity. The correct identification of these forces and the introduction of remedial policies is a complex task, and require careful conceptualization. A new food security policy needs to focus on individual and household level food security. Such a policy should address in a comprehensive manner, the availability, accessibility and utilization of food at a macro and a micro level.

(Food Security Working Group, 1997, pt.1.2)

This policy also established that for food security in the country to be achieved, the approach must be comprehensive and multisectorial.

Following upon these policies, the government developed the Integrated Food Security Strategy (IFSS) in 2002, which "defines food security as the physical, social and economic access by all households at all times to adequate, safe and nutritious food and clean water to meet their dietary and food preferences for a healthy and productive life" (Department: Agriculture. "The Integrated Food Security Strategy -South Africa", 2002, p. 6). Over the following years, a number of policies and programs have been implemented towards fulfilling this right, with varying degrees of success, failures and disappointments for the people who have most needed them: the poor, vulnerable and marginalized. Under the Integrated Sustainable Rural Development Programme (ISRDP), the Urban Renewal Programme (URP) and the Accelerated and Shared Growth Initiative for South Africa (AsgiSA), some of the objectives were to decrease levels of unemployment and poverty as well as accelerate rural and urban development respectively. The 2010 New Growth Plan (NGP) was focused on job creation, and, most recently, the NDP 2030 National Development Plan has the objective of eliminating poverty and reducing inequality by 2030 (National Planning Commission: National Development Plan 2030, 2013).

After several years of working towards ensuring food security, the government states that this has been achieved at a national level. Despite the numerous programs that have been implemented nonetheless, the government has also determined that household food security has not been achieved and over 12 million people – approximately one of every four people in the country – still face food insecurity (Department of Agriculture, Forestry and Fisheries – DAFF, "Interventions for food security", 2013). The South African National Health and Nutrition Examination Survey (SANHANES-1) (Shisana et al., 2013) determined that 26% of households nationwide are food insecure, while 28.3% are at risk of food insecurity. Framing this food insecurity, we can see that 56.8% of the population lives in poverty, with women being more impoverished than men: 58.6% of women as compared to 54.9% of men. The poverty gap is 27.9 percent, with a Gini coefficient based on HCE of 0.7% (Statistics South Africa: Poverty, 2016). These statistics clearly express the economic inequality of the population. In 1996, approximately 14 million South Africans faced food insecurity, and, 20 years later, the number of food insecure has only been reduced by approximately two million, despite the measures taken. Today, as was the case then, the majority of the food insecure are Black African, as well as many Coloreds. Over the years, however, there has also been a rise in White poverty, and there has been an increasing level of food insecurity among poor Whites.

With regard to the situation of food insecurity in the country, the South African government has established that beyond only aiming to solve food insecurity, the goal should be to achieve food sustainability, i.e., that people's access to food should be sustainable through their participation in the production of their own food. Toward this end, the government approved a Food Security and Nutrition Policy and initiated an intervention, the Fetsa Tlala Integrated Food Production Initiative, "which seeks to afford smallholder farmers, communities and households the ability to increase production of basic food, and increase access and availability of it to attain basic food security at household and local levels" (DAFF, "Securing access", 2013, p. 3). This initiative is now in process but has encountered a number of challenges.

The majority of the studies on food insecurity that have been conducted in South Africa have been on food insecurity in the rural areas, the former homelands where many Africans were restricted under apartheid, for these tend to be the poorest areas in the country, as well as in the more populated urban areas (e.g., see Twine and Hunter, 2011; Crush, Hovorka and Tevera, 2010). There has been less focus on food insecurity within some of the areas where food is produced in the country, despite the high levels of food insecurity in these areas. One such area is the Free State Province, one of the breadbaskets of the country and one of the two former Boer Republics that was historically governed by the Afrikaners and deeply segregated, politically, socially and economically until 1994. Over the last 20+ years of democratic government, the political landscape has changed in the province, as Black Africans now occupy the majority of the political offices and are in leadership positions. Notwithstanding, daily life in the province shows us that socially and economically, the societal structures have not changed as much as would be expected. Interestingly, the ANC was founded in Bloemfontein (the capital of the province) in 1912, two years after the National Party, which created the apartheid state, was founded in 1910.

In this state well known for its agriculture, as well as for its gold mining, there is a poverty level of 61.9%, higher than the national poverty level of 56.8% (Statistics South Africa: Poverty, 2014). According to the statistics of the Department of Agriculture, Forestry and Fisheries (DAFF), within the province, 8.0% of the households have severely inadequate access to food, 14.7% have inadequate access and 77.4% have adequate access (DAFF, "Fetsa Tlala integrated", 2013). These statistics show us that 22.7%, nearly one-fourth of the population, have inadequate access to food. How can this be possible in a province considered a breadbasket of the nation? What are the social, economic, political and even environmental circumstances within the province which may help to explicate this? And how do the food insecure perceive their inadequate access to food? How do they make meaning of it within their lives? These are intriguing questions that underlie people's narratives of their lives in this new South Africa.

There are a number of studies that examine food insecurity in South Africa through multiple lenses, including those using the capabilities approach, but there are still too few that do so through qualitative inquiry, examining the issue of food insecurity through the lenses of what meanings the people who face food insecurity make of their circumstances within the socioeconomic, political and cultural contexts of post-apartheid South Africa and, in particular, within the Free State. Food insecurity as lived by these people is an issue of gross social injustice. People who face food insecurity around the world are victims entrapped in the vise of structural poverty, created in large part by the policies of their past and present governments and/or those of external actors, such as multilateral organizations (e.g., the World Bank, International Monetary Fund). This has been the case of South Africa. The stories of food insecurity and unsustainability in South Africa, and particularly in the Free State, have been shaped by many factors, including: structural poverty, socioeconomic inequity and inequality; racism; historically discriminatory government policies, which increased significantly during apartheid; relatively well-conceptualized and in some ways poorly implemented government policies since 1994; trauma and attempts or non-attempts at reconciliation at an individual and societal level during and after apartheid; public health issues, such as HIV/AIDS and tuberculosis, and environmental circumstances, such as increasing drought and wildfires. As Meter (2012) explains, "Hunger is always caused by breakdowns in social connection and political inequality. There is no way to resolve hunger simply by producing more food, nor can technological improvement, by itself solve hunger" (p. 17).

Research, together with social-political experiences the world over, have demonstrated how important it is that the voices of people who live in poverty and/ or face food insecurity be included in the poverty alleviation and food security policy making processes. They need to be agents of these processes, not only the subjects of policies targeted at them. Notwithstanding the evidence building the case for this inclusive policy making, it has not been given the importance it deserves at international and national levels. Instead, too many organizations and governments have clung to old and often ineffective formulas for overcoming multidimensional poverty and achieving sustainable food security. The former UN Special Rapporteur for the Right to Food (2008–2014), Olivier De Schutter, however, was a strong advocate for this inclusion of the people. In his final report as UN Special Rapporteur, he explained that subsequent to the 2008 global food price crisis, a number of food production programs were implemented in countries to confront the crisis, but,

> while most of the initiatives that were adopted to strengthen the ability of countries to increase their own production and meet a greater share of their own food needs focused on supporting small-scale farmers, they did not include mechanisms for monitoring progress and accountability, *or for ensuring that food producers and consumers participated in policymaking processes.* They did not focus on the most vulnerable and they often failed to guarantee the transformation of support schemes into legal entitlements.
>
> (De Schutter, 2014, p. 3 4; italics are mine)

Such support for including the voices of the food insecure in the policymaking processes is heartening. They are all consumers, and some are food producers. It is ironic and distressing, as we will see in the following chapters, that small and family farmers are amongst the food insecure. The narratives of the people in this book make a strong case for this. They have been my co-researchers in helping me to understand their realities. As they narrate their stories, they make meaning of them.

It is imperative that we understand food insecurity in the Free State within the racial and socioeconomic dynamics of the province, which are in some regards different to those of other provinces. South Africa has three capital cities: Cape Town, Pretoria and Bloemfontein. Cape Town is the legislative capital, where Parliament sits, and Pretoria is the political capital, where the executive seat and ministries are. The Free State Province is home to the judicial capital of South Africa, the city of Bloemfontein, which is the seat of the Supreme Court of Appeal. Despite its political importance, it is still a largely agricultural province, shaped socially and economically by its Afrikaner farming and settlement history. In agriculture, it seems that the race relations have not changed; that is, the White farmer-Black farm laborer relationship remains in large part as it has been throughout the twentieth century. Moreover, despite over 20 years of Black African government in the province, one can perceive in daily life that some societal-racial structures and dynamics remain little changed and race relations remain rather tense, seething below the surface. One example of the little changed societal-racial structures is the townships. The poor Black Africans still mainly live in their townships and the Coloreds mainly live in theirs, separated from the Blacks, as was the case during apartheid. Interestingly, within these townships, a number of the Blacks and Coloreds who have achieved upward social mobility prefer to remain in the townships, simply remodeling their childhood homes and gentrifying their neighborhoods as such, instead of buying houses in the more affluent, mainly White neighborhoods. They say they do not feel welcome in these neighborhoods, and they do not feel safe.

In addition to lingering apartheid era social structures and customs, there have been a number of race crimes and race incidents over the past years in the Free

State. There have been serious race crimes, such as Black Africans attacking older White farmers and sometimes killing them. With regard to race incidents in recent years, I will give two cases that took place during my time there. In January of 2014, as students were coming back to campus to begin the new university year, both in a banner near the University of the Free State campus, and in the Afrikaans language newspaper, there was an advertisement in Afrikaans with the picture of a young White woman advertising flats for rental to female students, *"who want to be free from affirmative action policies and live in an affirmative action free environment"* (translation from Afrikaans). This ad caused a huge stir on campus, which has a 60% percent non-Afrikaans speaking Black student body. The rector of the university, Professor Jonathan Jansen, took action to address this discriminatory advertisement, including using it as an occasion to discuss racial tensions within the city and at the university.

One month later, in February 2014, on the Bloemfontein campus of the University of the Free State, there was an incident in which two male White students sideswiped a Black student, then supposedly beat him up and called him a kaffir.[2] Both incidents became nationally known, and the South African Human Rights Commission had to be brought in for the second case. The rector of the university suspended the two presumed attackers. What was sadly interesting to observe were the many nasty comments and opinions that were expressed among the people and in the media of the city about the first case and also within the province and nationwide in the media regarding the second one. It leads us to realizing that racial tensions are very much alive in South Africa and in the Free State. In September 2014, after reviewing the second case, the Human Rights Commission determined that it "was unable to find any corroborating evidence to make a conclusive finding of racism and violation of human rights" towards the Black student in the case (University of the Free State News Archive, September 9, 2014b, para.1). Furthermore, the Regional Magistrate found the two White students not guilty on all charges. The Black complainant's testimony turned out to have inconsistencies and exaggerations. He also demonstrated hostility throughout the trial and proved himself to be prejudiced and an unreliable witness. This case shows the other side of the coin of racism in the Free State: trumped-up charges on the basis of race and within the historical context of White discrimination and violence against Blacks. Within this context, it was easy to believe that the White students had beaten up the Black one. All of the above give a brief insight into some of the societal forces that have shaped life in the Free State Province and within which food insecurity is manifested.

This book contributes to the contemporary dialogue of what food security, food insecurity and food sustainability mean in the different societies worldwide. South Africa is still burning with the long-term impact of racism and violence. The former Boer Republic of the Orange Free State, now the Free State Province, still explodes with racial crimes of White–Black, Black–White (in this latter, especially against White farmers) and racial discrimination of Whites against Black, both subtle and overt. Even 23 years after the end of apartheid, the Free State in many ways still retains the societal forces that historically shaped the province and were part of life under apartheid. Within this framework, the issues of food security/insecurity and sustainability have a powerful place at the table of discussion.

Let us now understand the historical framework of South Africa, together with a description of the evolution of the politics, societal dynamics, economy and culture in the twentieth and twenty-first centuries to situate the importance of the people's stories.

Notes

1 This famous quote from Nelson Mandela's speech at the 2005 Campaign to Make Poverty History in Trafalgar Square for the campaign to end poverty in the developing world is placed at the beginning of the descriptive document of the No Student Hungry program of the University of the Free State.
2 Kaffir (kaffer in Afrikaans) is a term that was widely used in the past by Whites to refer to Blacks in South Africa. It is now considered an ethnic slur, and its use is condemned. It is derived from the Arabic term *kafir*, which means 'infidel' and was historically adopted by European traders to refer to non-Muslim Blacks.

References

African National Congress (ANC). (1994). *The reconstruction and development programme (RDP)*. Johannesburg: Aloe Communications.

BBC News. (2005, February 3). In full: Mandela's poverty speech. *BBC News*. Retrieved from http://news.bbc.co.uk/2/hi/uk_news/politics/4232603.stm

Calland, R. (2016, August 5). Sharp-tongued South African voters give ruling ANC a stiff rebuke. *The Conversation*. Retrieved from https://theconversation.com/sharp-tongued-south africanvoters-give-ruling-anc-a-stiff-rebuke-63606

Constitution of the Republic of South Africa. No. 108. (1996). *Statutes of the Republic of South Africa – constitutional law*. Retrieved from www.gov.za/documents/constitution/1996/a108-96.pdf

Crush, J., Hovorka, A., and Tevera, D. (2010). *Urban food production and household food security in Southern African cities*. Urban food security series no. 4. Kingston and Cape Town: Queen's University and AFSUN. Retrieved from www.afsun.org/wp content/uploads/2013/09/AFSUN_4.pdf

De Schutter, O. (2014, January 24). *The transformative potential of the right to food*. Report of the Special Rapporteur on the Right to Food. United Nations General Assembly, Human Rights Council, Twenty-fifth session. Retrieved from www.srfood.org/images/stories/pdf/officialreports/20140310_finalreport_en.pdf

Department: Agriculture, Forestry and Fisheries (DAFF). Republic of South Africa. (2013a). *Fetsa Tlala integrated food production initiative 2013/2014: An overview*. Retrieved from http://lgbn.co.za/home/attachments/article/71/FETSA%20TLALA%20%20INTERGRATED%20FOOD%20PRODUCTION%20INITIATIEV-%2012%20NOVEMBER%202013.pdf

Department: Agriculture, Forestry and Fisheries (DAFF). Republic of South Africa. (2013b, October 18–24). Securing access to food. *Mail & Guardian*, World Food Day, supplement, p. 3.

Department: Agriculture. Republic of South Africa. (2002, July 17). *The integrated food security strategy for South Africa*. Retrieved from www.nda.agric.za/doaDev/sideMenu/foodSecurity/policies.pdf

Food Security Working Group (Agricultural Policy Unit). (1997, November). *Food security policy for South Africa. A discussion document*. By the Food Security Working Group (Agricultural Policy Unit) for the Department of Agriculture and Land Affairs. Retrieved from www.nda.agric.za/docs/Foodsecurity/foodsecurity.htm

Graham-Harrison, E. (2016, August 6). Voters deliver stinging rebuke to ANC in South African election. *The Guardian*. Retrieved from www.theguardian.com/world/2016/aug/04/south-africansdeliver-stinging-rebuke-to-anc

Harrison, P. (2016, September 5). How South Africa's metropoles rose in revolt against the ANC on August 3. *Mail & Guardian*. Retrieved from https://mg.co.za/article/2016-09-05-the revolt-of-south-africas-metropoles-a-revolution-of-rising-expectations

The Integrated Food Security Strategy for South Africa. (2002). Retrieved from www.nda.agric.za/doaDev/sideMenu/foodSecurity/policies.pdf

Make Poverty History. (2005). *Mandela's speech*. Retrieved from www.makepovertyhistory.org/extras/mandela.shtml

Meter, K. (2012, January 18). *Hoosier farmer? Emergent food systems in Indiana: Tools for community self-determination*. Prepared for the Indiana State Department of Health. Minneapolis: Crossroads Resource Center.Retrieved from www.crcworks.org.

National Planning Commission. (2013). *National development plan 2030: Our future – make it work*. Retrieved from www.gov.za/issues/national-development-plan 2030

Reconstruction and Development Programme. (1994, September). *RDP white paper*. Discussion document. Retrieved from www.polity.org.za/polity/govdocs/white_papers/rdpwhite.html

Shisana, O., Labadarios, D., Rehle, T., Simbayi, L., Zuma, K., Dhansay, A., Reddy, P., Parker, W., Hoosain, E., Naidoo, P., Hongoro, C., Mchiza, Z., Steyn, N. P., Dwane, N., Makoae, M., Maluleke, T., Ramlagan, S., Zungu, N., Evans, M. G., Jacobs, L., Faber, M., and SANHANES-1 Team. (2013). *South African National Health and Nutrition Examination Survey (SANHANES-\ 1)*. Cape Town: HSRC Press.

South African History Online. Towards a people's history. (SAHO). (2014). *South Africa's key economic policies since 1993–2013*. Retrieved from www.sahistory.org.za/article/south africa%E2%80%99s-key-economic-policies-changes-1994-2013

Statistics South Africa. (2014). *Poverty*. Retrieved from www.statssa.gov.za/?page_id=739&id=1

Twine, W., and Hunter, L. M. (2011, October). Adult mortality and household food security in South Africa: Does AIDS represent a unique mortality shock? *Development Southern Africa*, 28(4), 431–444. DOI:10.1080/0376835X.2011.605559.

United Nations Development Programme (UNDP). (2017, March). *International human development report 2016. Human development for everyone*. Retrieved from http://hdr.undp.org/sites/default/files/2016_human_development_report.pdf

United Nations Development Programme (UNDP). (2015a). *International human development indicators. United Nations development programme human development reports*. Retrieved from http://hdr.undp.org/en/countries

United Nations Development Programme (UNDP). (2015b). *International human development report 2014. Sustaining human progress: Reducing vulnerabilities and building resilience*. Retrieved from http://hdr.undp.org/en/2014-report

United Nations Development Programme (UNDP). (2014). *Multidimensional poverty index (MPI). United Nations development programme human development reports.* Retrieved from http://hdr.undp.org/en/statistics/mpi

UN News Centre. (March 10, 2017). *UN aid chief urges global action as starvation, famine loom for 20 million across four countries.* Retrieved from www.un.org/apps/news/story. asp?NewsID=56339#.WMRNLRLytsM

United States Department of Agriculture Economic Research Service (USDA ERS). (2012, July). *International food security assessment, 2012–2022.* Retrieved from www.ers. usda.gov/media/849266/gfa23.pdf

University of the Free State. (2014a). *No student hungry programme (NSH).* Retrieved from http://giving.ufs.ac.za/dl/Userfiles/Documents/00000/13_eng.pdf

University of the Free State. (2014b, September 9). *UFS responds to the outcome of the court case in the alleged attack by Cobus Muller and Charl Blom on Gwebu.* News Archive item. Retrieved from www.ufs.ac.za/templates/news-archive-item?news=4116

World Food Programme. (2017). *Zero hunger.* Retrieved from http://www1.wfp.org/ zero-hunger

2 South Africa and the Free State Province

History, society, race and food

The stories of poverty and food insecurity in South Africa are situated within the history of the country, and this chapter delineates this history. It begins with a concise description of the political, socioeconomic and cultural history of the country, particularly with regard to the racial dynamics between the White and the non-White populations and the policies of the apartheid era. Thereafter, the social policies after apartheid, with a particular focus on the food programs established from 1994 onwards are described, together with the history of the Free State Province, as well as the food security and sustainability policies in the province.

A concise history of South Africa: politics, societal dynamics, economy and culture

As a country, South Africa has been shaped by several societal dynamics, including the consequences of Dutch and British use of the Cape of Good Hope as a trading post and then by colonization and the independent spirit of its early farmer settlers. Its history can be identified in five periods, which are not necessarily clear-cut but illustrate the historical development of the country. The first was the period of the VOC – the Dutch East India Company, approximately from 1652 to 1795. During this period of nearly 150 years, under Dutch rule, Afrikaner pastoral farms spread across what is today the Western Cape Province; the *Boer Commando* was the instrument of political power of these farms. *Boer* is the Afrikaans name for farmer. After waging war against the indigenous populations, the military leaders of this commando divided up the lands and bounties in an arbitrary manner, with very little regard for the economic plight of the impoverished Afrikaners, or subsistence farmers, of the Commando, thus creating strife amongst the groups (Terreblanche, 2012).

The second period was that of British Colonialism from 1795 to 1910, which began with Great Britain capturing the Cape of Good Hope from the Dutch in 1795. As Terreblanche (2012) explains of this period, "the economic interests of the Afrikaners were largely neglected, while large numbers of blacks were exploited by several repressive labour laws and by engagements in Frontier Wars" (p. 44). In 1867, diamonds were discovered in the colony and, in 1886, gold. With these discoveries began the British companies' extraction of mineral wealth in the country. During this period, the Cape and Natal (both ocean port areas) were British-controlled colonies, and the Transvaal and Free State were Boer-controlled republics. The Anglo-Boer War between the British and the two Boer Republics that had formed in the interior of the country during British rule was waged from 1899–1902, in large part for control over the gold. As a result of this war, the British took control of all the lands and expanded the mining. During this period, the Black population was dispersed throughout the country, many of whom had been forced off their tribal lands in the preceding years and whose rights were ignored. The Union of South Africa was created in 1910 (South Africa History Online: Land, Labour and Apartheid, 2014).

The extraction of mineral wealth led to the third period, that of the control that the Mineral Energy Complex and the several South African governments had during the first half of the twentieth century, from 1910 to 1948 (Terreblanche, 2012; Cameron and Spies, 1992). During this period, more lands were taken away from the indigenous peoples, a dire circumstance which was legalized through the enactment of the 1913 Native Land Act. With the growth of the mineral energy complex, this act also helped to institutionalize the highly exploitative migrant labor system for the gold mines. With this migrant labor system began the transformation of much of Black African life away from agriculture into cheap wage labor. The fourth period was that of the apartheid government, from 1948 until 1994; the fifth period is the post-apartheid period that began in 1994 with the election of the first democratic government, under Nelson Mandela. The stories of the people in this book are mainly contextualized within the third, fourth and fifth periods.

Before apartheid: the history of segregation and racial discrimination

The idea of White–Black African inequality was incorporated into the societal dynamics of South Africa since the very beginning of its colonization under the Dutch and then under the British and Afrikaner governments. Subsequent to the creation of the Union of South Africa in 1910, this idea of inequality became more pronounced through legislation, long before apartheid came into being in 1948. Some of the legislation promulgated the separation and segregation between the racial groups. One of the first was the *Mines and Works Act No 12 of 1911*, which "permitted the granting of certificates of competency for a number of skilled mining occupations to Whites and Coloreds only (South Africa History Online: Apartheid Legislation 1850s–1970s, para.2). This Act was then repealed by section 20 of the *Mines and Works Amendment Act No 27 of 1956*, during the deepening of segregation under the apartheid regime. There was rural racial segregation created through legislation such as the 1913 *Natives Land Act*, which delineated 8.9 million hectares, 7.5% of the country, as 'Native Reserves'. This act made it illegal for Africans (Blacks) to purchase land outside of these reserves. These reserves were "explicitly intended to set aside a labour pool that would provide low-paid workers when needed and otherwise contain 'excess Africans'" (Newman and De Lannoy, 2014, p. 20). This act created a problem for Black share-croppers, who worked on White-owned land but who also had their own piece of land. They were forced to decide between working for the White farmers and relocating to areas set aside for Blacks. The situation created by this act was only slightly improved by the 1936 *Native Trust and Land Act*, which increased the amount of land allocated to Blacks to just over 10% of the country (South Africa History Online: Land, Labour and Apartheid, 2014).

Indians were also subjected to repressive legislation and segregation. Indians first began arriving as slaves in 1634 during the Dutch Colonial era, and from 1690–1725, comprised 80% of the slaves in the Cape. The influx of Indian slaves continued until the end of slavery in 1838. By the 1880s, these Indians were fully integrated into the Cape White and Coloured communities. In the latter part of the nineteenth century and first decade of the twentieth, approximately from 1860 to 1914, there were two further migratory flows of Indians in two categories; first as indentured laborers to work for the Natal colonial government on the sugar plantations (which is today part of the province of KwaZulu-Natal, including the city of Durban) and then later came 'free' Indians, mainly traders looking for new opportunities abroad. The Indians in this last category came not only from India, but also from Mauritius and other lands, at their own expense. These migrations were stopped in 1914 (South Africa History Online: From Bondage to Freedom, 2014).

Among the repressive legislation and segregation the South African Indians were subjected to were the following: *The Durban Land Alienation Ordinance, No. 14 of 1922* enabled the Durban City Council to exclude Indians from ownership or occupation of property in White areas in the city of Durban. Further, this ordinance gave the Council the right to restrict ownership and occupation of land of any race group. The 1923 *Class Areas Bill* then proposed "compulsory residential and trading segregation for Indians throughout South Africa" (South Africa History Online: Apartheid Legislation 1850s–1970s, para. 6). This was followed by the 1924 *Rural Dealers Ordinance*, which carried the 1922 *Durban Land Alienation Ordinance*, further by preventing Indians from owning land in White areas. In 1925, through *The Areas Reservation and Immigration and Registration (Further Provision) Bill*, Indians were defined as aliens, and it recommended that their population be limited through repatriation.

Urban racial segregation was implemented through the 1923 *Natives Urban Areas Act No 21*, which required authorities to design separate neighborhoods for African people "and to exercise a measure of control over the migration of the African populations to towns". The 1934 *Slums Act* ensured that "inner-city neighborhoods and dilapidated suburbs would be demolished and that the displaced African communities, deported to areas on the periphery of the city, would be grouped separately by race" (p. 20).

Segregation during this period was not only geographical, with the Blacks and Whites living separately, but also emotional and physical, with Black families living apart, largely for economic reasons. The importance of to whom land was given and how the South African workforce was shaped is illustrated in the following excerpt.

> Land and labour are two very important elements of the economic development of a society, and the way they are used will influence how the society develops. In South African history there has always been a fight for the ownership of land and the need for cheap labour. Government policies over the years have tried to solve this problem in different ways.
>
> (South Africa History Online: Land, Labour and Apartheid, 2014, para. 1)

The White government needed cheap labor in the towns, mines and on the farms, so they needed to ensure that people would come to the White areas to work. Among other policies, the government implemented a tax system which the Blacks, through their chiefs, had to pay. There were few employment opportunities in the Black areas, so people were forced to go to the cities, and part of their earnings would then be turned over to their chief to pay the government taxes. Thus began the system that came to be known as the system of migrant labor, in which people travelled to different areas of the country, often far from home, to work temporarily, then returned to their families. Through this system, African societal dynamics began to change and problems arose. Among these were:

- Young men sometimes could not marry until they had done a certain amount of labour for the chief
- Families were disrupted
- Farms were left in the hands of women and young children
- Men in the cities became used to the Western way of life, and did not want to settle on the farms again
- The tribal and traditional society was broken up. (South Africa History Online: Land, Labour and Apartheid, 2014, para. 6)

The system of job reservation to protect White labor also began during this period, created through a number of laws which the government implemented, including the 1925 *Minimum Wages Act* and the 1926 *Mines and Works Act (Colour Bar Act) No. 25*. Under this system, certain better-paying jobs were reserved only for Whites, while the Blacks generally had lower-paying jobs. Notwithstanding, not all the Whites were wealthier than Blacks; there was also White poverty.

The apartheid regime

From 1948 onwards, the official apartheid state began to sharply increase the level of segregation, going towards total apartheid through a set of race legislations that created the legal, socioeconomic and geographical separateness between the different races, treating them very differently before the law. The original meaning of the term *Apartheid* in Dutch is 'separateness' or 'apartness'. Among these legislations was the 1950 *Population Registration Act*, which required every person to be classified by race, based on lineage and on 'physical appearance and social acceptability". Through this, people were to be labeled 'White', 'Indian', 'Colored' or 'Black'. Also in 1950, the *Group Areas Act* was promulgated, separating Blacks, Whites, Coloreds and Indians into unconnected areas. The act required redesigning cities to hinder all but the most instrumental forms of contact between the various population groups. The races had to be separated by at least 30 meters of land, with no roads linking them. It is important to note here that Black South Africans refer to themselves as Africans, which is a term that I will use interchangeably with Blacks from here onwards.

The homelands policy formulated by the apartheid government created an even greater level of segregation. Through the *Bantu Authority Act, Act 68* of 1951, the homelands, or Bantustans, were established, as were the regional authorities for the same. The *Bantu Education Act No. 47* of 1953, which was a fundamental part of the apartheid project, deepened what would become the generational educational disadvantages of the Blacks with regard to the Whites in South Africa. Through this act, African students were not allowed the same education as White students. Instead, African children were to receive an inferior education, one that would provide them with skills to work within their own communities in their respective homelands or in manual labor jobs under Whites. This Bantu Education system was dictated by the Black Education Department in the Department of Native Affairs, which was tasked with compiling a curriculum "that suited the nature and requirements of the black people" (Bantu Education Act No. 47 of 1953), with the same act indicating that African students "were to be educated in a way that was appropriate for their culture". The apartheid government took it upon itself to define what culture meant, what should be taught and at what educational levels, and what the purpose and outcomes of the Bantu Education System should be. The implementation of this education system,

> this cornerstone of apartheid ideology-in-practice wreaked havoc on the education of black people in South Africa, and deprived and disadvantaged millions for decades. Its devastating personal, political and economic effects continue to be felt and wrestled with today.
>
> (South Africa History Online: Bantu Education
> Act No. 47 of 1953, 2014)

The truth underlying this statement will be very much understood through the stories of the food insecure within their socioeconomic contexts and the interpretation of the meanings they make of their food insecurity.

Through the *Promotion of Bantu Self-Government Act 46* of 1959, the homelands were established by ethnicity: Venda, Lebowa, QwaQwa, Ciskei, KwaZulu, KaNgwane, Transkei, Gazankulu, KwaNdeble and Bophuthatswana. They were areas to which the apartheid government moved a number of the Blacks and had the intention of moving all of them, according to their different cultures. This meant for example, that the Xhosa, no matter where they had been living, were assigned to go to Ciskei and Transkei, KwaZulu was for the Zulu, Lebowa for the Pedi and Northern Ndebele, Gazankulu for the Shagaan and Tsonga and Venda for the Venda. Two of these homelands were in what is today the Free State Province: Boputhatswana for the Tswana and QwaQwa for the Basotho (New History: "Homelands or dumping grounds?" 2014; South African History Online: "The Homelands", 2014, para. 6).

The objective was to separate the Africans from the Whites, as well as from each other, and to make them responsible for governing themselves independently. The goal of the apartheid government was to make South Africa only for Whites and independent homelands for Blacks, meaning that the Blacks would be forced to support themselves in these areas. Between 1963 and 1971, all the homelands received a legislative assembly and a form of self-government. Furthermore, through the *Bantu Homelands Citizenship Act* of 1970, the apartheid government promulgated that Blacks living throughout South Africa become legal citizens of their particular homeland, even though they did not live there. Blacks could then only exercise their rights through their homeland governments and did not have citizenship of South Africa or civil or political rights in the country.

Despite the original purpose of the developmental policy as formulated by the apartheid government to foster self-sustainable development in the homelands, this did not come to pass. Development in the areas was slow for, among other factors, the African governments lacked resources and the homelands were situated in areas that were economically unproductive. Moreover, they were densely populated; there were too many people in not-too-fertile lands, making it difficult for the people to feed themselves (Newman and De Lannoy, 2014). In its focus on getting Blacks out of South Africa, the apartheid government forcibly removed Black rural settlers, redundant farm laborers and unemployed urban Blacks to the homelands, as well as group areas removals in the towns, and evictions of farm laborers, to a total of approximately 3.5 million people (New History: "Homelands or dumping grounds?" 2014). Many Blacks who had been born in the urban areas were suddenly forced to live in a 'homeland' that was created for them by the White government. Moreover, even those who continued to live in the townships had citizenship and rights only in their respective homeland. The economic struggles in the homelands were depicted through the fact that

> . . . millions of Blacks had to leave the Bantustans daily and work in the mines, for White farmers and other industries in the cities. The homelands served as labour reservoirs, housing the unemployed and releasing them when their labour was needed in White South Africa.
> (South African History Online: The Homelands, 2014, para. 6)

During apartheid, the system of migrant labor continued, but despite the Bantu Homeland policy and the forced removals of Blacks from the cities, the townships remained, for the Blacks, as well as Coloreds and Indians, in different areas of the country. They also provided cheap labor for the Whites. Families continued to be separated, as men lived in the cities without their wives, and miners lived on the mine premises where their wives and children could not stay with them. More and more women came into the towns and cities to work as domestic workers, further disrupting the family structure as they left their children behind under the care of their extended family members (South African History Online: Land, Labour and Apartheid, 2014).

The apartheid regime began to suffer serious setbacks in the 1980s, leading to some reforms. These were not sufficient to quell opposition to it, nonetheless. In 1990, President Frederik De Klerk began negotiations with the opposition to end the regime. The apartheid regime formally ended in 1994 with the first multiracial elections, which were won by the ANC, leading to Nelson Mandela becoming the first Black president of the country.

On April 27, 1994, with the new government of a democratic South Africa in power, the homelands or Bantustans ceased to exist and became part of the nine new provinces of South Africa: Western Cape, Eastern Cape, Northern Cape, Free State, North West, Gauteng, Limpopo, KwaZulu-Natal and Mpumalanga. There are also two impoverished independent kingdoms within the borders of the country: Lesotho, bordering with the Free State, Eastern Cape and KwaZulu-Natal Provinces; and Swaziland, bordering with KwaZulu-Natal and Mpumalanga Provinces, as well as with Mozambique. The economies of these kingdoms are closely intertwined with that of South Africa, and their peoples travel frequently between the nations.

The post-1994 republic of South Africa: poverty alleviation and food security programs

Over 20 years after the formal end of apartheid, household food insecurity is still rampant in South Africa, despite the implementation of the national and regional policies to achieve food security. When South Africa's first Black president, Nelson Mandela, came to power in 1994, he expressed the desire to create a more socially, economically and politically just nation inclusive of all its peoples. Several analysts of the process have explained, in detail, how the very process of transformation was corrupted from its conception (see, for example, Terreblanche, 2012; DuPreez, 2013), and this corruption led to the various national plans and programs not always being conceptualized in the best interests of the people and, furthermore, being implemented in the best ways possible. Numerous analysts have expressed that part of this failure has been a consequence of not joining the forces of the most qualified people – majority White – in the different sectors who were part of the economy during the apartheid era with the incoming generations of Black Africans who needed to be educated to eventually take over the economy. The constant lament and preoccupation in different sectors of the economy, especially over the last decade, is the realization that too many poorly qualified people have been placed in strategic positions in the public sector.

Most were placed because of political affiliation with the ANC, which has led to endemic corruption and poor government. One of the sectors that have been gravely affected by this is the agriculture and food production, distribution and trading sector. This realization has led to more overtures in recent times to create collaborations with some of the qualified people of the past. But let us focus on the issues of poverty alleviation and food security/insecurity, which are the themes of this book.

The first national plan that the ANC coalition government created in its first year of government to address the numerous social and economic problems that the poorer peoples of the country, majority African, were facing as a result of the years of apartheid was the 1994 RDP. Some of the most severe of these problems were: a failing economy; inadequate education and health care; a high rate of unemployment as a result of a lack of jobs; grossly insufficient housing; and a high rate of violence. As we shall see through people's stories in the following chapters, today, over 20 years later, these very same problems continue, albeit within the sociopolitical context of democracy, despite the numerous programs that have been implemented over the years.

The aim of the RDP was to bring together the people of the country and use the country's resources to confront the negative consequences of apartheid and create a democratic, non-racist and non-sexist future (African National Congress: Reconstruction and Development Programme, 1994). Beginning with the RDP, a number of priority policy objectives have been formulated by the successive governments, each with their corresponding programs focused on alleviating poverty in South Africa, restitution for the historically disadvantaged and building a stronger country. One of these programs was the Land Reform Programme. This program had three branches: land restitution; land redistribution (redistribution of lands to the Black Africans who had been deprived of land during greater part of the twentieth century); and land tenure reform.

In the RDP, food security was identified as a priority policy objective, and, over the following years, a number of programs directed towards improving the food security conditions of historically disadvantaged people were created. Improving their access to food was one part of these (African National Congress: Reconstruction and Development Programme, 1994). In the first ten years of beginning the path to democracy (1994–2004), among other things, the government used to give out food parcels to the needy. These parcels helped them greatly, and there was much improvement in alleviating poverty. In 2004, this monthly parcel consisted in 12.5 kg of mealie meal, 10 kg of rice, 12.5 kg of samp, 2 kg of beans and 2.5 litres of cooking oil, soap and toiletries. However, over the last decade, people in the Free State Province report that there has not been much improvement, and food parcels are neither monthly, nor do they contain the same amounts of food and other goods. They are much more irregular and smaller than they used to be.

The objective of food security was also enshrined as a fundamental right in the 1996 Constitution of the Republic of South Africa, which states that every citizen has the right to have access to sufficient food and water, and that the state will ensure the realization of this right (Constitution of the Republic of South Africa: "Statutes", 1996, Provision 27). Other social programs implemented through the different spheres of government were: child support grants; free health services for children between 0–6 years and pregnant and lactating women; pension funds for the elderly; and working for water and community public works. In the area of food security per se were: the Integrated Nutrition Programme; the Primary School Nutrition Programme; provincial community food garden initiatives such as Kgora and Xoshindlala; production loans scheme for small farmers; infrastructure grants for smallholder farmers; and the presidential tractor mechanization scheme (The Integrated Food Security Strategy for South Africa, 2002; Friedman and Bhengu, 2008). Building on the Land Reform Programme, in 2000, the Land Redistribution for Agriculture Development Programme (LRAD) was created. It aimed at redistributing land for farming purposes, intended to assist people in acquiring lease land for agricultural purposes.

In 2001, the government identified a number of areas in the country, which were gravely underdeveloped, areas it declared poverty nodes, or Nodal areas. Nodal areas are those that are,

> characterised by underdevelopment, contributing little to the GDP, absorbing the largest percentage of the country's population, incorporating the poorest of the rural and urban poor, structurally disconnected from both the First World and the global economy, and incapable of self-generated growth.
>
> (Department of Provincial and Local Government
> Programme of Action, 2005)

Subsequent to identifying these areas, the government indicated that they needed to focus on formulating strategies to overcome these conditions of underdevelopment and poverty within them. Toward this end, the Urban Renewal and Integrated Sustainable Rural Development Programmes were launched. Through these programs, the government's objective was to foster an integrated approach to policy and planning through intergovernmental cooperation in these poverty nodes. Afterwards, the Integrated Sustainable Rural Development Strategy and the War on Poverty Programme were also established. The Presidential Nodal Zones were part of these. In 2009, the government departments were reconfigured and the nodal areas were then integrated into the Comprehensive Rural Development Programme.

The objectives of all of these programs, and numerous others, were commendable, because of the government's objective to improve the living, health, social and economic conditions of the populace. Notwithstanding their commendable intentions, their implementation was disjointed because there were too many programs carried out simultaneously by too many different government departments, at times overlapping each other, creating an unsatisfactory situation. To correct this and refocus on food security as a priority objective, the South African government decided to formulate a national food security program "that would streamline, harmonize and integrate the diverse food security programmes into the Integrated Food Security Strategy" (IFSS)(Department: Agriculture. "The Integrated Food Security Strategy – South Africa", 2002, p. 5).

National food policies and programs

The IFSS document established that South Africa at the beginning of the twenty-first century faced five fundamental food security challenges: (i) to ensure the sufficient availability of food for all the population, in the present and the future; (ii) to foster the conditions for the matching of people's incomes to prices so as to ensure that each citizen have access to sufficient food; (iii) to empower citizens so that they make the best choices for nutritious and safe food; (iv) to create adequate safety nets and food emergency systems throughout the country so that people who are unable to meet their food needs from their own efforts may be provided for and to mitigate the extreme impact of natural and other disasters on people and (v) to have adequate and relevant information so as to be able to analyze, communicate, monitor, evaluate and report on the impact that the food security programs are having on the target population. In this document, food security is defined as "the physical, social and economic access by all households at all times to adequate, safe and nutritious food and clean water to meet their dietary and food preferences for a healthy and productive life" (Department: Agriculture. "The Integrated Food Security Strategy – South Africa", 2002, p. 6). This definition draws upon the definition of food security by the Food and Agriculture Organization of the United Nations (FAO) and corresponds to the definitions generally adopted by different multilateral organizations. The goal of the IFSS is to "eradicate hunger, malnutrition and food insecurity over 2015" (Department: Agriculture, "The Integrated Food Security Strategy – South Africa", 2002, p. 6).

Over the following years, through the IFSS, a number of policies and programs have been implemented towards achieving this goal, with varying degrees of success, failures and disappointments for the people who have most needed them: the impoverished and marginalized peoples of the society. After two decades of working towards ensuring food security, the government has stated that this has been achieved at a national level, but not at the household level. To achieve the objective of sustainable food security, all of the government departments in the country have a food security mandate, but not all of them comply with it. The rise in food prices around the world especially over the last decade, with the often-mentioned 2007–2008 food price crisis among these, has affected developing nations. South Africa has been hard hit with these price rises. The prices of staples such as wheat, corn, soybeans and rice have been rising significantly (Food and Agriculture Organization: The State of Food and Agriculture, 2014). Moreover, the neoliberal economic policies that the government implemented, for example, through the much-criticized macroeconomic policy framework, the GEAR strategy in 1996, have affected the production, trade, distribution and consumption of food for the people of South Africa.

Every year on October 16, World Food Day, attention is drawn to the situation of food security in South Africa in the South African media. One of the leading weekly newspapers, the *Mail & Guardian*, dedicates a special supplement to this issue in its edition of the World Food Day week. In its October 18 to 24, 2013, edition in celebration of World Food Day, the Department of Agriculture, Forestry and Fisheries (DAFF) dedicated this supplement to discussing the food situation in the country. In it, they explained that, "The reality is that 12-million South Africans have severely inadequate access to food. Even more distressing is the fact that while these South Africans suffer, the country, at a national level, is food secured" (DAFF, "Sustainable food systems", 2013, p. 1). These 12 million people represent 24% of the population. The department admitted that there is a structural household food insecurity problem in the country and that the main causes are the widespread chronic poverty and unemployment. The department also pointed to the importance of the IFSS and stated that "to address global food security challenges", the IFSS helps "to streamline, harmonize and integrate the diverse food security programmes" (DAFF, "Securing access", 2013, p. 3).

One recent strategy the South African government has formulated to combat the food insecurity problem is by motivating and supporting people in rural and urban areas to grow the food for their households and their communities so that they could have sustainable access to food. To this end, the government approved a Food Security and Nutrition Policy and initiated an intervention, *the Fetsa Tlala Integrated Food Production Initiative*, "which seeks to afford smallholder farmers, communities and households the ability to increase production of basic food, and increase access and availability of it to attain basic food security at household and local levels" (DAFF, "Securing access", 2013, p. 3).

This is an interesting turn of events in a country which, like many other countries in the Global South, has struggled with ensuring that its people have sustainable access to healthy food. As a result of its historical economic development, first shaped by colonization, then by apartheid, through which the agrarian sector declined and people in rural areas who historically produced their own food were forced off their lands and many went to the cities, the South African economy has been turned into a wage economy and most households today purchase food. Consequently, with rampant poverty and structural inequalities, the poorer households are the ones which have the least access to food. Like populations in many other parts of the world that had been previously colonized, then subject to bad governance and economic mismanagement, a dependency mentality was created in South Africa. The South African professor, novelist and playwright, Zakes Mda, in his novel *The Heart of Redness*, brilliantly illustrates, through his fictionalized, yet very real, depiction of contemporary rural South African society, how the dependency mentality that has been created has been detrimental for rural communities in this country. The following excerpt explains this well.

"That is the danger of doing things for the people instead of with the people" adds Camagu "it is happening throughout the country. The government talks of delivery and of upliftment . . . The notions of delivery and upliftment have turned our people into passive recipients of programs conceived by so-called experts who know nothing about the lives of rural communities. People are denied the right to shape their own destiny. Things are done for them. The world owes them a living. A dependency mentality is reinforced in their minds".

(Mda, 2000, p. 180)

Talking with people throughout the country, one comes to realize that this dependency mentality is not only evident among some people of rural communities, as Mda describes, but also among those in poor urban and semi-urban areas. The government seemingly now wants to reverse this trend by motivating people to produce food and not only provide food to them. This is interesting because it goes beyond what the definition of food security stipulates, which emphasizes that people should have sustainable access to healthy food and clean water, but not necessarily that people must *produce* their own food. Within the conceptualization of food security that is more widely known and accepted (see Appendix), a government needs to provide its people with this food, be it from national production or imported. Further highlighting the importance of food security in the country, the South African Human Rights Commission, which oversees the provision of economic and social rights to the people of the nation, between November 2013 and February 2014 embarked on the Right to Food Campaign (South African Human Rights Commission, 2014). This campaign had already been conceptualized in March 2003 at a seminar organized by FIAN International (FoodFirst Action Network), at which the array of participating South African organizations came together to discuss approaches to implementing the right to food in the country. Central to their discussions was the need to create a campaign to co-ordinate activities that would assert and advance the right to food.

Consequently, it is quite remarkable that DAFF explained the underlying reasoning of the Fetsa Tlala Integrated Food Production Initiative as the following: "feeding the nation is not about providing food; it is also about providing the means, through policies, for citizens to take part in the production of their own food" (DAFF, "Sustainable food systems", 2013, p. 1). This is of fundamental importance to understand the context of people's struggles within poverty, and with sustainable access to healthy food in South Africa, because it seems to highlight that the government realizes that it is essential that people need to participate in producing their own food, but will it help them sufficiently to not only alleviate their food insecurity, but also to achieve household food security, which is the objective established by the government? This is an important question one needs to ask in the discussion on food insecurity in the country.

Two years later, in the *Mail & Guardian* October 16, 2015, World Food Day celebration supplement, the analysis of food insecurity focused directly on the relationship between poverty and access to food in the nation. Despite the implementation of the food security policies described above, statistics showed that approximately 29 million people faced food insecurity. Fourteen million of these could not afford food, and 15 million had to choose between eating three meals or paying their basic expenses (Pugh, October 16, 2015). This is over half the population of South Africa. Every year, old and new programs to achieve household food security and sustainability are proposed, some of which are implemented and are successful, whereas others are not.

To better understand the situation of food insecurity/security, it is important to examine the policies of DAFF, the main – but not only – torchbearer for food security in the country, further. In the *2012/13–2016/17 Strategic Development Plan* of DAFF, Food Security and Agrarian Reform constitute one category of the five 'programme deliverables' established. The other four deliverables are: Agricultural Production, Health and Food Safety; Economic Development, Trade and Marketing; Forestry and Natural Resources Management; and Fisheries Management (DAFF, 2012). Within the program deliverables, food security is a sub-program which

> provides national frameworks to promote the Sustainable Household Food Security Programme through improving the production systems of subsistence and smallholder producers in the agriculture, forestry and fishery sector to achieve food security livelihoods and facilitate the provision of outputs, implements and infrastructure support.
>
> (DAFF, 2012, p. 47)

To achieve its objective of ensuring food security, the department states that it "plays a critical role in ensuring agricultural production by means of promoting entrepreneurship and providing support to smallholder farmers" (DAFF, "Sustainable food systems", 2013, p. 1). The mantra of the department, as it joins with provincial departments of agriculture, is "one family, one food garden" to ensure increased access to food production, so people in rural and urban areas can sustain themselves and their families. Another idea underlying this is that South Africa's population in 2014 was approximately 50 million and grain consumption is about 14 million tons. By 2030, however, the population is expected to be about 59 million, and they calculate that a minimum grain stock of about 25 million tons will be required to feed this population; thus, there is a need to increase food production. What is interesting about this is that they are not following the policy that has been used in both South Africa in the past and in other countries, where what has been done is to increase the production of commercial farming. To the contrary, the government states that the objective now is to move away from thinking that producing food is the responsibility only of commercial farmers. Following this line of reasoning, DAFF further explains that "to ease pressure on farmers . . . South Africans must cultivate and nurture a small scale farming sector and cooperatives to assist us in firstly, creating employment, and secondly, helping us create sustainable SMMEs" (p. 1).

Elucidating the reasoning underlying its sustainable food security policies, the government delineated some of the challenges South Africa faces: "South Africa, as is the case in many developing countries, is facing challenges of poverty, unemployment, climate change, crime/safety on farms, increases in the cost of living, economic recession, the Aids pandemic and surging food prices, among others" (p. 1). They are also conscious of the fact that food insecurity and environmental degradation are inherently linked. To this end, they explained that "As the world's population is growing and the pressure on food supplies increases, people are forced to use practices which increase yield in the short term but are devastating for land in the medium or long term" (p. 1). The importance of the government understanding and elucidating the significance of this linkage cannot be emphasized enough. This is fundamental in achieving food security as well as protecting the agricultural lands for present and future generations, which are an essential part of constructing food sovereignty.

Another important explanation is achieving food security through interrelationships between different actors in the food system. As the Minister for Agriculture, Forestry and Fisheries, Tina Joemat-Pettersson, stated in that 2013 *Mail & Guardian* article, "Food security will only be achieved through links between other government programs, the agri-industry, the agro-processing and retail sectors, the research-based institutions, the NGOs and civil society" (p. 1). This is a very eloquent statement, and the minister seems to be conscious of the need for these necessary interrelationships to be created. The question remains, however, are these other actors in the food system willing to work together on these programs? What would be their incentives to do so? History has shown us that agri-industry and the agro-processing sectors do not necessarily want any of their power – and, moreover, their profits – to decrease.

As explained above, all of the government departments have the mandate to work together to achieve food security, but not all of them necessarily comply with this mandate. Some of the departments work on their own, some collaborate, and some have no food security programs. The Department of Agriculture, Forestry and Fisheries, together with its provincial departments, also works with the Department of Rural Development and Land Reform, the Department of Health, and the Department of Social Development to fulfill this mandate. In Chapter 5, where people who live in rural areas tell their stories, is explained how these departments are developing these mandates in the Free State Province.

In the Department of Social Development's *2009–2013 Strategic Development Plan*, one of the core objectives is *Food for All*. To fulfill this objective, the department formulated that

> Dealing with malnutrition in very deprived areas as identified by the Department of Health is an urgent challenge. As lead department of the Social Protection and Community Development Cluster, we will continue to work with the Department of Agriculture, Forestry and Fisheries and the Department of Rural Development and Land Reform to co-ordinate the government's efforts

to addressing citizens' rights to food. Plans for rolling the "Food for All" programme are far advanced, and implementation will begin in areas where levels of malnutrition are very high.

(Department of Social Development, 2008, p. 4)

In recent years, an Inter-Ministerial Committee (IMC) on Food Security, which is jointly led by the Ministers of Social Development and of Agriculture, Forestry and Fisheries, has been formed, with the focus on fighting food insecurity, hunger and malnutrition. In its 2012–2015 Strategic Development Plan, the Department of Social Development delineates under the objective of *Food for All* that

The IMC has been tasked with delivering an integrated, intersectoral food security programme based on the Brazilian "Fome Zero" (Zero Hunger) programme which has played a key role in addressing citizens' rights to food. Efforts to observe this right will generate demand for the supply of nutritious food, and the government intends to use the state procurement of food as a catalyst for local food production and procurement. Female-headed households, children, people with disabilities, and people who are falling prey to gaps in social assistance will form part of the primary target.

(Department of Social Development, 2012, p. 13, pt. 3.4.1)

Overall, the government initiatives and programs to achieve food security in South Africa are certainly commendable. It is indeed very important for a government to understand that food security does not only mean ensuring that people have sustainable access to healthy food, whether this be produced nationally or imported, but that food insecurity is shaped by numerous factors, including structural poverty, social and economic inequalities and inequities, as well as land degradation and climate change, among others. The measures explained above that they are using to carve the path towards household and community food security are important. We have to ask certain questions, however. When we look at the policies and programs the government is implementing to achieve household food security, we need to ask, are these fostering democratic agency in the people of South Africa? Moreover, why would it be necessary to foster this agency?

In the October 2013 overview DAFF gave of the household food insecurity in South Africa, it cited former president and lifelong freedom fighter Nelson Mandela as saying, "We do not want freedom without bread, nor do we want bread without freedom. We must provide for all the fundamental rights and freedoms associated with a democratic society" (DAFF, "Sustainable food systems", 2013, p. 1). The department cites this as support for its food security initiatives. Thus, we can say that the government *seems* to consider democracy as a fundamental part of achieving its goal of food security.

Based on this, should we not ask ourselves if it is important to understand whether, in the meaning that people make of their own food insecurity, and that of others, they have fostered any democratic agency to overcome their food insecurity challenges? Furthermore, we should highlight understanding the importance of centering on the food insecure as important agents, not only in their own food systems, but also those of their communities and regions. There are several food programs which are already essential to the lives of food insecure South Africans today. One of these is the National School Nutrition Programme.

The National School Nutrition Programme

The National School Nutrition Programme, or the school feeding scheme, as it is popularly known in South Africa, is a food program initiated by the Department of Basic Education that touches the lives of many poor South Africans who have children attending school. Through it, children are given one hot cooked meal a day at school, thus ensuring that the most food insecure children have at least that one meal. It also helps their parents to be able to stretch out their meager incomes a little further. It is directed at the public schools in the country, and its objectives are:

- to contribute to enhanced learning capacity through school feeding programms
- to promote and support food production and improve food security in school communities
- to strengthen nutrition education in schools and communities (Department of Basic Education: National School Nutrition Programme, 2014)

All the learners at the schools are beneficiaries of the program in recent years, not only the poorest learners in each school, as used to be in the first years of the program's implementation. Moreover, since 2009, the program has expanded to secondary schools. Even though the program is an initiative of the Department of Basic Education, its implementation and success have been the result of the cooperation between the National Department, the Provincial Departments, District Offices and other partners.

The Statistics South Africa General Household Survey of 2013 shows that almost three-quarters of public school learners were benefitting from feeding schemes, with the percentage of learners steadily increasing over three years, from 67.8% in 2010 to 74.5% in 2013. In the Free State Province, this percentage increased from 64.7 in 2010 to 77.3 in 2013 and to 78.1 in 2015 (Statistics South Africa: "General household survey 2013", 2014; "General household survey", 2016).

The social grants

Within the South African government's policy of social benefits, formulated with the objective of being a direct means to combat poverty, the government provides a number of social grants for lower income people through the South African Social Security Agency (SASSA). This social assistance system is one of the largest on the African continent. The Treasury's National Budget Review for 2013/14 revealed that 3% of the country's gross domestic product is dedicated to spending on social grants. Furthermore, this spending was projected to rise from R118 billion in 2013/14 to R145 billion by 2016, as more people are covered (National Treasury, 2014). In 2016, over 16 million people in South Africa who are vulnerable to poverty and need state support received social grants. Not only South African citizens are eligible for grants; so are permanent residents and refugees who are living in South Africa. The grants available include: child support grant; older person's grant; disability grant; grant-in-aid; care dependency grant; war veteran's grant; and foster child grant. To be able to qualify for any of the grants, among other requirements beneficiaries have to have or demonstrate to have applied for a government-issued ID and, in the cases of children, for their caregivers to have or demonstrate to have applied for the children's birth certificates. Unfortunately, these requirements sometimes prevent people from receiving the grants because, for a number of reasons, they did not have this documentation. All of these grants, except for the war veteran's and grant-in-aid, are the most commonly received grants among the people whose stories are told in this book.

To receive the disability grant, in addition to the ID and other requirements, the beneficiary cannot have an income of more than R5 150 per month if single, and R10 300 as combined income if married. The grant is conferred for a maximum of R1 350 per month. For the foster child grant, together with the ID and child's birth certificate, among other requirements, the court has to legally place the child in your care. This grant is for R830 per child. It is important to mention, however, that while the legal placement is being processed and if the child is already in the home, with the satisfactory assessment of the home conditions by a social worker, the foster parent(s) can receive a temporary foster care stipend of about R300 per child. The care dependency grant is to care for a child who has a severe disability and is in need of full-time and special care. Similar to the foster child grant, the child must be legally placed with the caregiver by the court. The caretaker must not have an income over R13 500 per month if single and must not have a combined income of over R27 000 per month if married. Notwithstanding, this income limit does not apply to foster parents.

The child support grant is directed to a child/children's primary caregiver, be it a parent or a relative, who is in need. It is provided as help to raise the child the caregiver is looking after. The caregiver must earn no more than R3 100 per month if single and have a combined income of no more than R6 200 per month if married. This grant cannot be given for more than six children who are not the caregiver's biological or legally adopted children. This grant is R320 per child per month. A number of the lower-income people throughout the province I became acquainted with received this grant. All grants for children are given until they are 18 years old. The older person's grant used to be called the Old Age Pension and is paid to people 60 years and older. To qualify for the grant, the beneficiary cannot be earning more than R5 150 per month if single and more than R10 300 in combined income if married. This grant is for R1 350 per month from ages 60–75 and R1 370 per month from age 75 onwards (South African Government: Social Benefits, 2014).

Many lower-income older people around the country receive this grant, and many of their younger relatives, children, grandchildren, nieces, nephews etc. live with them and benefit from it. Over the years since these social benefits were granted, the number of beneficiaries has grown, and, at present, almost one-third of the population receives at least one social grant. Statistics South Africa's 2015 General Household Survey found that over the 12-year period 2003–2015, the number of beneficiaries of social grants grew from 12.7% to 30.1%. Over the same period, the number of households in the country receiving at least one social grant grew from 29.9% to 45.5%. A little over a quarter of the Black population, 33.5%, and Colored population, 27%, received a social grant, compared to 12% of the Indian/Asian and 6.3% of the White population. These are telling indicators of poverty along the racial lines; however, they must be read with caution, for they only indicate persons who actively sought grants, not those who are necessarily most in need of them. In the Free State Province, 31.0% of individual beneficiaries received social grants and 52.4% of households. (Statistics South Africa: "General household survey 2015", 2016).

Social grants have undoubtedly benefitted the lower-income population of the country, for they provide the people with monies to assist them with their living costs. To **assist** them is the operational word here, for the grants were never meant to constitute the entirety, or almost the entirety of people's income, as they have become in the case of many throughout the country. It is important to understand that the poor in South Africa are living within multidimensional poverty, as explained in the introduction. The levels of unemployment and underemployment are high, the level of education among the African population remains low, salaries for the lesser educated are low and the cost of living is continually rising. Within this context, the social grants are not achieving their objective of supporting people as they make a better future for themselves and their families, until they would not need the grants any longer. To the contrary, they have become in many instances the sole source of income and are stretched to cover expenses that they were not conceptualized for. The child support grant is a good case to illustrate this.

Recent research from the University of Johannesburg Centre for Social Development in Africa determined that while this grant has definitely been beneficial for the disadvantaged children and youth in South Africa, its full benefit has been undermined because other services, which are meant to be free, such as education and primary health care, have been failing. Consequently, families have had to use the money from the grant to cover these costs. As Dr. Tessa Hochfeld, University of Johannesburg Centre for Social Development in Africa Senior Researcher explained in a September 5, 2016, article in the *Mail & Guardian*, "the grant is failing to deliver social justice because it is doing more than what it is meant to do," (Skosana, 2016, "Working too hard: Social grants stretched thin within a failing system"). These findings are supported by numerous other studies through-out the country and beyond of the social grants, poverty, and other social and economic issues in South Africa.

Having understood the background of these social programs that shape the new South African society, let us turn to the place which is the home to the people whose stories are told here: the Free State Province.

The Free State Province: history and contemporary societal dynamics

The Free State Province that we know today was formerly known as the Orange Free State and was created through the Great Trek (*Groot Trek* in Afrikaans), which took place from 1835 to the early 1840s, shaping the history of South Africa. About 12 000–14 000 Boers, who became known as the *Voortrekker* (which in Afrikaans means 'the forerunners of the Trek'), were the pioneers in their quest to move away from the Cape Colony, and the policies of the British government, forging their way into the interior of the country, with some settling in the area just north of the Orange River. At the time, the Orange River deline-ated the border between the Cape Colony and the rest of what became South Africa. In their intent to settle in the area and found a number of towns and farms, the Voortrekkers came into conflict with the indigenous groups, and in particular with the Basotho under the leadership of their king, Moshoeshoe. By 1848, the Voortrekkers declared part of this area that they had settled in as the Orange Free Sovereignty. After sovereignty was granted to the Transvaal Republic, which was to the north, it became the Boer Sovereign republic, ZAR (*Zuid-Afrikaansche Republiek*, in Afrikaans, or *South African Republic*, in English). The British rec-ognized the independence of the Orange River Sovereignty in 1854, and, thus, the Orange Free State (*Oranje – Vrystaat* in Afrikaans) was born. This Boer Republic incorporated both the former Orange River Sovereignty and the traditions of the Winburg – Potchefstroom Republic. It had numerous conflicts with the Basotho, mainly over who owned the land and where to delineate the border between the Orange Free State and the Basotho Kingdom, as well as with the British. It was the British, however, who ended up determining the border, after the Basotho Kingdom became a British Protectorate and the Second Basotho War came to an end in 1868. To conciliate with the Boers, the British decided to give the Orange Free State much of the most fertile Basotho lands, consequently drawing the cur-rent border between the Kingdom of Lesotho and the Free State Province.

The Second Anglo-Boer war (1899–1902) further determined the history of the province. During the war, the Orange Free State joined forces with the ZAR in their battle against the British. Nonetheless, the Boers lost the war in 1902 and the Boer republics became British colonies. After the war, the name of the Orange Free State was changed to the Orange River Colony, and in 1910 the Orange River Colony became one of the provinces of what became known as the Union of South Africa. With its inclusion as a province, the name was changed back to the

Orange Free State. It remained with this name for the following decades, through the times of apartheid and after the country became the Republic of South Africa in 1961 (Cameron and Spies, 1992). After South Africa's transition to democracy in 1994, the Orange Free State became a South African province and the name was changed once again, now to the Free State Province, as it is known today.

The establishment of the Union of South Africa in 1910 was the founding of the country that we know today as the Republic of South Africa. Through this establishment, the colonies of the Cape, Natal, Transvaal and the Orange Free State, which were previously separate, became provinces of the Union. The Union, however, was not an independent entity; it was established with dominion status under the British, which meant that even though it was no longer a colony, it was not free to leave the British Empire, nor ignore the monarchy. It finally achieved its independence in 1961, under the apartheid regime (Cameron and Spies, 1992; South African History Online: National Party, 2014).

The Free State covers 10.6% of the total land area of the country, and at last count in the 2011 Census, has a population of 2.7 million in its four district municipalities and one metropolitan municipality. It is the second least populated province in the country. The least populated province is the Northern Cape, with a population of 1.1 million people, and the most populated is Gauteng (home to Johannesburg), bordering on the north with the Free State, with 13.2 million people (Statistics South Africa: "General household survey 2015", 2016). The province is home to the judicial capital of South Africa, the city of Bloemfontein. In addition to its political importance, it is a largely agricultural province, shaped socially and economically by its Afrikaner farming history (Free State Online: Free State, 2013) and has historically been considered the breadbasket of South Africa (The Local Government Handbook: Free State, 2013). Its economy is still mainly based on agriculture, and many of the farms are still in the hands of Whites, but it also has a number of goldfields. Bothaville, in the Lejweleputswa District, is one of the most important maize centers of the country.

Approximately 87.6% of the population is Black African, 8.7% White, 3.1% Colored and 0.4% Indian, Asian or other ethnic groups (Statistics South Africa: Census in brief, 2012). During the years of apartheid, Indians were prohibited from living in the Free State, but since the period of democracy began in 1994, a growing number of Indians have been making the province their home. As we will see from the demographic tables in the following chapters, however, even today they have a small presence in the province. They are more known for being merchants in the city, and in the townships there has been an influx of other South East Asians, such as Bangladeshis, who have tuck shops there. Coloreds have also held a rather different cultural space to Blacks and Indians in South Africa because, of the three non-White racial groups, they are the only ones who speak Afrikaans as their mother tongue. They were also politically oppressed by the Whites, forcibly segregated into their own residential areas, as were all non-White populations, so they shared some of the same struggles of the others, but not all, which is evident in the societal dynamics of the country. In the later years of apartheid, Coloreds and Indians were allowed some political representation – but not effective power – through the formation of the Tricameral Parliament in 1985, in which they were included in the Houses of Representatives and Delegates, respectively. Blacks were excluded under the pretext that that they had political power in their respective homelands, whereas Coloreds and Indians had no homelands (South Africa History Online: Tricameral Parliament, 2014).

The most widely spoken languages in the Free State Province as the first language are Sesotho (64.2%) and Afrikaans (12.7%), followed by IsiXhosa (7.5%), Tswana (5.2%) and Zulu (4.4%). English is the first language of 2.9% of the population, followed by sign language (1.2%), IsiNdebele (0.4%), Sepedi (0.3%), Xitsonga (0.3%) and other languages (0.6%) (Statistics South Africa: Census in brief, 2012; South African Government: Provinces, 2014). Due to the province being historically an Afrikaner dominated one, most Blacks over the age of 40 speak Afrikaans. English is also widely spoken as a second or third language, and it is taught at school from fourth grade onwards. Classes at university level throughout the province are taught in English and the University of the Free State, formerly an Afrikaans-language-only university until 1994, is today a dual-language institution (English-Afrikaans). The issue of this, and other universities continuing to dictate lectures in Afrikaans, is a major issue in the country. The capital of the province is Bloemfontein, which, together with its semi-urban areas of Botshabelo, Mangaung and Thaba Nchu, has a population of 747 431, of which 83.3% are Black African (Statistics South Africa: Mangaung, 2013).

The food situation and food programs in the Free State Province

Since its time as a Boer Republic, the Free State was always quite successful as an agricultural region. This situation continued throughout the twentieth century as part of Union and during the apartheid government. During this time. the province was a major contributor to the national agricultural economy, by 1994 producing 40% of the maize that went to market and 50% of the wheat in the country. It was also a significant producer of sorghum, peanuts, red meat, cotton and wool, with an increasing horticultural production (Free State Mission on Rural Investment, 1997). With the land reform, rural development and other economic and social policies that have gone into effect since 1994, the economy of the Free State has changed substantially. While it still remains agricultural, the agricultural production has decreased. Today, only 24.4% of the households are agricultural, while 75.6% of the households are not (Statistics South Africa: Agricultural Statistics, 2013), and a considerable percentage of the impoverished population is unemployed and is living off social grants.

The Free State today has a poverty level of 61.9%. We need to place this level of poverty in context in South Africa: Guateng has the lowest level of poverty (33%), the Western Cape (35.4%), North West (61.4%), then the Free State (61.9%), Northern Cape (63%), KwaZulu-Natal (65%), Mpumalanga (67.1%), Eastern

Cape (70.6%) and Limpopo (78.9%) (Statistics South Africa: Poverty, 2016). Of the Free State population living in poverty that is employed, many receive very low wages that barely allow them to survive. In Mangaung Metropolitan Municipality, for example, which comprises Bloemfontein and Mangaung, as well as the semi-urban areas of Botshabelo and Thaba Nchu, 27.7% of the economically active (employed or unemployed but looking or work) people are unemployed, while 37.2% of the 150 128 economically active youth (15–34 years) in the area are unemployed (Statistics South Africa: Mangaung, 2016). In the province, 5.4% of the inhabitants have severely inadequate access to food, and 21.1% have inadequate access (Statistics South Africa: "General household survey 2015", 2016).

Despite 20 years of Black African government in the province, one can perceive in daily life that some societal-racial structures and dynamics remain relatively unchanged, and race relations remain rather tense. One example of the relatively unchanged societal-racial structures is in the townships and other poor areas. The poor Black Africans there still mainly live in their Black townships, the Colored live mainly in theirs, somewhat separated from the Blacks, and the poor Whites mainly live in their own sections of the cities and towns, as was the case during apartheid. There are also some lower-income areas where Blacks, Whites and Coloreds do live together. Another example is that the more affluent Whites still occupy a superior place in the provincial society, as they are the majority of farmers, skilled laborers and professionals. Further, there have been a number of race crimes and incidents over the past few years in the Free State. These include Black Africans attacking older White farmers and sometimes killing them. These crimes and other incidents have exacerbated White fear of Blacks, not helping the cause of improving race relations in the province at a time when this is sorely needed as Whites and Blacks learn to live with each other and engage in societal dynamics quite different to those they were historically accustomed to.

As I have explained both in Chapter 1 and above, nearly one-fourth of the people in the province have inadequate access to food, and the provincial government has been implementing food programs and initiatives to confront this situation. In 2015, 15.7% of households in the province reported missing a meal (Statistics South Africa: "Free State Community Survey results 2016", 2017). In my view, the issues of food security/insecurity and sustainability in this province have a powerful place at the table of discussion because within them, the structural poverty and socioeconomic, political and cultural inequities that oppress the people are manifested.

As was the case of all the provinces in South Africa, the Free State has been subject to the food security policies and programs I have described above that the government has implemented since 1994, the most recent of which has been to formulate sustainable food security policies and programs. Discussing the reasoning underlying its sustainable food security policies, the government delineates some of the challenges South Africa faces: "South Africa, as is the case in many developing countries, is facing challenges of poverty, unemployment, climate change, crime/safety on farms, increases in the cost of living, economic recession, the Aids pandemic and surging food prices, among others" (DAFF, "Sustainable food systems", 2013, p. 1). The government is also conscious of the fact that food insecurity and environmental degradation are inherently linked. To this end, officials explain that "As the world's population is growing and the pressure on food supplies increases, people are forced to use practices which increase yield in the short term but are devastating for land in the medium or long term" (DAFF, "Sustainable food systems", 2013, p. 1).

Following the directives of the national government to decrease poverty and improve food security and sustainability in the province, the Free State provincial Department of Agriculture and Rural Development has created several programs to achieve these goals. The programs and initiatives of the Department are to contribute to the following five strategic goals: (i) vibrant, equitable and sustainable rural communities contributing towards food security for all; (ii) sustainable rural and agricultural development; (iii) animal and plant health, food safety and effective risk management; (iv) optimizing stakeholder relations; and (v) sustainable resource management (Department of Agriculture and Rural Development: Strategic objectives, 2013).

Among the programs it has developed specifically in the province to achieve its goals are *ReKgaba Ka Diratswana* and *Mohoma Mobung*. *ReKgaba Ka Diratswana* is "a household food production program that promotes the establishment of food gardens for personal consumption in addressing food insecurity and poverty alleviation" (Department of Agriculture and Rural Development, "Qabathe bolster", 2013, para.12). This program is directed to the most vulnerable households in the province and has the objective of helping to create more than 2 800 households food gardens, by providing these households with agricultural starter packs (seeds, some equipment and know-how) (Department of Agriculture and Rural Development, "Qabathe bolster", 2013). In Chapter 5, I describe how this program is being carried out in Thabo Mofutsanyana Municipality. Mohoma Mobung is directed to addressing the national government's Zero Hunger Strategy. As formulated by the Department, this initiative is:

> a multi-year mega Public and Private Partnership business concept, which revolves around income generation through farming in the rural area of the province, and the creation of on and off-farm agribusiness, value chain enterprises and Black Economic Empowerment. It is a strategic approach that aims at addressing low household incomes by increasing agricultural production, value and profitability of household agricultural production, Agroprocessing and Marketing. It includes crop, fisheries and livestock, related agro-processing and agribusiness enterprises and market access concerns . . . The total budget required is more than R 1.2 billion and has the potential of creating more than 10 000 decent permanent jobs and more than 100 000 indirect jobs.
>
> (Department of Agriculture and Rural Development, 2013, para. 1, 3)

Further to its own initiatives, the Free State Department of Agriculture and Rural Development has joined forces with the Department of Social Development to implement greater access to food for the poor and vulnerable. Furthermore, academic institutions in the province and in other provinces also focus on improving food security in the Free State. One of these institutions is the University of the Free State, which mainly, but not exclusively, through its Faculty of Natural and Agricultural Sciences, has been doing research and establishing programs and other initiatives towards combatting food insecurity.

There have been a number of studies on food security done in South Africa in recent years. The majority of these have focused on the urban areas, such as in Western Cape, Guateng and KwaZulu-Natal Provinces, which are two of the most populated provinces – with KwaZulu-Natal being one of the breadbaskets of the country – as well as in the poorest and most rural provinces such as the Northern Cape, Limpopo, Mpumalanga and the Eastern Cape. The Free State is a province that has been relatively understudied in comparison. Nonetheless, in recent years, in line with the national objective of achieving food security for all, there has been increasing research, as well as a number of programs and initiatives. These have mainly followed three trends. The largest trend is with regard to finding ways to increase food production, as well as food production and sustainability. The second trend is to understand food security as related to nutrition and public health, and the third is situating food security within the realm of poverty and community development.

Some of the studies done have been nationwide surveys, such as the 2013 and 2015 Statistics South Africa General Household Surveys mentioned above. The 2013 survey, for example, determined that in terms of *vulnerability to hunger*, the percentage of households in the country decreased from 23.8% in 2002 to 11.4% in 2013. During this period, there was, however, an increase in 2008 to 16%, which was concomitant with the worldwide trend of greater food insecurity as a consequence of the 2007–2008 global food crisis, which caused a sharp rise in food prices. With regard to households that *had limited access to food*, the percentage of these declined from 23.9% in 2010 to 23.1% in 2013. This was only 0.8%, which is minimal, especially in light of the number of food security programs that the government has been carrying out since 1994, and as a more focused effort, since 2002 through the IFSS. The households with *more limited access to food* decreased from 28.6% in 2010 to 26.0% in 2013 and 22.6% in 2015. North West Province had the most serious problems of access to food, where 37.3% of its households had inadequate or severely inadequate access in 2013 and 39% in 2015. The Free State Province was the fifth province with serious food insecurity problems, where 25.8% of the households suffered from inadequate or severely inadequate access to food (Statistics South Africa: "General Household Survey 2015", 2016).

Other studies, as well as research and policy papers, focus on urban food insecurity, which has become a more urgent issue because of the influx to inner-city urban areas, such as Capetown, Johannesburg and Durban. Quite a few have been done with regard to urban food security in the major cities by the African Food Security Urban Network (AFSUN), an institute at the University of Capetown, which has produced a series of policy and research papers specifically focused on raising the profile of urban food security issues in Africa (e.g. Crush and Frayne, 2010; Crush, Hovorka and Tevera, 2010; Battersby, 2012). These papers focus on bringing to the fore the urgency of understanding and addressing food insecurity among the urban dwellers, particularly the poor and vulnerable. They focus on the large urban areas both in South Africa (Capetown, Johannesburg, Durban) and in the rest of Africa, particularly Southern Africa. Bloemfontein, which is the largest city in the Free State, is not considered in these studies. Labadarios et al. (2011), on their part, did a review of national surveys of food security in South Africa. Other universities also have centers that are focused on insecurity, such as the African Centre for Food Security at the University of KwaZulu-Natal. The University of the Free State is also focusing on food insecurity among its students, as it has found that many students do not have enough food and often skip meals. I describe this situation in Chapter 4.

SANHANES-1 (Shisana et al., 2013) investigated food security as related to adequate nutrition and health. The findings showed that with a 95% Confidence Interval (CI), in the Free State Province, 39.3% of the population was food secure, 31.9% was at risk of hunger and 28.8% experienced hunger. The instrument used in this study to evaluate hunger was the Community Childhood Hunger Identification Project (CCHIP), which attempts to quantitatively capture through a survey predictable reactions and responses based on the following feelings:

- Feelings of uncertainty or anxiety over food (situation, resources, or supply);
- Perceptions that food is of insufficient quantity (for adults and children);
- Perceptions that food is of insufficient quality (includes aspects of dietary diversity, nutritional adequacy, preference);
- Reported reductions of food intake (for adults and children);
- Reported consequences of reduced food intake (for adults and children); and
- Feelings of shame for resorting to socially unacceptable means to obtain food resources (Coates et al., 2007 in Shisana et al., 2013, p. 145).

These feelings are very prominent in the stories that people told about their food insecurity and the meanings they make of the same. SANHANES – 1 also found that in the Free State Province, 8.9% of the population have low general nutrition knowledge, whereas 61.7% has medium general nutrition knowledge and 29.4% have high nutrition knowledge, making it second in nutrition knowledge only to the Western Cape, where 35.7% of the population have high nutrition knowledge. This is a very interesting finding; that the overwhelming majority of the people of the Free State have a medium to high knowledge of what good nutrition is and how it is related to health and in particular to non-communicable diseases (NCDs), such as hypertension, cardiac illnesses, cancer and obesity, of which there are high rates in the country. I perceived this as well in my own research.

My analysis, however, is not quantitative, but qualitative and focused on people facing food insecurity within some areas in the Free State Province. In the next chapter, I begin to narrate some of the stories of these people.

References

African National Congress (ANC). (1994). *The reconstruction and development programme (RDP)*. Johannesburg: Aloe Communications.

Battersby, J. (2012). Beyond the food desert: Finding ways to speak about urban food security in South Africa. *Geografiska Annaler: Series B, Human Geography*, 94, 141–159. doi:10.1111/j.1468-0467.2012.00401.x

Cameron, T., and Spies, S. B. (Eds.). (1992). *A new illustrated history of South Africa*. Johannesburg: Southern Book Publishers; Cape Town and Johannesburg: Human & Rousseau.

Constitution of the Republic of South Africa. No. 108. (1996). Statutes of the Republic of South Africa – Constitutional Law. Retrieved from http://www.gov.za/documents/constitution/1996/a108-96.pdf

Crush, J., and Frayne, B. (2010). *The invisible crisis: Urban food security in Southern Africa*. Urban food security series no. 1. Queen's University and AFSUN: Kingston and Capetown. Retrieved from www.afsun.org/wp-content/uploads/2013/09/AFSUN_1.pdf

Crush, J., Hovorka, A., and Tevera, D. (2010). *Urban food production and household food security in Southern African cities*. Urban food security series no. 4. Kingston and Cape Town: Queen's University and AFSUN. Retrieved from www.afsun.org/wp content/uploads/2013/09/AFSUN_4.pdf

Department: Agriculture, Forestry and Fisheries (DAFF). Republic of South Africa. (2013b, October 18–24). Securing access to food. *Mail & Guardian*, World Food Day supplement, p. 3.

Department: Agriculture, Forestry and Fisheries (DAFF). Republic of South Africa. (2013c, October 18–24). Sustainable food systems. *Mail & Guardian*, World Food Day supplement, p.1.

Department: Agriculture, Forestry and Fisheries (DAFF). Republic of South Africa. (2013d). *Fetsa Tlala integrated food production initiative 2013/2014: An overview*. Retrieved from http://lgbn.co.za/home/attachments/article/71/FETSA%20TLALA%20%20INTERGRATED%20FOOD%20PRODUCTION%20INITIATIEV-%2012%20NOVEMBER%202013.pdf

Department of Agriculture, Forestry and Fisheries (DAFF). Republic of South Africa. (2012). *Strategic plan 2012/13–2016/17*. Retrieved from www.nda.agric.za/doaDev/topMenu/StratPlan201213 201617.pdf

Department: Agriculture, Forestry and Fisheries (DAFF) and Department of Social Development. Republic of South Africa. (2013, August). *National policy on food and nutrition security*. Retrieved from www.nda.agric.za/docs/media/NATIONAL%20POLICYon%20food%20and%20nutrirition%20security.pdf

Department: Agriculture. Republic of South Africa. (2002, July 17). *The integrated food security strategy for South Africa*. Retrieved from www.nda.agric.za/doaDev/sideMenu/foodSecurity/policies.pdf

Department of Agriculture and Rural Development. Free State Province. (2013, March 27). *Qabathe bolster farmer support programmes*. Retrieved from www.ard.fs.gov.za/?p=1631

Department of Basic Education. (2014). *National School nutrition programme*. Retrieved from www.education.gov.za/Programmes/NationalSchoolNutritionProgramme/tabid/440/Default.aspx

Department of Provincial and Local Government. Republic of South Africa. (2005). *Programme of action. Nodal areas.*

Department: Social Development. Republic of South Africa. (2012). *Strategic plan 2012–2015*. Retrieved from www.dsd.gov.za/index2.php?option=com_docman&task=doc_view&gid=283&Itemid=39

Department: Social Development. Republic of South Africa. (2008). *Strategic plan 2009–2013.*

Du Preez, M. (2013). *A rumour of spring, South Africa after 20 years of democracy*. Cape Town, South Africa: Zebra Press.

Food and Agriculture Organization of the United Nations (FAO). (2014). *The state of food and agriculture 2014: Innovation in family farming*. Retrieved from www.fao.org/3/a-i4040e.pdf

Food and Agriculture Organization of the United Nations (FAO), International Fund for Agricultural Development (IFAD), and World Food Programme (WFO). (2014). *The state of food insecurity in the world 2014: Strengthening the enabling environment for food security and nutrition*. Retrieved from www.fao.org/3/a-i4030e.pdf

Free State mission on rural investment. (1997). *Action programme for the creation of the sustainable livelihoods in the rural and peri-urban economy (1996–1999)*. Prepared by a joint task team of the Department of Agriculture, The Rural Strategy Unity and the World Bank. Free State Province: Rural Strategy Unit.

Free State Online. (2013). Free State. Retrieved from http://www.freestateonline.fs.gov.za/?page_id=744

Labadarios, D., Mchiza, Z. J.-R., Steyn, N. P., Gericke, G., Maunder, E. M. W., Davids, Y. D., and Parker, W. (2011). Food security in South Africa: A review of national surveys. *Bull World Health Organ*, 89, 891–899. doi:10.2471/BLT.11.089243. Database: Academic Search Complete.

The Local Government Handbook. A Complete Guide to Municipalities in South Africa. (2013). *Free state*. Retrieved from www.localgovernment.co.za/provinces/view/2/free-state

Mda, Z. (2000). *The heart of redness*. Oxford University Press.

National Treasury. Department: National Treasury. Republic of South Africa. (2014). *National budget review*. Retrieved from www.treasury.gov.za/documents/national%20budget/2014/review/FullReview.pdf

New History. (2014). *Homelands or the dumping grounds?* Retrieved from http://newhistory.co.za/Part-4-Chapter-14-A-state-of-change-Homelands-or-dumping grounds/

Newman, K. S., and De Lannoy, A. (2014). *After freedom: The rise of the post-apartheid generation in democratic South Africa*. Boston, MA: Beacon Press.

Pugh, H. (2016, October). Be part of the food solution. *Mail & Guardian*, Special report. Retrieved from http://mg.co.za/article/2015-10-16-00-be-part-of-the-food-solution

Shisana, O., Labadarios, D., Rehle, T., Simbayi, L., Zuma, K., Dhansay, A., Reddy, P., Parker, W., Hoosain, E., Naidoo, P., Hongoro, C., Mchiza, Z., Steyn, N. P., Dwane, N., Makoae, M., Maluleke, T., Ramlagan, S., Zungu, N., Evans, M. G., Jacobs, L., Faber, M., and SANHANES-1 Team. (2013). *South African National Health and Nutrition Examination Survey (SANHANES- 1)*. Cape Town: HSRC Press.

Skosana, I. (2016). Working too hard: Social grants stretched thin within a failing system. *Mail & Guardian*, Bhekisisa Centre for Health Journalism. Retrieved from http://bhekisisa.org/article/2016-09-05-00-working-too-hard-social-grants-stretched-thin within-a-failing-system

South African Government. (2014). Provinces: Free State. Retrieved from http://www.gov.za/aboutsa/south-africas-provinces#fs

South African Government. (2014). *Social benefits*. Retrieved from www.gov.za/services/servicesresidents/social-benefits

South African History Online. Towards a People's History. (SAHO). (2014a). *Apartheid legislation 1850s–1870s*. Retrieved from www.sahistory.org.za/politics-and-society/apartheid legislation-1850s-1970s

South African History Online. Towards a People's History. (SAHO). (2014b). *Bantu Education Act No. 47 of 1953*. Retrieved from www.sahistory.org.za/bantu-education-act-no-47-1953

South African History Online. Towards a People's History. (SAHO). (2014c). *From bondage to freedom the 150th anniversary of the arrival of Indian workers in South Africa.* Retrieved from www.sahistory.org.za/people-south-africa/indian-south-africans

South African History Online. Towards a People's History. (SAHO). (2014d). *Land, labour and apartheid*. Retrieved from www.sahistory.org.za/article/land-labour-and-apartheid

South African History Online. Towards a people's history. (SAHO). (2014e). *The homelands*. Retrieved from http://www.sahistory.org.za/article/homelands

South African History Online. Towards a People's History. (SAHO). (2014f) *Tricameral parliament*. Retrieved from www.sahistory.org.za/archive/tricameral-parliament

South African Human Rights Commission. (2014). *Right to food is also a human right*. Retrieved from www.sahrc.org.za/home/indexe9b8.html?ipkMenuID=92&ipkArticl eID=270

Statistics South Africa. (2017). *Free state community survey 2016 results*. Retrieved from www.statssa.gov.za/?p=7993

Statistics South Africa. (2016, June 2). *General household survey 2015*. Retrieved from www.statssa.gov.za/publications/P0318/P03182015.pdf

Statistics South Africa. (2014, June 18). *General household survey 2013*. Retrieved from http://beta2.statssa.gov.za/publications/P0318/P03182013.pdf

Statistics South Africa. (2012). *Census in brief*. Retrieved from www.statssa.gov.za/Census2011/Products/Census_2011_Census_in_brief.pdf

Statistics South Africa. (2013). Mangaung. Retrieved from http://www.statssa.gov.za/?page_id=1021&id=manguang-municipality

Terreblanche, S. (2012). *Lost in transformation*. Johannesburg, SA: KMM Review Publishing Company (PTY) Ltd.

Terreblanche, S. (2002). *A history of inequality in South Africa 1652–2002*. Scottsville and Johannesburg, South Africa: University of KwaZulu-Natal Press and KMM Review Publishing Company (PTY) Ltd.

3   The city and the townships

South Africa is a country that has been undergoing political change, carving the path toward democracy, since the 1990s. In spite of the ongoing and progressive approaches to overcoming the systemic racism that shaped the South African society throughout its history, and particularly under the apartheid regime, this racism still permeates much of the everyday lives of its people. To understand food insecurity/security in the country, we need to be conscious of the fact that these situations are shaped by structural social, economic and political inequities and inequalities within a society undergoing not only political change, but also racial retribution. As one of the few provinces where Afrikaners still dominate the economy, where Afrikaans is still widely spoken and the structure of apartheid is still deeply felt, the Free State Province is a particularly fascinating place to understand the complexity of how poverty and food security/insecurity are lived and perceived in the country.

Understanding food security/insecurity and expressions of agency through people's stories are here framed within the theoretical-methodological constructs of narrative inquiry (Chase, 2005; Hollway and Jefferson, 2001) and storytelling as meaning-making. Narrative inquiry constructs delineate understanding the narrative as making meaning of one's experiences through reflection and within sociohistorical and political contexts. As Chase (2005) explains, "a narrative communicates the narrator's point of view, including why the narrative is worth telling in the first place. Thus, in addition to describing what happened, narratives also express emotions, thoughts, and interpretations" (p. 656).

I was particularly interested in the stories of the food insecure in poor rural and urban communities of the Free State, what they make of their food situation, the personal narratives through which they express their viewpoints about this situation and, among other elements, its characteristics and conditionalities as seen through their eyes, as well as their agency to confront this situation. As I got to know the participants whose stories I tell in this book, it was fundamental for me to understand that their narratives emerged from their life experiences, and that both of these are framed within South African epistemologies of this province which has historically been mainly Sesotho (the main tribal people of the province) and Afrikaner (White), as well as Tswana, isiXhosa and other cultural groups. Their historical experiences, epistemologies and ways of thinking about and living their worlds have shaped their histories and their lives and the meanings they make of food security/insecurity and sustainability. My time in the Free State Province made me realize that interweaved within the fiber of these epistemologies is the way they tell their stories, what elements frame their stories, what is important to them; telling their stories is one of their ways of being in the world.

Underlying people's stories is their learning throughout their lives how to survive, or to live, in their societies. In the academic field of adult education, through critical theory we examine the economic, historical, sociocultural and political contexts within which adult learning takes place, as we question and critique our assumptions about the perspectives, societal dynamics, social structures and institutions of the society in which we live (Merriam, Caffarella and Baumgartner, 2007; Foley, 2002). In the case of the participants in this book, I found it fascinating to understand how their non-formal and informal learning to live within the post-apartheid South Africa informed their perceptions of their own lives, and their society. Some questions underlying this learning were: How have the food insecure in the Free State learned to cope with the challenges they face with regard to their limited access to food? Are these coping strategies interrelated to their history of segregation and apartheid? And if they are, what is the nature of this interrelation? Moreover, how are they interconnected with the contemporary societal dynamics, including racial, economic and political dynamics, of the post-apartheid Free State Province? I came to understand the food insecure as theorists in their own right and of their own socioeconomic, political and cultural circumstances. Some, but not all, of the people who face food insecurity tend to be among the poor and vulnerable groups, marginalized in different ways within their own societies, so a fundamental question underlying my inquiry was: How do these people theorize their food security within their marginal spaces? With them, I explored the possibilities that meaning making through narratives may elucidate the critical awareness that is necessary for the democratic transformation of society, which is one of the declared main goals of the post-1994 South Africa. Together with this, I came to realize that this critical awareness is possibly being restricted by the urgency of their survival.

Many of the participants lived in Mangaung Metropolitan Municipality, the central and most populated municipality of the province, which comprises urban and semi-urban areas, and Thabo Mofutsanyana Municipality, which mainly comprises rural areas. Both municipalities encompass areas of economic importance. In both municipalities, my focus was on areas where many of the poor and vulnerable live. In Mangaung Municipality, these were the inner city areas and townships of Bloemfontein, as well as the large semi-urban town of Botshabelo. In Thabo Mofutsanyana Municipality, the focus was on the small town of Kestell and the large, more urbanized town of Harrismith, which is at the crossroads between the provinces of the Free State, Gauteng (home to Johannesburg) and KwaZulu-Natal (home to Durban).

Understanding the history and lives of the people in the Free State Province, including its human, social and physical geography in the present and in the time of apartheid, was fundamental to the framing of my work. In which geographical areas, what dimensions of the life of the province I would study, who I would have conversations with and how I would interpret these conversations and the societal dynamics of the province were all framed by and continually shaped this understanding. Whatever richness this book has comes from this understanding.

The places

Mangaung Metropolitan Municipality

Mangaung means 'place of the cheetah' in Sesotho, the most widely spoken African language of the province. Mangaung Metropolitan Municipality is the eighth largest municipality in the country and has a population of 747 431, of which 83.3% are Black African, 11.0% are White, 5.0% are Colored and other groups are 0.7%. In this municipality, 4.3% of the population 20 years and older have no formal schooling, while 4.7% have completed primary education. So almost a tenth of the population have little or no education. Approximately a third of the population, 33.2% have some secondary education, 30.3% have completed matric and 14.2 % have some form of higher education. Almost 68 % of the population is between the working ages of 15–64, and the unemployment rate of this population is 27.7 %. The youth unemployment rate (ages 15–34 years) is 37.2% (Statistics South Africa: Mangaung municipality, People, 2014c). The most widely spoken language as a first language in the municipality is Sesotho, followed by Afrikaans, then Setswana and IsiXhosa. English is the most widely spoken language of communication among the different populations. A little over a tenth, 11.4%, of the population derives no income, while 4.6% earns under R4 800 (R means rand, the South African currency). A slightly higher percentage, 6.8%, has an income between R4 801 and R9 600 (Statistics South Africa: Mangaung municipality, Economy, 2014b). This means that approximately 22% of the population is eligible to receive government social grants. These data are revealing of the population in the municipality for they provide us with a portrait of the racial and cultural-linguistic composition of the province, as well as the levels of education and of unemployment.

The importance of this municipality as a focal point of research is that it comprises the capital city of Bloemfontein and the large semi-urban towns of Botshabelo and Thaba Nchu, with the challenges that arise from their historical and contemporary societal dynamics. A number of people in the municipality, as in the rest of the country, receive social grants from the government, but there is still a relatively high level of food insecurity. Created by the segregation policies of apartheid, Botshabelo and Thaba Nchu even today remain overwhelmingly Black and impoverished.

As the judicial capital of the country and the capital of the former Orange Free State, one of the two former Afrikaner Republics of the country, Bloemfontein was one of the centers of Afrikaner domination in South Africa, with its ensuing societal dynamics of racial segregation and social and economic oppression of the Blacks and Coloreds. Created through the segregation policies, there are still a number of Black African and Colored townships in Bloemfontein, which even today remain segregated by color. White people generally do not live in the townships or the semi-urban areas of the municipality. The impoverished Whites tend to live in mainly white areas or in mixed neighborhoods in Bloemfontein and its outskirts. The impoverished peoples of different racial groupings also live in the inner city areas of Bloemfontein.

Thabo Mofutsanyana Municipality

My focus in the Eastern Free State was within the rural Thabo Mofutsanyana Municipality; Kestell, Harrismith and QwaQwa rural villages in the Maluti-A-Phofung Local Municipality in the QwaQwa region. It is a district through which two National Roads, the N3 and N5, pass, connecting different regions of the country. It is also home to the famous Golden Gate Highlands National Park, a major tourist attraction for lovers of nature, hiking and mountain climbing on the slopes of the Drakensburg Mountains. It is an area of great scenic beauty and rich cultural heritage and has enormous potential for tourism development. The main economic sectors are agriculture and tourism (The Local Government Handbook. Thabo Mofutsanyana District Municipality, 2014).

These towns had benefitted under the Regional Industrial Development Programme of the apartheid government, but after the subsidies were no longer given, the socioeconomic situation of the area became critical (Department of Rural Development and Land Reform: Free State CRDP, 2009). Maluti-A- Phofung was declared a nodal area in 2001, one of the 22 Nodal areas of the country at that time. As I explained in Chapter 2, a Nodal area is a severely impoverished area to which the successive governments directed *The Urban Renewal and Integrated Sustainable Rural Development Programme*, *War on Poverty Programme* and then the *Comprehensive Rural Development Programme* to address underdevelopment in the area. QwaQwa was also a homeland during apartheid, a rocky, infertile land which could not sustain the thousands of Black Africans forced to live on it.

Maluti-A-Phofung is the third most densely populated area in the province and has a high rate of poverty and unemployment. The majority of the population lives in the rural areas. It has a population of 335 784, of which 98.2% are Black African, 0.2% are Colored, 0.2% are Indian/Asian, 1.3% are White and 0.1% are of other ethnic/cultural groups. Over two thirds, 81.7%, of the people speak Sesotho as their first language, followed by 10.7% who speak IsiZulu (because of the area's proximity to KwaZulu-Natal Province, home to the IsiZulu peoples). A very small percentage, 2% of the people speak Afrikaans as their first language, and 1.5% speak English as theirs. Over half, 62.8% of its population is of working age (15–64 years) with an unemployment rate of 41.8%, and a youth unemployment rate (15–34 years) of 53%. A little less than a tenth, 8.9% of the population 20 years and older have no formal schooling, 26.8% have completed matric, and 7.9 % have some form of higher education (Statistics South Africa: Maluti-a-Phofung, 2014a). The key nodal challenges of the municipality are:

> Poverty, Inadequate provision and maintenance of basic infrastructure, Informal housing and insecurity of tenure, Inadequate public transport, Lack of economic opportunities, High illiteracy and innumeracy, Non-payment of services, Droughts, HIV/AIDS, Unemployment and Crime.
>
> (Department of Agriculture and Rural Development.
> Free State Province: "Agricultural land", 2012, p. 3)

Interestingly, despite being a Nodal area, there are a number of commercial farms and major nature conservation centers in the region. Through its farms, it significantly contributes to the gross agricultural income for the province, and its beef production is highly regarded (Statistics South Africa: Maluti-a-Phofung, 2014a). This situation expresses some of the contradictions of food insecurity; hunger in the midst of plenty.

The people

The people of this book are women and men who face varying degrees of food insecurity within the Free State Province. Living in South Africa, I met many people and had multiple informal conversations. Through these conversations, I chose 12 participants for in-depth semi-structured interviews. The spectrum of participant and non-participant observations and conversations created a rich world of knowledge which have shaped this book. The majority of these people live in the poor Black, Colored and White neighborhoods. I was very interested in hearing the stories of these persons, because I believe that the food insecure are theorists in their own right. Moreover, their voices need to be heard, and they need to be invited to participate in the formulation of policies that are directed towards them, to achieve their food security.

I had conversations, but not interviews, with some peasant farmers who are no longer food insecure, but who work in subsistence farming and contribute to overcoming the challenges of food insecurity and joblessness within their communities. I met with agricultural economists and professors who work in rural sustainable ecologies, others who are in different ways involved in research on food insecurity, as well as officials from the Department of Agriculture and Rural Development, and the Department of Social Development, who implement the provincial food security policies. My conversations with these persons, as well as other research and literature, led me to understanding some dimensions of food insecurity in the province from their perspectives, richly interrelating to my findings.

The agricultural economists are some of the professionals who are advising the farmers and the government departments, with regard to improving food production in the state. It is they who are formulating and/or are helping to formulate the programs on social capital and entrepreneurship. The policy implementers are the persons who implement the government policies and programs. I found it essential and interesting to speak with them to understand their perspectives on implementing the policies and on the food situations experienced in the communities

As defined by the South African government, following the World Food Program definition, the food insecure are persons who have inadequate access to food. The 2013 statistics showed that 8.0% of the households in the Free State had severely inadequate access to food, and 14.7% had inadequate access to food, 22.4% of the population of the province. In 2015, 6.8% of the households had severely inadequate access to food, and 18.0% had inadequate access, 24.8% of the population, an overall increase of 2.4%. When we look at these statistics, we can see that the percentage with severely inadequate access decreased slightly (1.2%), but the percentage with inadequate access increased 3.3%. This, despite the number of food programs, both governmental and non-governmental, that exist throughout the province.

The 12 participants whose stories are narrated here are six men and six women, Black and White, ages 23 to 62. Intertwined contextually are narratives of a number of other persons, including those of a few Colored persons who face food insecurity. There are still few Indians in the province, even after the apartheid ban on them was abolished, much less poor and vulnerable ones. I did not meet any impoverished and economically vulnerable Indians, so their narratives are not included here. Of the 12 participants whose stories are narrated here, two are White Afrikaans men, four are Black men (three Sesotho and one Xhosa) and six Black Sesotho women. I would have liked to interview a White woman, but never interacted with any for a substantial enough length of time to establish sufficient rapport to have deeper conversations with them. I did do a substantial amount of non-participant observation with both White men and women in Bloemfontein, nonetheless, for the streets of the city are filled with White beggars of both genders. There are few Black beggars. Blacks on the streets tend to be street vendors, hustling up quick sales at the *robots* (the traffic lights), whereas the poor Whites beg at the robots. I explain this in detail in the sections below. The stories here are also contextualized by the narratives of people who do not face food insecurity to understand the meanings they attribute to the situations of food insecurity and food unsustainability (Duneier, 2011). Understanding the perspectives of these different participants has allowed me to paint a more complete portrait of the issues around food in the Free State.

The faces of poverty and food insecurity in Bloemfontein

"Hunger has many faces. Across the world, it manifests itself in a myriad of ways, through people having substantially varying levels of access to food, in many cases with this access not being sustainable". This was the sentence with which I began Chapter 1, and it emphasizes two of the main elements at the core of impoverished people's experiences. The first is that structural poverty is a vise that is strangling the poor and vulnerable, and the second is that hunger is not a monolithic concept; it indeed manifests itself in a myriad of ways and, moreover, obscures social and economic injustices. There is much more to hunger than meets the naked eye.

In the following sections, we will see the situations of food insecurity as situated within the structural poverty and abundance of Bloemfontein, in particular with regard to the poor and vulnerable of the townships. Here, I tell the stories of people who face challenges around food. These stories are powerful narratives of people's experiences, as told in their own voices. The following questions underlay the framing of my inquiry into their lives: (i) How do the social, economic, cultural, political and economic contexts of the people who face food insecurity influence their perspectives of their experiences of food insecurity? and (ii) Does their meaning-making lead to agency in their own lives and that of their communities?

Where our people live

The people whose stories I narrate here live mainly in the townships of the periphery of the city of Bloemfontein and work in the city. In Chapter 4, I focus on persons from the food markets, the inner city and the University of the Free State. Here, I describe the lives of the low-wage workers who live in the townships and the challenges they face with regard to their access to food. Some of them work at the University of the Free State and others at a Christian NGO in the inner city, which works with the poor and vulnerable people of the city and its townships. From these, I chose six men and women to interview, whose perspectives illustrate some of their challenges. I also describe the perspectives of some unemployed men and women in Phase 9, a very poor area of the township and the challenges they face in this regard, as well as those of Sister Electa from the Lesedi Centre of Hope, in Turflaagte, in the township, where HIV/AIDS and TB patients are cared for.

Most of these situations described are in the lives of Blacks and some Coloreds, because the townships are overwhelmingly Black, with some historically Coloured areas. There are many poor Whites in Bloemfontein, however, who live in different sectors in the city and on its outskirts, whose stories are also important. Two of these stories are told in the next chapter; that of a White man who works at a food market and a White homeless man who is a beneficiary of the inner-city Christian NGO. Most of the businesses, offices, government ministries and the main theatre of Bloemfontein are in the city center, but most of the middle- and higher-income people do not live there. They live in the areas off the center and in the suburbs. Lower-income people and the homeless live in the city center. The townships encompass the periphery of the city, and there are also poor neighborhoods, White as well as mixed Black, White and Coloured, in the holdings on the outskirts of the city. The University of the Free State Bloemfontein campus is in the city.

In Chapter 2, I gave the percentages of the demographics and languages spoken in the Free State and Mangaung Metropolitan Municipality. Let us look at the percentages of these side by side with those of Bloemfontein. As we can see in Table 3.1, Bloemfontein has the highest percentage of Whites and Coloreds in the province, making up nearly half the population in the city, as compared to their percentages in the rest of the province. Moreover, it is these percentages that contribute to Afrikaans being the most widely spoken first language in the city (42.5%), as compared to in the rest of the province (12.7%).

To understand life within poverty, I engaged with people in the townships and in the city. Three of the people I met at the university served as my points of entry to communities in the townships. Two are cleaning ladies, Esther and Jenny, with whom I spent a lot of time and got to know quite well. The other is a professor of nutrition and dietetics, Dr. Lucia Meko, who introduced me to the people of Phase 9, an area in the *location*, as the inhabitants call the townships. The name *location* comes from the Afrikaans term *lokasie*, which means 'place', used to refer to the segregation of the non-Whites from the Whites in South Africa. In the township today, informal settlements are interspersed among the formal set-tlements. I focused on Mangaung, which is one of the largest Black townships in the province. It comprises the sub-townships of Batho, Botjhabela, Phahameng, Phelindaba and Kagisanong (Rocklands) (South African History Online: Growth of informal settlements, 2014). These sub-townships are in turn subdivided into different areas and Phases, such as Freedom Square, Chris Hani and Phases 1 to 9.

Table 3.1 Comparative Demographics Free State – Mangaung Metropolitan Municipality – Bloemfontein

Demographics (in percentage)	Free State Province (pop. 2.7 million)	Mangaung Metropolitan Muncipality (pop. 747 431)	Bloemfontein (pop. 256 185)
Black African	87.6	83.3	56.1
White	8.7	11.0	29.8
Colored	3.1	5.0	12.8
Indian/Asian			0.8
Other racial groups	0.4	1.7	0.5
Languages (in percentage)			
Sesotho	64.2	51.9	33.4
Afrikaans	12.7	15.8	42.5
English	2.9	4.2	7.5
IsiXhosa	7.5	9.6	7.1
Setswana	5.2	12.3	
Other languages	7.5	6.2	9.5%

Source of demographics: South Africa Census 2011. Table is of my elaboration. (Statistics South Africa, 2012)

In the food markets, I became acquainted with the workers and car watchers, and in the City Centre, I volunteered at a Christian NGO which works with the poor and vulnerable people of the city. Many of them are homeless men and youth, as well as the unemployed men from the townships who come into town to look for 'piece jobs', that is, temporary tasks they can do for a few hours or days just to make ends meet. I also spent months walking and driving around the streets of the city, observing its people and the places and getting to know some of them. These rich interactions and observations allowed me to understand the rich tapestry of life in the city, albeit through the eyes of a foreigner.

The townships and the city: living between two worlds

Place, where we are situated geographically, emotionally, historically, culturally and politically, shapes the meanings we make of our own lives and those of others, as well as our interpretation of events. As I explained in earlier chapters, the Free State Province is a unique place geographically, historically, culturally and politically. In this chapter, I carry this further, delving into what emotional meanings place holds for the people of this province, within the historical, cultural and political contexts.

To understand life in this province, I began with the place where I was situated, the University of the Free State Bloemfontein campus, to begin to appreciate the societal dynamics within this place and some of the people of the province. From there, I expanded my network of contacts, communication and understanding. I spent a lot of time going around the Free State, getting to know people, observing their interactions in daily life in the different places and learning more about the places, people and societal dynamics of the province. Getting to know people and gaining access to certain places also allowed for participant observation as I engaged with the participants in different activities. Some of these were, for example, activities as simple, yet rich in engagement as cooking together or teaching and learning. An example of one person I got to know well is Esther, a cleaning lady, who taught me Sesotho, and I, in turn, helped her to improve her English, as well as gave her children English classes and helped them with their homework. We also cooked together, teaching each other recipes from our respective cultures. Esther then introduced me to several people in her community in the township, including her pastor and fellow church members, who shared some of their lives and struggles with me.

I got to know several of the cleaning ladies of the residences where I was living, as we chatted on a daily basis. They loved it when I would greet them in Sesotho and would correct my pronunciation and teach me more. One of them, who is isiXhosa, was also determined that I learn her language, not only Sesotho, so she also taught me a little isiXhosa. They were surprised at my interest in them and intrigued at my research, not quite always understanding why I was interested in their lives, but, over time, we became very friendly, and we would talk about their lives and their struggles. I cooked for them on occasion, which shocked them at the beginning, but it helped to establish deeper rapport between us. Before I go deeper into their stories, I will briefly describe the contexts of the low-wage workers at the University of the Free State, at the Christian NGO, a group of unemployed people of Phase 9 and the Lesedi Centre of Hope.

Low-wage workers: the cleaning women

During my time living on the University of the Free State campus, I became well acquainted with a group of eight cleaning women. The maintenance staff at the university, i.e., cleaning men and women, grounds men, gardeners and other staff who do manual labor, are mostly Black, and the majority live in the townships on the periphery of Bloemfontein and in the semi-urban towns of Botshabelo and Thaba Nchu, which are 57 km and 66 km away from Bloemfontein, respectively. All of these areas were formed as segregated areas during apartheid for the non-Whites to live, and even today, their populations remain mainly non-White. I came to understand that these workers are part of the working poor of the Free State province; people who are part of the labor force, but whose incomes fall below the poverty level. They earn very low wages that barely cover their living expenses, and they face difficulties covering their basic needs, including food.

The eight cleaning women are Dineo, Othusitse, Pinky, Onalena, Mputho, Sylvia, Esther and Jenny, as well as their supervisor, Valentine. I was able to speak and establish rapport with all of them, because like many of the working poor in the city under the age of 60, they speak a fair amount of English, as well as being fluent in Afrikaans and their native languages. All of them live in the townships and travel to work by bus or taxi (minivan). Three are married or live with their partners and children, three are single mothers with children and/or grandchildren living at home, one is single without children and lives with her parents and one lives alone. Of the ones with children, only three receive child support grants. All of these women struggle to survive, for even though two have partners who work, their combined salaries still keep them below the threshold of living wages. As a supervisor, Valentine earns significantly more than the other women and her husband also works, so their joint income is above the level of poverty and they live comfortably. Their comfortable life, however, is quite recent. Until 2013, when she got her promotion, Valentine was a cleaning woman, earning the same as the others, so she is well aware of the challenges they face in their daily lives and does her best to support the women in many different ways.

Low-wage workers: the staff at the Christian NGO

This NGO is deeply imbued with Christian beliefs of the progressive branch of the Dutch Reformed Church, and its inner-city location is affiliated with what used to be an important center of White Afrikaner worship until its congregation moved away to the suburbs of Bloemfontein after 1994. The church continues today, but its congregation is now made up of the inner-city people: the poor, the homeless, the vulnerable. The organization has several programs: food; basic medical assistance; clothing; youth; needlework skills training and job creation; weekly outreach with women trapped in prostitution; and temporary work. Underlying each one of these programs are the core values of assisting vulnerable people to meet their immediate needs, while at the same time, helping them to realize, in the words of the Managing Director of the organization, "through the grace of God, their God-given dignity" and to become agents of their own change. In this way, the vision is to transform communities from vulnerability to ability.

I worked mainly with the food program, but also collaborated with the needlework and temporary work programs, as well as the life skills sessions, through which the Pastoral Manager and Outreach Program Manager worked on a weekly basis with the beneficiaries of the programs to help them develop skills to confront challenges in their daily lives. Through the food program, there is a daily soup kitchen at 3 p.m. from Monday to Friday and at 11 a.m. on Sunday after the church service, as well as weekly food parcels for the lower-level staff and the beneficiaries who are deemed to be taking responsibility for their lives. All the staff is involved in the daily soup kitchen. The needlework skills training and job creation program provides the unemployed with the opportunity to utilize the skills that they are acquiring to earn an income. In the temporary work program, men are employed in small teams as part of regular clean-up campaigns in the city, with the commitment of making Bloemfontein a cleaner and more beautiful city.

The soup kitchen serves on a daily basis between 45–80 or sometimes even 100 people, mainly all men, with the rare appearance of a woman. The staff uses this time to engage with the beneficiaries. These beneficiaries who come to the soup kitchen tend to be in one of four situations: (a) They are living on the streets and have no jobs; (b) they have homes but are very poor and cannot afford to buy food for themselves and their families, so they come to eat at the soup kitchen; (c) they are in town looking for 'piece jobs' (temporary work) and have not eaten all day, so they pass by to eat before heading home again; and (d) they are from semi-urban areas, such as Botshabelo and Thaba Nchu, have come into town to find work, get piece jobs and sleep on the streets to save their money to take back to their families on the weekend or once a month, and so come to have their one meal a day at the soup kitchen.

My interest in the organization derived from wanting to comprehend how the people who work in, and those who are the beneficiaries of, an organization that addresses food insecurity and some of the different dimensions of poverty understand food insecurity as they perceive and/or live it. When I was there, the organization had 12 staff members and three to five rotating part-time workers. Seven of the staff were White, four were Black and one was Colored. The rotating part-time workers were all Black men. All of the Black staff and part-time workers lived in the townships and came from similar backgrounds as the beneficiaries. Several of the staff would like to further their education to improve their lives and those of their families. When I first arrived at the NGO, and during my first weeks there, I did not think I would ask any of the staff members for interviews as such, because I took it for granted that they would be food secure, in view of the fact that they are working in an organization with a social justice mission, and a soup kitchen. Over time, however, as I spent more time with them working side by side, I realized that seemingly paradoxically, some of them do face food insecurity. This led me to realize that it would be important to understand their situations much better through focused in depth conversations, which I did with two staff members, Ruth and Abraham, and two part-time workers, Tumelo and Thabo. In Chapter 4, where I discuss White poverty in the city, I include the experiences of David, a homeless man who is a beneficiary of this organization.

The unemployed of Phase 9

The two sections above are of the working poor in the townships, but it is essential to include the voices of the people who have lost their jobs and can no longer find work, or those who are now ready to begin their working lives and cannot find jobs. To this end, I focused on a group of about 18–20 women and three men, the majority of whom do not work, in Phase 9, a very poor area in the townships. It is one of the oldest settlements, and when the houses were built during apartheid, they had no toilets and no water, and most people do not even have an address. It is also an area that has no RDP houses, and the drainage systems are precarious. When it rains, there is a great deal of flooding. Dr. Lucia Meko, from the Department of Nutrition and Dietetics at UFS, had been working with the people of this community for about two years, establishing a program with them to improve their eating habits, their access to food and create some community initiatives to improve their lives. Through this program, she brings her 3rd- and 4th-year undergraduate students in nutrition and dietetics so that they can gain experience and learn about the kinds of patients that they will be seeing in the hospitals when they begin their professional lives. They go house to house, trying to establish people's levels of food security/insecurity and assessing their nutritional status, as well as checking for and controlling their diabetes and hypertension. There is a high incidence of both of these illnesses in the communities. To assist them in understanding the importance of healthy eating, the students give the members of the community nutritional counseling. As part of the program, Dr, Meko has also been helping people to grow household and community gardens. I explain these gardens further in Chapter 4.

Lesedi Centre of Hope

This center is part of the Partnerships for the Delivery of Primary Health Care, including HIV and AIDS (PDPHC) Programme, Motheo District. It coordinates the HIV/AIDS projects in the Archdiocese of Bloemfontein. The Sisters and other members of the Centre care for the sick, the poor and the Orphaned and Vulnerable Children (OVCs) in the townships and across the Free State. The Centre gives primary care to the poor and vulnerable of the townships who are ill and in need of help. Part of this care is helping them with seemingly simple, yet vital things for people who live in dire poverty, such as providing them with transportation from their homes to the hospitals, to the South African Social Security Agency (SASSA) to get their social grants and providing them with home-based care and hospice, among other things. The person I spent the most time with at the Centre in its work in the township was Sister Electa, a German nun who has been living and working with the poor and vulnerable of the Free State for 40 years. Her perspective of the issues that the people in the townships suffer is unique, because she has dedicated her life to them both during apartheid and now in the 20 plus years of democracy.

Life in the townships

To understand the environment of structural poverty in some of the poorer areas of the townships and the challenges the people there face, I bring into dialogue the global perspectives of the UFS cleaning women, the unemployed of Phase 9 and that of Sister Electa from the Lesedi Centre of Hope with the specific perspectives of the six participants I had in-depth interviews with: two cleaning women (Esther and Jenny) and four members of the staff of the Christian NGO (Ruth, Tumelo, Thabo and Abraham). Table 3.2 succinctly describes some of the characteristics of these six participants. Further to these details, I give their brief bios below.

Esther

Esther and Jenny work together as cleaning women in the student and visiting professor residences at UFS, and both live in the *location* (township) in economically depressed areas. They share some of the same challenges, such as providing for their families within their context of structural poverty, but their lives are somewhat different. Esther is 37 years old, married with three biological children and a foster child who is HIV positive. Her biological children range in age from 11 to 15 and her foster child, Kiki, is four. Her husband, Bernard, is a security guard at the university. They live in Phahameng location in the township. Many of the houses in their neighborhood are mkukhus (flimsily made houses) and unfinished brick houses. Their home is a tiny, two-bedroom, unfinished brick house with an indoor bathroom and toilet, a small kitchen and running water. These last details are important because there are many people who do not have these luxuries in the township. Their home has no living room or dining room, but they do have indoor plumbing and running water, even though they suffer from severe water shortages, as do many people in many areas of the township.

Esther grew up in Botshabelo, the semi-urban area I discuss in Chapter 5. Her mother has been working as a domestic worker all her life and her father as a laborer. Her biological father abandoned Esther's mother when Esther was

Table 3.2 Participants' demographics: Bloemfontein and its townships

Participants	Race and gender	Age	Occupation	Family configuration	Monthly income
Esther	Black woman	37	UFS Cleaning woman	Married, working husband, three biological children, one HIV + foster child	She: R2 000 Husband: R 3 200
Jenny	Black woman	44	UFS Cleaning woman	Single, non-contributing adult son, one foster daughter in school	R2 000
Ruth	Black woman	44	Christian NGO cook	Living with her unemployed partner, is HIV+, has one adult stepson, three young children	R2 400
Tumelo	Black man	31	Christian NGO part-time worker	Married, but separated from working wife, one child	Approx. R 500–600
Thabo	Black man	34	Christian NGO part-time worker	Single, two children	Approx. R 500–600
Abraham	Black man	33	Christian NGO Program Coordinator	Married, working wife, one child	Over 3 000

a baby, and when Esther was four years old, her mom married the man who became Esther's father, and who she loves dearly. They worked hard to send Esther to school so that she could have a better life than they did. Esther was doing well at school and studying towards her matric when she fell in love with Bernard, a much older, divorced man with three children, and got pregnant. To her parents' dismay, she dropped out of school in grade 11 and got married after her baby was born and went on to have two more children. Her parents did not want her to get married and told her that they would help her raise her baby so she could finish her education, an offer she declined to live with Bernard. She has always worked as an unskilled laborer since she dropped out of school. Esther and Bernard's joint income is R5 000, but despite being below the poverty level and the minimum income level to get the child support grant, they do not get this grant for their three biological children. They only used to get R320 as the child support care of their foster child, Kiki. This amount changed in May 2014 to R830 when Kiki was finally legally placed in their care after her biological father sent them her birth certificate, two years after abandoning Kiki.

Jenny

Jenny is a 44-year-old divorcée, a single mother with a 16-year-old foster daughter and 26-year-old son who came to live with her after being kicked out of his paternal grandmother's home. He did not grow up with Jenny, because when she left his father, who used to abuse her physically, verbally and emotionally, he decided to stay with his father. After Jenny left her husband, her mother rejected her, and with nowhere to go, one of her uncles offered her a small plot of land that he had in Phase 6, an area of the township, to build a mkukhu for herself, which she did. She built it with her own hands, starting with a few sheets of zinc, pieces of wood and cardboard, improving it little by little over the years since, and it is now a two-bedroom mkhukhu with mud floors and two windows. Her toilet is a pit latrine in an outhouse, and she has no shower or bathroom. She, her son and her daughter bathe with large buckets using washcloths in their bedrooms. The only running water they have is a tap in the yard. They wash their clothes and dishes out in the yard and bring a bucket of water in for cooking on their two-burner electric hotplate. It is bitterly cold in the winter and very hot in the summer, so Jenny and her children are often uncomfortable, but they make do with what they have. Despite all the lack of convenience, Jenny has made out of her zinc shack a very neat and clean home, filled with love.

Jenny has had little formal education, only up to grade 6 under the Bantu Education system of apartheid. She has worked as an unskilled laborer all her life and aspires to a better life for herself and her daughter. She suffers from chronic arthritis and is in constant pain, but cannot miss a day of work, because, for each day she misses, R100 is discounted from her salary. The same applies to all the cleaning women at the university, which is a grave injustice to them, for they cannot afford to lose any amount of their very low salary. Jenny's meager monthly income of R2 000 supports her household, for her daughter goes to school and her son was unemployed for a long time. He only got a job as a construction worker at the beginning of 2014. Even after obtaining employment, he never contributed to the household expenses, expecting his mother to provide him with food and home amenities. Different to Esther's case, Jenny has not been receiving a foster care grant for her foster daughter Sunny, because Sunny's former foster mother, who is an alcoholic, has refused to give Jenny Sunny's birth certificate. That foster mother was still receiving the R830 foster child grant for Sunny and did not want to give it up.

Ruth

Ruth is a 44-year-old Black woman. She is the cook at the Christian organization and also does the general daily cleaning. She lives in Batho location (in the township), in an RDP house with her husband, stepson and two of her three children. Her eldest son, who is 16 years old, lives in Bothsabelo with her father and stepmother. Her father is paralyzed, so her son helps his grandfather, and his grandparents raise him, provide for him and send him to school.

Ruth is HIV positive and is in good health. She takes her medication daily, which the government provides for free. None of her children are HIV positive, and neither is her partner. She is working to obtain her matric, for her studies were interrupted when she was a teenager. She wants to further her studies, to be able to improve her life for herself and her family. Her partner is not working. She is the only person working, so with her salary, and the grants she receives for her three children, she supports her partner, children and adult stepson, who does not have a job. Her salary is not always enough. She was born during apartheid and, like Jenny, was in her early twenties when Nelson Mandela became president of South Africa. She was 10 years old when her mother passed away, and her father quickly remarried. She and her younger brother then entered a life of verbal, physical and psychological abuse by their stepmother, with their father ignoring the abuse. They did, however, have aunts and a grandmother who looked out for them but couldn't always help them. This life of abuse led her to never having stability in her life growing up, but she discovered her Christian faith as an adolescent and has clung to it as the pillar of her existence.

Tumelo

Tumelo is a 31-year-old Black man, who works part time at the same organization as Ruth. He is married and has a three-year-old son, but is separated from his wife and son at the moment. He really wants to get them back. He now lives by himself in a mkhuku in the Chris Hani area of the township. He grew up in Thaba Nchu, a former homeland for Tswana people in the Free State, with his maternal grandparents and dropped out of school in Grade 9. He has worked as an unskilled laborer all his life, but is determined to go to trade school to learn a trade and make a better life for himself and his family. He is a soft-spoken and kind young man who always has a ready smile and is always very willing to help others. He is well liked at the organization. He arrived there one day, to the soup kitchen, because he was hungry and had no food or money, while he was looking for a job. He was a beneficiary of the soup kitchen for about two weeks when the opportunity came up to be part of a work crew, organized by the NGO, working on a part-time basis, which he gladly accepted. Then they offered him to also work part time as a guard at the gates of the organization, as well as helping with the soup kitchen, which he has also been doing. With these part-time jobs, he barely makes ends meet, so he merely survives.

Thabo

Thabo grew up in Batho location, in the township of Bloemfontein, where he still lives, in a small brick house that belonged to his parents. Thabo has a high school education, having passed his matric. Passing their matric is a big deal for poor

Africans. Not everybody gets to matric, even today, and moreover passes them. Tumelo, for example, dropped out of school and did not do matric. Of the Black Africans who were working at the organization, Abraham, Abongile and Thabo did, and passed matric, Ruth is doing her matric and Tumelo dropped out of high school. Abraham and Abongile went on to college, but Thabo didn't, even though he is a very intellectually curious man. He has two daughters from a long-term relationship, but he is no longer with their mother. His daughters live with their mother, and he does not economically support them.

After passing his matric, Thabo began working as a laborer in temporary jobs, including gardening, painting and construction and also briefly as a hospital patient care worker, which he enjoyed. After being unemployed for about eight months and barely surviving, Thabo started coming to the soup kitchen on a daily basis, relieved at being able to alleviate his hunger, while he continued to look for work. Thabo's enthusiasm and desire to work led him to joining the clean-up program and to Abraham offering him part-time work at the organization, tending to the gate, assisting in the soup kitchen and general support in whatever needed to be done. Tumelo and Thabo do the same part-time jobs.

Abraham

Abraham is the Program Coordinator of the organization. He is a 31-year-old Black Xhosa man and is married with a child. Abraham is the only Black in the organization in a mid-level administrative position, even though he, like them, comes from humble beginnings. He is also the only one of the participants with a university degree. He was born and raised in the Free State by a single mother, who has been a domestic worker all her adult life. He grew up in the township, in an area called Freedom Square, where he still lives today, now in a home of his own, with his wife and child. Abraham's mother was a live-in domestic worker who could not have her children living with her at work. From the age of seven onward, Abraham and his brother lived by themselves in a mkhukhu. Their mother would come on a fortnightly or monthly basis to check up on them, buy them food and pay for electricity and other household and living expenses. This was not an uncommon situation in South Africa during apartheid, and there are still instances where this happens.

He went to a public elementary school for Blacks in the township, but after 1994, when schools nationwide began their integration process, his mother made the huge financial sacrifice to send him to a private formerly all-White school where he felt totally out of place and struggled to keep up with the other students. After failing many times, he transferred himself to a Black public school where he excelled and passed his matric (Grade 12 nationwide examinations) at 23 years old. He then worked at a series of jobs, improving his skills and knowledge as he was also going to university part time. He began as a part-time worker in the clothing program at the organization, and worked his way up to become the Youth Outreach worker, then the Program Coordinator. He finished his undergraduate university studies at age 30 but has been unable to receive his degree because he owes the university a lot of money in tuition, which he is hoping to be able to pay off little by little.

Making meaning of their own lives

Getting to know the participants and understanding how they make meaning of their world within their contexts permits us to identify several themes. Analyzing these themes through the confluence and divergence of the perspectives of the participants is fascinating. Doing a deeper level of analysis of these themes by bringing them into critical dialogue with lived experiences and theories of poverty and food insecurity allows us to understand this dialogue as one of power, critical consciousness and survival, of which food insecurity is only one manifestation. The reality is that food insecurity, and especially the kinds of food insecurity experienced by these people, is never only about whether you have food or not.

The time I spent in the townships and with people from the townships made me realize that the situations in people's lives there are complex. Within the realities of structural poverty that they live are intertwined the issues of social and economic inequity and inequality, attitudes towards gender roles, their agency, food insecurity in its different levels and forms and public health issues such as HIV/AIDS, tuberculosis, alcoholism, drug abuse, teenage and multiple pregnancies, as well as social violence, such as domestic abuse, child prostitution and rape. Some of these issues are expressed in the themes below. These themes are: their economic difficulties and survival; their food situation; their perspectives of the food situation in the Free State; their awareness of government food programs and non-governmental programs; work opportunities in the province; their perspectives of the government; their conceptualizations of people's desire to work; the value of education; differences in the food situation during times of apartheid and now; their faith; what poverty means to them; White poverty from the Black perspective; HIV/AIDS, poverty and food security; about racial differences with regard to people caring for each other; working with the poor and vulnerable; and their agency.

Their economic difficulties and survival

All of the participants who live in the township, with the exception of Abraham, struggle to survive. Abraham faces economic constraints, but he makes a little more money than the cleaning women and Ruth do and much more than Tumelo and Thabo do as part-time workers. Moreover, his wife works, so with two salaries, they are able to cover their living expenses and provide for their baby. The cases of the cleaning women are quite different. Their income of R2 000 barely covers their living expenses for themselves and their families. Some of them receive child support social grants, which helps them a little, and two have working husbands, but even so, it is never nearly enough, and those like Jenny, who do not receive a grant, really struggle. Ruth's situation is a little better, because in addition to the child support social grants for her three children, she receives a weekly food parcel from the organization where she works and clothing. Nonetheless, with an unemployed husband and adult stepson who depend on her and do not contribute to the household income, she also experiences grave economic difficulties. The child support social grants are only for children until the age of 18. So for those parents who have children over 18 who are still at school doing their matric, such as is the case of some of the unemployed women of Phase 9, it becomes very challenging for their families to maintain them.

Among the monthly expenses of these participants are transportation costs, approximately R380 per person (except for the unemployed) and electricity, which is approximately R300, and this electricity does not last all month. In South Africa, many of the homes in poor areas have pre-paid electricity. Towards the end of the month they often have to buy R20–R30 more in electricity to get to the end of the month. Their toiletries cost between R300–R400, depending on the size of the family. They also have their children's school fees (between R100–R200 per month) and transportation fees (between R50 and R90 per week), as well as clothing for the family. In Esther's case, she sends her children to private school, which costs R300 per month per child, and she has three children, there goes R900 of her and Bernard's joint salaries of R5 000. Moreover, most of them have funeral policy monthly installments for the members of their family. Funerals among Africans are a big and expensive affair, and for most poor people, part of their dignity lies in being able to provide their families with a good funeral. Then there are the expenses for food, as well as money set aside to improve their houses. Some of them live in RDP[1] houses, but others live in mkhukhus[2] and houses they have built or are still building themselves. Their expenses vary according to their family size and needs, obviously, but these are the basic expenses. Then, in the winter, which is very cold in the Free State, they have the added expense of heating (mostly with paraffin heaters) and extra clothing, while their salaries remain the same. Paraffin costs between R9–R12 per liter, and a liter lasts about a day and a half. This creates an additional expense of approximately R200 per month for them for three to four months per year.

As they come towards the end of the month, their difficulties increase because they start to run out of food, electricity and basic things. In Tumelo and Thabo's cases, their expenses are considerably lower, because they have no school expenses or funeral policy; neither do they have families who live with them. They do, however, also have much lower incomes. They receive their clothing from the donations at the organization where they work, as well as one meal a day, and a weekly food parcel with essential goods, which helps them. In the view of the cleaning women, the economy is weak. Their cost of living has been going up exponentially every year, but their salaries do not improve at the same rate. The costs of transport and food, for example, have been increasing considerably over the last few years. Their salaries go up once a year, but this is not equivalent to increases in food, transport and their other essential expenses. Their increase in salary is only R70 per year, but this amount is nowhere near to being enough to cover the rising cost of living. These women, Ruth and Abraham would buy food in bulk from the cheap supermarket chain Shoprite, but then have to carry it home on public transportation. There are shops in the townships that sell items by units, e.g., one roll of toilet paper, one tomato, one onion, which, when summed up, are more expensive for the people, but buying only a unit at a time is sometimes all they can afford. There is a high level of unemployment in the township communities, with people who live exclusively off the social grants, among whom are a number of single mothers. There are also entire families, for example, who live off the old age grant of the grandmother or grandfather, which is barely enough to sustain one person.

Within the conversations of the cleaning women, a fiery issue of discussion was the difficulties they experienced in their daily lives and what they see in the society in which they live. They acknowledge that they live in a land of plenty, but the question that these women ask over and over again is: *Of what use is living within plenty if you cannot really access it?* This is a fundamental question in their lives and to the issue of the meanings they make of the struggles they endure, among which is their food insecurity. All of these people have difficult lives, but they try to keep their heads above water. As is the case of many poor South Africans, the majority of them are devout Christians and find their emotional and spiritual support in their faith.

Their food situation

Food is often one of the last items on the list of expenses of the poor, which is very true in the case of all of the participants: the cleaning women, the unemployed of Phase 9 and the staff at the Christian organization. Food for them, like for so many other poor South Africans, is something to fill one's stomach. Being able to have something to eat, even if it is bread and tea, not to feel the hunger pangs and be able to continue working, is their daily life. Their school-aged children have lunch at school, under the national school-feeding program. All of the mothers, both employed and unemployed, try their best for their children not to go to school hungry, so even if it is just a piece of bread and tea or a small portion of pap and milk, at the very least "the children have something in their stomachs", as the women of Phase 9 said, a sentiment repeated by the other mothers.

As is generally the case among lower income families in the province, they buy mainly mealie (maize) to make pap,[3] samp,[4] as well as rice and potatoes, which they accompany with inexpensive vegetables, such as spinach, squash and pumpkin, with chicken perhaps once or twice a week and other meat much less frequently. Fish is quite expensive for them, so they also eat it infrequently. Sometimes, they can only afford to have tea and bread. Tea is very important to them. Many South Africans drink tea, and having several cups of tea per day is part of their lives. As both Thabo and Jenny affirmed, for them, not being able to afford to buy tea and sugar is considered an indignity.

The Black staff at the Christian organization live a particularly paradoxical experience. At their workplace, they are surrounded by food as part of the soup kitchen, yet Ruth, Tumelo and Thabo and, to a lesser extent, Abraham face difficulty in having sufficient food in their own homes. As the cost of living in South Africa rises, food is becoming more and more expensive, and their salaries/income are insufficient to meet their essential needs. Ruth is HIV positive and has to take her antiretrovirals (ARVs) daily, so she needs to eat at least two meals. Due a new rule implemented in early 2014 that the staff could only eat one meal at and provided by the organization, she had to go out and buy extra food to supplement that one meal so that her medication could work properly, which cuts into the money that she sets aside for transportation and her other expenses. The staff had been told that the food is for the beneficiaries and that they have to use their salaries to buy food. But their income is already stretched thin by their monthly expenses, and they do not have sufficient extra money to buy food every day, so they have been living in a paradoxical situation: living Christian values with the poor and vulnerable and surrounded by food, but going hungry. In a conversation one day, Abongile (the Youth Outreach worker) and Ruth told me, "Because we are not beneficiaries, must we go hungry, working on an empty stomach?" In further conversation, Ruth added that she really wanted to tell the Managing Director, "If you care about your staff, talk to us, listen to us and help us out", but she had not done so because she thought he should have already realized that his staff is experiencing grave economic difficulties.

As I got to know the Managing Director and the management of the organization better, I realized that these middle- to upper-middle-class Whites did not really understand life for the Blacks and Coloreds in the township or even much about the realities of the poor Whites. They did not realize the difficulties that their staff was experiencing because they did not really understand the realities that these were living, and their staff had never really explained these difficulties to them. Within this situation are embodied the racial misunderstandings and power dynamics that have in part shaped the difficulties for Whites and Blacks to enter into meaningful dialogue in South Africa.

Of all the Black staff, Abraham is in the best socioeconomic position, but food is still not a priority for him. Both he and his wife work and between them, they can cover their basic needs and a little more. Nonetheless, their first priority is to pay their bills and spend some money on improving their home. They do not spend much money on food. Abraham explains his perspective on food through the following:

> Yes, so eventually food does become a problem . . . But I think, I'd rather eat to fill up my stomach and then buy something else which is much more important with my money, like saving, like buying some tiles (for his house) because I know even tomorrow, when I do not have a job, I will be secured. I will be pleased that I can say but I did work in the past, look at what I have

done, rather than say, I did work in the past, I'm eating the money (*he laughs*). Money is gone!

What Abraham is saying here is very important because he voices an opinion, variants of which I heard time and time again. It illustrates the fact that food is not a priority for people who are facing challenges in their lives; having a roof over their heads and that their children eat, are clothed and having their basic needs met are much more important for them.

Interestingly enough, both Thabo and Tumelo, who are the ones with the lowest incomes at the organization, feel comfortable with their food situation. For both of them, the fact that they are now working, even though it is low-wage work, is most important to them. Both of these men are separated from their partners and their children. Thabo stated happily that his food situation has improved and is now "normal", even though, as he expressed, "I don't eat what I want to eat at a time I want to eat it, but at least I can be able now to, every day". They both get a meal a day at the organization and a weekly food parcel, as all the staff do, and Thabo stated that he is able to cover his living expenses and buy food for himself. When he was not working, however, he suffered a lot. He was hungry, obviously, but not being able to buy simple and relatively cheap items like tea and sugar, for him as a man who loves tea, was degrading. He said it also affected his social relations, for it made him feel that he could not visit people for fear that they would think he was visiting only to have some food. As he explained to me,

> And it also have a social impact. Like when you visit people and they know that you are not working, esh, even if you visit them on a social or like a friendly visit, just visiting them, they tend to think you are there for food. So that is one of the social impacts that that has on one. So I was even afraid to visit people because I was thinking that, "man, this person is gonna think I am here for food", so it just isn't good.

To him, not working represents that there is something wrong in your life, "that there's an element of abnormality in your life; there's something that's just not going right in your life, one way or the other".

Listening to Thabo, Tumelo, Ruth and Abraham's stories of the pain they have suffered from their poverty and hunger, I came to realize that there is so much more beneath their ever-smiling faces. In their day to day, they always have a big beaming smile and greet in the friendliest ways, and when I chat with them in the day-to-day activities, the conversations are always engaging. Speaking to them about these issues in particular, however, in their own lives, they revealed the pain they have lived, and in some regards are still living through. Their sunny outward attitude hides the anguish in their lives, and they hide their hunger. As Tumelo put it eloquently, "Even somebody will never see that I am poor or I not eat, because I am always happy, I am always smiling.

People not gonna say, this man eat pap without maybe a fish or whatever". Thabo in turn said,

> I remember when I was still like growing up, my . . . mother liked to say, "look, even after you have eaten porridge with nothing . . . or even if you have nothing to eat, just take a Vaseline and apply it to your mouth and that people are gonna interpret that as maybe the fat of the meat, so that they think you have eaten meat".

This is an important issue within their context of need. It illustrates that their pride and their dignity are foremost, that no one should really see that they are suffering.

Their perspectives of the food situation in the Free State

Most of these people believe that there is a lot of food in the province, enough for everyone, but that for many, including themselves, there is not enough money to buy it. From the cleaning women's perspectives, even though some people, such as themselves, work, they still live in poverty. Even with the social grants that many people, employed and unemployed, receive, these monies are insufficient to cover their living expenses and buy food. Tumelo agreed that there is a lot of food in the Free State, but he specified that it was "especially for the people who have, who works or who are rich". For him, the irony is that while there is a lot of food, and people who have the money can buy enough food, there are others who are struggling, in a worse situation than he is in. He explained this as

> There are people here in the village, even there in my village (the township) if I am having so many things, I can't throw them, I give maybe to my next door neighbors, they other people who are struggling more than me . . . Even they have no porridge. They are struggling, struggling . . .

Thabo's view differs from those of the other participants in that he does not think there is enough food in the Free State, for which he believes there are multiple reasons. He said that the first evidence for him there is not enough food is that there are close to 100 people who come to the organization's soup kitchen every day, and this soup kitchen is only one of many. He summed up some of these factors through the following:

> So there's many factors which contribute to this thing: the issue of land, unemployment, to manage to buy seeds, not to have money to buy equipment to prepare the land to plant there. So there is a whole range of issues. And then another thing is also, other people who make, who doesn't have kids, who doesn't want to do nothing.

Sister Electa, from the Lesedi Centre of Hope, is of the opinion that one of the problems in the Free State is that maize is being imported, even though 40% of the maize for the country comes from the Free State. Moreover, much of the wheat production in the province is being changed over to sunflower crops and potatoes. She points out furthermore to the effects of climate change and lack of resources:

> The seasons are changing. The rains do not come when they should; they come later and the crops are damaged. The lack of water is also a huge problem. Unless a farmer has underground water and an irrigation scheme, his crops are not going to grow well.

Moreover, maize prices in the country are strictly controlled by the government, and farmers do not seem to be getting their fair share. She also explained that based on the severe difficulties they have been facing in recent years, farmers in the province have been known to commit suicide because their livelihoods are being destroyed.

This despair permeates the experiences and narratives of farmers throughout the country. South Africa has both well-established commercial farming developed historically by White farmers and subsistence farming in rural areas, mainly by Black peasant farmers. However, with the advent of democracy, through land restitution and redistribution legislation, a number of large farms are in the hands of Blacks, who do not know how to work them. This has been one of the factors that has led to a decline in agricultural production. In the Free State, most of the farms are still in the hands of White farmers. In recent years, in the hope of validating retribution and redistribution, as well as improving the agricultural production, the government created a program to partner established White farmers with younger Black farmers, for these to learn from the more established farmers.

Their awareness of food programs: government and non-government

One would think that people who live in situations of need and are beneficiaries of government programs to help them alleviate their poverty within their young democracy would be aware of programs that exist to help people confront their problems regarding their access to food. Especially so in South Africa, where the right to food is written into the constitution and quite a number of government food security programs have been formulated and implemented since 1994, as I described in Chapter 2. Interestingly, this is an erroneous assumption, for none of the participants were sure how many of these government programs exist. Most of them thought that there are no programs per se, but instead just occasionally handing out of food, especially around election time. Thabo is adamant that the government is doing nothing for the people, that it is merely using them, because the food parcels that it gives out during electoral campaigns, as well as giving people their long-awaited title deeds to their lands and properties, are used as "as political tools, for electioneering", he expressed with anger.

Some of the cleaning women said that they had also heard about food parcels, which they believe may be from the government, occasionally being given to the very poor, mainly orphans and street children. They expressed that they were not exactly sure what the food parcel consists of, but they have heard that it includes a bag of mealie meal, tinned stuff, fish oil, washing powder, soaps and some other household items, which they have heard are mostly expired. It is interesting to notice how they distanced themselves from knowledge about these parcels, which seemed to signify dire poverty to them; only for the very poor and underprivileged, which they did not consider themselves to be. Further to the food parcels, they indicated that the government has also given seeds, hosepipes, wheelbarrows and spades to some people to help them plant their gardens.

The issue about growing vegetables was a polemic one for these women, however. As Valentine, the matron, said quite heatedly, "you may have food in the garden, but if you don't have paraffin or electricity to cook it, then what do you do with the food? You can go and buy R.10 in electricity, but it is still too little". This is a very interesting point, for it elucidates how growing your own food is not necessarily the solution in itself to food insecurity, for it needs to be accompanied comparatively with the means to preparing this food on a sustainable basis. Growing the food is only part of the equation to alleviating food insecurity. Alleviating food insecurity must be carried out within the context of being able to also have the means to preparing this food for consumption on a sustainable basis, without having to worry about where you get the money to pay for the electricity, gas or paraffin to cook it. This is part of what it means to overcome structural poverty and achieve food security.

In Sister Electa's view, the discussion and programs on achieving food security for the poor people of South Africa, including the Free State Province, have to be analyzed by issue, for the challenges they face cannot be addressed as if they were homogeneous in nature. She explained that the food garden program, for example, needs to take into account that there is a lack of water in the poor areas, the soil is poor and that the birds and other animals eat the vegetables. So the government giving the people seeds and tools, and even fertilizer in some cases, does not solve the problem.

Most of the participants were aware of, and some are, or have been beneficiaries of some food donations or programs that were not from the government. Ruth, Tumelo, Thabo, Abraham and Abongile, the Youth Outreach worker, all receive a weekly food parcel from their organization. The cleaning women and the unemployed of Phase 9 said that they had either received or heard of food parcels from churches, and the Lesedi Centre of Hope gives out food parcels once a month. They give them to those who attend the support group they have created for people who are ill, in need and have little or no income, as well as people who are about to get social grants, to bide them over until they receive their grants. Within these parcels, people get 5 kilos of maize meal, 1 kilo of cake flour, 1 kilo of sugar, 1 bottle of oil, 1 tin of fish, 2 packets of soya toppers for pap, face soap, toothpaste and 1 packet of powdered soap (laundry soap). Furthermore, every Thursday, a bakery brings bread to the Centre, which they then use for meals for the people of their community or distribute to them.

Thabo knows of some soup kitchens in other areas, run by churches, such as the Christian Revival Church which has a truck that goes to areas in the location to give children soup and bread. As he stated, "Yah, that's the church that I know which is trying to do something about this starvation of poverty in terms of . . . in this food issues". He also knows of some other churches which give out food parcels to people in need. Throughout the province, and the country, churches tend to provide food to people in need, whether through soup kitchens or through distribution. This is a trend that we also see in many other parts of the world.

Work opportunities in the province

The opinions of the participants were divided on the issue of whether there are enough work opportunities in the Free State. Some of them, such as Ruth and Abraham, believe that there are job opportunities, whereas others, such as Tumelo, believe that there are not. What they are all unanimous about is that the system is rife with corruption. Their differing views on how this corruption is manifested are important to understand. One manifestation of this corruption is with the labor brokers. In South Africa in recent years, there has been a severe problem with these brokers. There are a number of labor brokers all around the country that companies outsource their vacancies to, and a number of them take advantage of the people. Many of them only offer people the jobs if they give them a bribe. Ruth and Abraham said that in Bloemfontein, the bribe is around R500. The bribe is called a 'drink' and if you do not give the brokers a 'drink', you do not get the job. Ruth's husband, who has been unemployed since January, asked her to give some brokers a 'drink' for him, but she refused. She says it goes against her Christian faith.

The Congress of South African Trade Unions (COSATU) has been fighting for these brokers and brokering agencies to be eliminated, and in August 2014, President Zuma signed the *Labour Relations Amendment Act*, which, as the ANC declared, "deals decisively with the untenable exploitation of workers through labour brokers" (SABC, "Labour Act", 2014, para. 3). In this vein, government spokesperson Mac Maharaj expressed that the act "sought to respond to the increased informalization of labour, to ensure that vulnerable groups received adequate protection and were given decent work" (para. 6).

Tumelo, on the other hand, believes that people are struggling because of poverty and the lack of job creation. He is unsure why there is a lack of job creation, but his thoughts on it are that maybe the province is overpopulated or that there are more people who are not working, as compared to the past. Statistics South Africa 2016 shows that the province is the second least populated in the country, with 2 817 900 inhabitants, 5.1% of the total population of the country, having declined 0.7% since 2002, so overpopulation in itself is not the problem.

Thabo believes that there are employment opportunities, but in his own case, attributes his inability to get a full time job to a number of factors. Two of the foremost are first that most of the jobs are based on short-term contracts, whereby you only work for a few months at a time, and second, that the economy wants skilled labor. He believes that because he does not have any technical or commercial skills, it is more difficult for him to find a job. He does not consider himself "a choosy person" when it comes to work but explained that the type of work that he does depends on his ability, on whether he is able to do the job. He explained that when he is offered a job, he first deliberates whether he is able to do the job, and then if he determines that he is, he takes it. In this regard, his attitude is very different to Abraham's, who believes that he can do any job he is asked to do. Abraham's motto is "if you can do it, I can do it".

Abraham believes that the employment opportunities in the province are different depending on whether it is the private or public sector. He considers that there are job opportunities in the private sector, but that these depend on one's educational level and the time one is working, for as he said, "Most of the things you want, you will acquire after a very long time". In his view, it will be difficult for the unskilled laborers or those who only have matric to get well-paying jobs so as to build a better life for themselves. Their incomes will be only sufficient for them to survive, not to flourish. With regard to the public sector, he believes there are also jobs, but getting them depends on whom you know. In his opinion, only well connected individuals get jobs. This was a view shared by several of the participants.

Thabo elaborated on this by stating that even with job reservation during apartheid, where certain jobs were reserved for Whites and certain jobs for Blacks, everyone had jobs. In his view, job reservation is still very present today, albeit in a different way, for there are jobs which cannot be accessed by certain people, but by others. He believes that this job reservation is no longer based on the criteria of race, but is,

> . . . more of a tribal thing. People are being given jobs on a tribe basis. On a homeboy basis; are you my homeboy? Do we come from the same town? That's what we see now. So I think there's a thin line between job reservation and that was existing in apartheid, and what we see now. There is a small line. I think it is the same thing. So, one can say alright, it's true, there's not much difference.

Sister Electa is of the opinion that there is about a 40% unemployment rate in the townships and about a 60% rate for women. Her experience has shown her that there are more job opportunities for men because of the ongoing construction in the province. Successive South Africa Statistics Quarterly Labour Force Surveys show that unemployment for women is indeed higher than that for men. But this does not matter when viewed in the light of the meaning people make of their own and other people's experiences. What matters is that in the eyes of this woman, who has spent the better part of 40 years working in the townships, the unemployment situation is grave, and she can clearly perceive that fewer women who desire or need jobs are unemployed, worsening their living situations.

There is yet another side to the story of unemployment, further complicating it, which is that people who are ill also have difficulty finding employment. A number of the ill in the township have HIV-related tuberculosis (TB), making it more problematic for them to work. This leads to the problem of survival, because for a person with TB to apply for a disability grant on the basis of having TB is quite challenging. According to the SASSA parameters, if you are HIV positive, you are not sick, despite the fact that the Lesedi Centre of Hope workers see so many people on a daily basis, year after year, who are so sick that they cannot stand. So they cannot work because they are sick and they cannot receive a disability grant, because they are not disabled. Consequently, they get caught in the vise of chronic illness and chronic poverty. Sister Electa told the story of a woman who suffered from epileptic seizures, sometimes two to three times per week. She was unable to get a grant to help alleviate her poverty, because the authorities said, "she needs to get a job", but who would employ her as she is prone to epileptic seizures? It became a vicious circle of hopelessness for her.

Another dimension to unemployment, especially for some men, is the indignity of unemployment. For Thabo, not having a job was demeaning to him as a man, for it robbed him of his dignity. In this regard he said,

> I mean it's a disgrace Mama. It's an embarrassment, it's painful, because like sometimes, there are some things that you want and you not working manifests itself in so many ways. You become thin, you become dirty . . . it's like these things they happen automatically to you . . . It's demoralizing, Mama; it's just not good for a man not to work.

It was also painful and embarrassing for him as a parent because he could not buy his children even simple things like ice cream or sweets, which they asked him for when they saw other children with these.

It is very interesting to see how our South African friends above make meaning of the employment/unemployment in the province, as we compare these with recent statistics. The Statistics South Africa July–September Quarterly Labour Force Survey (published November 22, 2016) showed that employment levels in all metropolitan provinces in the country grew, except in Mangaung Metropolitan Municipality in the Free State Province, which declined by 7 000. The province also had the highest unemployment rate in the country –34.2% – having grown 2.6% from July–September 2015 to July–September 2016. Unemployment includes discouraged job seekers. In light of these statistics, we can see that Tumelo's thoughts that there may not be many sources of employment is true, but hidden within these figures are the many people who have stopped looking for work, because they perceive that there are not many sources of employment. It has become a double-edged sword, both for people's hope and dignity, as well as for government policy. In a 2016 newspaper article, Roy Jankielsohn of the Democratic Alliance in the Free State, the main opposition party, blamed the ANC-led government of Premier Ace Magashule for not committing sufficiently to creating an environment that was conducive to investment in the province, consequently leading to the increase in unemployment figures. Moreover, placing food security at the center of this situation, he stated that in the province, "the reality is that more than a million people struggle every day against great odds just to put food on the table", (Setena, 2016, "Unemployment in FS escalating"). Politicians are indeed aware that economic security and food security are interrelated, but when we look at how employment opportunities in the province are decreasing, one cannot help but wonder if the government, and many politicians, realize just how interwoven employment, economic security, food security and human dignity are.

Their perspectives of the government

Many of the poorer people in the townships want to believe in the ANC because of the political rights they are now enjoying but are angered by what they view as the corruption in the government. Government corruption is a much discussed, much lamented issue in South Africa today, and a number of people are aghast at the level of corruption.

Some of them have a hard time understanding why the government has not been helping the people more. Esther's perspective illustrates this well. Esther deeply believes in what Mandela and the other freedom fighters achieved for South Africa and she would not consider, thus far, voting for any other party aside from the ANC, because as she told me one day when we were chatting before the 2014 presidential election, "it is Mandela's party. If Mandela believed in it, then I have to believe in it". Nonetheless, she, like many other South Africans, is angry with the party because of the endemic corruption that has pervaded it over the years. She has no desire to ever go back to the times of apartheid, but she does compare some aspects of life under that regime in a favorable light when compared to the present day circumstances. She explained that many people rightfully state that apartheid was not right, because now they are starting to get jobs. Notwithstanding, she regards life today as expensive, for as she expressed heatedly one day in frustration, "all things high – petrol, food, transport, everything is money! During apartheid, the cost of living not high!"

Valentine also deeply believes in the ANC government, but does not question it the way Esther does. To the contrary, she states that the government has said that South Africans must help each other. Abraham, on the other hand, despises everything that has to do with the government and considers it immensely corrupt. Onalena (another of the cleaning women) feels open anger at the president and her frank talk about the corruption in his government frequently created some interesting, and often heated, discussions within her group of workmates. Some of the cleaning women want the ANC to succeed, despite the corruption that they acknowledge exists in the government, at both the provincial and national levels.

Some of them lay the blame for corruption more at the provincial government level rather than at the presidential level.

In an interesting turn, Valentine explained the issue of corruption as a consequence of what she considers the ineptitude on the part of Blacks in power. In her view as a young Black woman, Black Africans were hungry for authority when democracy came, but they were not prepared. She is of the opinion that "White people know what to do". She considers that Black people are clever, but that they did not have opportunities until the Black government came to power. Consequently, they do not know how to manage this power. This is a very interesting observation with regard to how she perceives Whites and Blacks and their relation to being in positions of power. In her view, their history has shaped these relations. This is a view I found to be shared by other poor Blacks. Through my work, I came to realize that how poor Blacks and Coloreds in the Free State perceive positionality and capability often differs from how Blacks and Coloreds who have been able to experience social mobility perceive these. The social mobility of these latter groups has mostly been through education and/or through political and economic advantages in the post-apartheid South Africa. There are, nonetheless, cases of a small number of Blacks who were able to experience some privilege within the apartheid era.

Sister Electa, the German nun who has lived in South Africa for over 40 years, believes that the culture of corruption has become so profoundly engrained in the South African administration today that "if you don't steal, you are not normal". She also pointed to another dimension of the issue of corruption, which is that the money in the province is not going to the projects that would benefit the people who are the most needy. Looking at the provincial government administration through the lenses of the needs of the poor communities in the province, she believes that the province has been wasting money instead of using its resources to benefit the health of the people. In her view, which I came to realize over time is shared by many people, the political environment also influences how monies are distributed and when. There is a big difference, for instance, between whether the monies are distributed before elections or afterwards. Before elections, for example, government food parcels abound and food programs are rolled out, but these do not always continue on a sustainable basis after the elections are over.

The issue of Blacks being in positions formerly occupied by Whites, building on what Valentine expressed above, is also entwined with corruption to a certain point in the view of some. As they see it, corruption is rampant, but not only with regard to financial misdemeanors, but also with regard to personnel. Sister Electa explained this by stating that sometimes Blacks are employed not because they are capable, but just because they are Black, and that in her view, this is detrimental to the cause of creating networks of support for the vulnerable. This is an interesting point that is very present in the discussions one has in the Free State, and all over South Africa today, with regard to affirmative action in post-apartheid South Africa. With the coming to power of the Black government, many Blacks have been placed in positions held before by Whites. Unfortunately, a number of them have been ill prepared for the positions they hold. In the mid-1990s, when this started taking place, there were few Blacks who were qualified to assume the positions held by the Whites during apartheid. The inferior education system that many Blacks historically had access to was worsened by the implementation of the Bantu Education system, which atrophied the education of the Black population. In the last 20 years, millions of Blacks have been able to experience better education, but some of the best qualified people are still not in the positions they should be in, for cronyism and nepotism reign in many places, putting a number of people in power because of personal or political connections.

In Thabo and Abraham's view, which is shared by others, the Black government is perpetuating the oppression of the Afrikaner government during apartheid. This oppression is experienced through the dire poverty many people are victims of today, despite the improvements that have been implemented. Thabo stated that he sees the freedom that they live, but he also sees poverty, and quoting Nelson Mandela, he said, "All that I see is the freedom and as the late Nelson Mandela said, 'where poverty exists there is no true freedom'".

"People are lazy"

This is a phrase I heard over and over again: Black people complaining about the laziness of others, mainly Blacks. There seems to be the collective belief that Black people are lazy. Esther and the unemployed women of Phase 9 explained people being lazy as their having no initiative and not wanting to work. Some of them gave as an example that there are people who live on farms but are not planting. Esther in turn, gave as an example that a woman who stays at home, who does not have a job, can grow spinach in her yard and sell a bunch for five rand (in the supermarket it is generally sold for approximately eight rand), but she would not do it. In Esther's view, this woman would prefer to complain and envy her neighbor who does grow vegetables. She said that the government takes care of the people now through social grants, but even though these are not enough, some people prefer not to work. There is a view among some that a culture of dependency on the government has been created in South Africa today.

The value of education

In general, education is valued among the people in the townships and they endeavor to send their children to school so that they can aspire to a better future. In this way, Esther and Bernard make the sacrifice to send their children to private school so that they can get a better education and be able to go on to university. They want their children to have the opportunities that Esther denied herself and that Bernard, as a 55-year-old poor Black man who grew up during apartheid, did not have. Sunny, Jenny's 16-year-old foster daughter, is studying very hard to do well at school, because she wants to earn a bursary (scholarship) to go to university to study accounting. She wants to become an accountant to make money and give her mother a better life. Thabo agreed with these views and expressed that if people do not have training and experience, then it is unlikely that they will be able to find a way to get themselves out of their situation of poverty. Emily, in turn, not only ensures that her children get a good education, but she is also furthering her own education by studying for her matric at age 44, aspiring to then go the University of the Free State to study nursing. Tumelo, on his part, wants to go to trade school to be formally trained in a trade, and then he wants to do his matric. They both want to complete their interrupted high school education, for their own pleasure, as well as to prepare themselves for a better future.

For Abraham, pursuing education is a form of self-discipline. He enjoys education because of his love of learning and because he believes that education helps to shape a person's intellect, not necessarily because it will guarantee one a job. He explained this through the following:

> Now I see in the township, people, I see how uneducated people live like *(he pounds his fist into his palm again for emphasis)* you understand? It doesn't mean that when you are educated, it's a guarantee that you'll find top job. It's not a guarantee. I pursue education as a self-discipline; it disciplines you, you understand? That's how I pursue it. I don't even think that when we have this degree or diploma, there's 100% chances that you will be rich, in that sense. There are a lot of people in my neighbourhood that they have diplomas and degrees, and they are unemployed for many years, many, many years, I'm telling you.

Echoing this last point that Abraham has made about education and unemployment, education is an important, yet somewhat frustrating issue for the unemployed women of Phase 9. They want their children to be educated so that they can have better opportunities in life than they, who all grew up under apartheid. To this end, they expressed that "today, if you are not educated, then you can't work". Notwithstanding, paradoxically, in the socioeconomic situation that the country is facing, they find it terribly frustrating that even those who have matric cannot find work. One of the women, Suzy, gave the example of her son, who has an information technology diploma but cannot find work. Like so many other people, he has prepared his CV and given it out, but cannot find work. She said it sometimes "takes more than ten years knocking on doors with your CV". In the vein of the point made in the section above of bribes, job brokers and connections, they were all of the opinion that "finding a job depends on who you know. You give them your CV and you find work".

Difference in the food situation during times of apartheid and now

"Times are different now". This is a statement I heard over and over again throughout the country and from all the participants. Everyone, without exception, said that the food and economic situations have changed from the times of apartheid to the present. All of the participants expressed that, in their own experience, during apartheid the money was very little, but there was food for everyone. In their view, the rise in food prices has also made access to food much more difficult.

All of the group of the unemployed people of Phase 9 that I spoke with are Black, with the exception of one, Mariette, who is Colored, but most said that during apartheid, times were better. They agreed that people were oppressed, had no rights and could not do what they wanted, but that clothes and food were not expensive. "During apartheid wasn't nice", they said, "but you get food and clothes". Now housing is better, but food and clothes are more expensive and "life is not good; no food, no good life". In Mariette's opinion, today they are living 'the new apartheid', and in this new apartheid, you must fend for yourself. In this way, she is echoing what Thabo said in the section above about Blacks in power re-creating the oppression the Whites had implemented through apartheid. The cleaning women stated that during apartheid and during Mandela's presidency, food was cheap, but since 2000 – and Onalena was adamant about this – things have changed. This was under the presidency of Thabo Mbeki, the president who followed Nelson Mandela. They hold the authorities of the Free State responsible for the deterioration of their situation, even though Onalena insisted that South African President Jacob Zuma is also responsible. With regard to the issue of hunger, most of the participants expressed that there was hunger during apartheid, but not like there is now. They are of the opinion that there is more hunger now, which both saddens and angers them.

Tumelo pointed to the issue of education as being an instrument that makes the present day circumstances more difficult, "because you have to learn more, you have to go to school". He is referring here to the fact that under apartheid, Blacks had an inferior education and were not allowed into skilled labor and so as unskilled laborers for Whites, they got jobs. In the post-apartheid South Africa, in the push to create a more educated Black workforce, Black people need to be educated to get a job, to learn a trade or study for a profession.

Apartheid is still very much in the national psyche, for both those who experienced it as adults, such as Ruth, some of the cleaning women and the unemployed of Phase 9, and those who were merely children when it ended, as is the case of Abraham, Thabo and Tumelo. Even though it has formally ended, they invariably compare contemporary times to the past, whether this be through experience, as we saw above, or through hearsay. With regard to this, Thabo said that he has heard over and over again and remembers that during apartheid, everybody was working and that people did not go hungry or want for shelter, for

> the government of the day would make sure that that at least each and every household has 50 kg of mealie meal and other necessary things, like the coffee and sugar and everything. And no one slept on the streets; everyone had some shelter over his or her head. That's what I remember.

Thabo went on to voice an opinion which I heard several times during my conversations with people throughout the province; that some older people say that apartheid was better than the situation they are living today. I have heard this from other older people too; people over the age of 40, who were already work-ing adults towards the end of apartheid. With regard to what changes have taken place in these 20 years, Thabo believes that the only difference between apartheid and now is that today everybody has rights and that the only thing that is better now is the issue of one being able to be what one wants to be. Elaborating on this, he said:

> Like now we have an open society, whereby one can become anything that one wants to become. If one wants to become a lawyer, a doctor, the jobs that were not, the careers that were perceived to be, the careers that were only by the White people, today even Black people can do it. So there is a small dif-ference. Not such a big difference. The other day I was listening to this on the radio, and the same thing repeated itself on TV.

Further to this, the cleaning women brought up some other social issues that are important to them, such as rape. They said that in the past, rape was not as preva-lent as it is in the present. The rape of women and children has become one of the most widespread and urgent social issues in South Africa. Statistics show that in 2012, for instance, there were 64 514 reported incidents of sexual offences in the country. Notwithstanding, many cases go unreported to the police and some stud-ies estimate that if all the cases had been reported, the number would have been over 500 000 for the country (Rape in South Africa, 2015). The reported cases of rape have decreased a little over the years. In the 2013/2014 period, there were 46 253 and in 2015/2016, 42 596 (Africa Check: Rape Statistics in South Africa, 2016). This decrease is actually worrisome for organizations focused on treating victims of rape in the country, as well as for the government, because it does not necessarily indicate that there have been fewer rapes, but instead that fewer peo-ple are reporting cases of rape.

The South African Medical Research Council has estimated that only one in nine rapes is reported to the police (Africa Check, 2014). Among the rea-sons why rapes are not reported are: mistrust in the police; the humiliation within the person's community as being exposed as a victim of rape; the fact that oftentimes the offender is known to or part of the victim's family; fear or retaliation or intimidation on the part of the perpetrator; and "the possibility of negative financial consequences, particularly if the victim is a child and her family relies on the perpetrator's income to survive" ("Rape in South Africa", 2015, para. 3). These reasons illustrate that rape affects the victim in more ways than only enduring physical and emotional harm. Financial harm can also be inflicted upon her, or him, for there are also cases of rape of boys. This last reason highlights how rape and poverty within food insecurity is framed and sadly interrelated. When talking about these social issues, the women all became quite animated because these are social issues of concern to them, as women and mothers. Pointing to this, they said boys and girls used to play together and were not afraid like they are now. Moreover, in the present, people are scared to be out and about, for they get robbed. Crime and violence are endemic in today's South Africa.

Their faith

For many poor South Africans, faith is central to their lives and most of the participants beamed when they spoke about God and their church. One cleaning woman, Mputho, is not as devout as the others and this causes some discomfort between her and her coworkers. They believe that God has a plan for them, while she questions what this plan is and why there needs to be suffering. Abraham believes in God, but is not as devout as many of the others. Jenny and Ruth are good examples that illustrate the importance of faith in people's lives. Notwithstanding the difficult life they both have, they are devout Christians and feel that God is protecting them and guiding them, and that He has his reasons why he has given them the challenges they face in life. Their faith is unwavering and they go to church every Sunday, rain or shine.

Most of the unemployed women and men are religious and their faith helps them, because when they pray, they feel that God gives them what they need; not necessarily what they *want*, but what they *need*. They made sure that they clarified that distinction for me. In many ways, some of them feel that despite their socioeconomic situation, "things are not as bad as they could be without God". They gave as an example that even though they do not have much food, they do not go to bed without eating. They say they are never hungry, for as long as there is a little mealie meal and spinach, or even bread and tea, there is food. Thabo believes in God as the Creator of our world and the force behind all that exists and everything we do. His faith is not blind and bound to asking for his immediate needs, but is quite philosophical and filled with wonderment:

> I believe in God. I look around, I look at the landforms, the sky, the sea, and I look at what people can do as a human being. There are many people around and there's nothing that surprises me that is being done by human beings. So, there is this thing that there is someone who is very, very powerful behind some of the big things that I see, for example the sea, the sky and other land forms. So I believe in God . . . and I think that is God is behind these things and also I like . . . the other I was just asking myself, why is it that when they say we live with a, we have a wonder such a lot of air here. Why is it that in the ultimate end we die? Why is it that our air just stops? Why is it that we just stop breathing when there is such a lot of air? And then I came to the fact that we . . . there is some specialty behind us. So I believe in God, I believe that someone very, very powerful behind things that are here. So I believe, I believe.

Further to this, he believes that his faith in God has helped him to understand his circumstances. Interestingly, he also said that his faith has helped him to realize that "there are people, most especially the government who deliberately doesn't want to change the situation of South Africa".

What poverty means to them

There are a number of people, including children, in the townships who are very poor and homeless, and in the eyes of the cleaning women, this is a sad consequence of life in today's South Africa. Poverty is an essential issue for them, because it is what they struggle with every day of their lives. Five out of the eight women are over 40, so they came of age and began their working lives under the apartheid system, which they remember well and compare with the present, as I explained above.

The unemployed women and men of Phase 9 conceptualize poverty as struggle. For them, it is "when people struggle to eat, to get something to wear, if you struggle for your children to go to school. Poverty is struggle". In my conversations with Abraham, Abongile, Tumelo and Thabo, I came to realize that for an African man, poverty is shame; the man feels robbed of his manhood, not being able to provide for himself and his family. Tumelo, for example, struggles with poverty, but he finds some satisfaction in being able to have a roof over his head and some food to eat. To him, poverty means "struggling, job creation, that there are more people who are not working". Struggle is the main strand running through Tumelo's narrative; people struggling to make ends meet, people struggling to survive amidst plentiful resources which they cannot access because they are poor.

For Abraham, there are two kinds of poverty: financial poverty and mental poverty. In his view, mentally poor people are those who do not break away from their mindset of poverty and dependency and do not face the challenges in their lives by trying to help themselves. He has no patience with them. He acknowledges that there are people who do not have money and barely survive, but firmly believes, based on his own experience, that they have to find ways to overcome this challenge. For Thabo, poverty is the inability to do things, to have things, to have access to things, for one's life. Further to this, for him, poverty

> means a rawness, it means . . . because there are different types of poverty. There is the poverty of ideas, like ideas maybe to take one (out) of a situation that one is in. It means so many things, it means a rawness . . . One other thing I can also say, to me it . . . a person who doesn't have experience, a raw mind, who hasn't experienced everything . . . A person, like for instance, if you do not have any training, of some sort, if you don't have any training, that you haven't experienced anything that can take you out of your situation . . .

White poverty from the Black perspective

For Black Africans, especially those who grew up under the apartheid regime, the omnipresence of White poverty is bewildering. Having grown up under the oppressive system of apartheid as poor Blacks, the majority of the participants are somewhat confused about the abundance of poor Whites today. The cleaning women are not quite sure as to why there are so many poor Whites today; people who can be seen begging on the streets of Bloemfontein, for example, whereas one hardly sees Black Africans begging, for they are instead street hawkers. They think that Whites beg because "they are used to quick money", as compared to Black Africans, "who are used to working for their money".

This is an opinion with several variations that I heard quite a lot from Blacks and Coloreds: that Blacks are accustomed to working hard, but Whites are not. In the opinion of the unemployed of Phase 9, despite what they see on the streets, few Whites struggle; they believe that only some of them do. Nonetheless, they do believe that more affluent people treat poor Blacks and Whites with the same disdain. Thabo, on the other hand, has no sympathy for poor Whites, for he believes that if they are poor today, it is because they have squandered the money that they had accumulated during apartheid. He and Tumelo even dispute the argument that some Whites are poor. They believe that "White poverty is a smokescreen, it is pure propaganda".

Abraham's view of poor Whites is quite different from that of the others, and it is one that he has built through his work at the organization. There, he has gotten to know White people better and has come to realize, similar to the unemployed of Phase 9, that there is no color difference in poverty. He explained that all his life before coming to the organization, he always thought that there were no poor White people, that even after apartheid ended Whites were still in superior socio-economic positions to Blacks. Before coming to the organization, whenever he saw a White person, he felt that this person was superior to him just because he/she is White. I also perceived this in other places and in conversations with other people; that the perception many poor Blacks have of Whites being superior to them is still ingrained in them, similar to the times of apartheid. Abraham explained this perception as following:

> You see White person being poor standing with the board at the robot,[5] "I have no job, no nothing". . . No what? No what? Us as Black people, you understand, ehh, we think "how can a White person be poor?" It's such a shame eh. But now for you as a Black person, you see another Black man being poor, it's normal, it's nothing. It's normal, man, we are Black, we are poor, (but) seeing White people being poor, you are so amazed *(he laughs)*, such a shame. But now here, we are all together, we are all equal. Whether you are Black or you are White, you understand? You have the same thing; you are rich, you are poor, you are Black, you are White. Black poor, White poor, one is the same thing. Which means there is no that, coming to your question, neh, there is not perception that only only only poverty affects eh . . . Black people. It does not only affect, nowadays, it does not only affect Black people; it affects White people as well.

As we can see here, for Abraham, the Black poor and the White poor are equally poor, so interestingly, within the context of this post-apartheid society, they are equal in their poverty.

"Blacks know how to work"

This was an interesting trend of thought I found, which seemingly contradicts the trend I describe above *"Black people are lazy"*. I say seemingly contradict, because I realized that what it really means for these people is that Blacks know what it means to struggle, to have worked hard in the past. The unemployed of Phase 9 consider that as Blacks, they were 'made to struggle'. In their view, Blacks know what it means to struggle because they have been struggling for so long; they are accustomed to having a hard life. In my conversations with other poor Blacks, and as Abraham expressed above, I heard the same theme again and again: *We know what it's like to have a hard life*. So for them, being poor and having to struggle is not the problem. The problem is the *kind* of poverty that they are living in and the *kind* of struggle that they are being forced to engage in; it is poverty and struggle within the first freedom and the first democracy they have ever had as South Africans. They have rights, but they do not have a life with dignity. I explain this issue in detail in Chapter 6.

HIV/AIDS, poverty and food security

HIV is an epidemic in South Africa today which has touched the lives of millions. South Africa has the largest HIV/AIDS treatment program in the world, covering millions of people. In April 2004, free ARVs were introduced in the public sector in the country, after a prolonged battle between activists and former President Thabo Mbeki and Health Minister Dr. Manto Tshabalala-Msimang, both of whom continually questioned the interrelationship between HIV and AIDS and the effectiveness of ARVs to combat these. This Health Minister advocated for the consumption of African potatoes, garlic and beetroots as nutritional supplements to fight AIDS, pointing to ARVs as being not effective in fighting the virus, as well as their side effects. This put her in direct conflict with AIDS activists and experts and led her to being infamously dubbed 'Dr. Beetroot', 'The Potato Doctor' and other names by her critics. Interestingly enough, this controversial doctor was one of the people who focused on healthy nutrition as one of the major instruments in the fight against AIDS.

Since the policy implementation in 2004, however, for over a decade, only people with a CD4 count of 500 would qualify for these free antiretrovirals, leaving out a huge swathe of the HIV-positive population with CD4 counts below 500. Impoverished persons with low CD4 counts were impacted the most by this policy. The struggle for access to all continued over the years, yielding fruit in May 2016 when the South African government updated the HIV policy to allow treatment for all HIV positive South Africans, regardless of their CD4 count (Child, 2016). This new policy follows the World Health Organization's recommendation, based on long-term research, that people should start treatment with ARVs as soon as they tested HIV positive, even if they are healthy. This research shows that the earlier a person starts ARV treatment, the less likely they are to get sick and the more likely they are to live longer.

Both Ruth and Esther's foster child Kiki are HIV positive. Fortunately, they are on ARVs and are doing well. Notwithstanding, they need nutritious food to keep them healthy. Despite being HIV positive, Ruth is healthy. She takes her ARVs on a daily basis and gets them for free, from a clinic in Bainsvlei, Bloemfontein. She has never been gravely ill as a consequence of being HIV positive and explained that she feels 'so normal' that she sometimes forgets her medical condition. Ruth tries to eat as well as she can, but she always gives preference to her children's nutrition first. On her part, Esther tries to give Kiki as much nutritious food as she can, but on her and her husband Bernard's salary, they cannot always give her what she needs, for they have three other children to feed. Esther is aware that Kiki should be eating eggs, yogurt, fruit and milk – Kiki should be drinking a glass of milk a day as mandated by the doctors and nutritionists – but she cannot always give it to her. Kiki's story is one of many children in South Africa: children abandoned by their parents and raised by other family members. Kiki is one of the lucky ones, because she has been embraced by a family who loves her and takes care of her as well they can. Many other HIV-positive children have been rejected by their family members and have been put in orphanages or thrown out onto the streets to fend for themselves. The streets and shelters are filled with these children, which is an issue I discuss below in the section on the Christian organization.

The poor and vulnerable are the ones who have suffered the most, for they are those who have the fewest resources with which to combat the epidemic. Fortunately, as I explained above, the government in recent years has been providing poor people with free ARVs, and there are many prevention and care campaigns throughout the country. Nonetheless, the epidemic continues, creating many HIV/AIDS orphans who become financial burdens on their extended families after their parents pass away, or, as I mentioned above, are put into overflowing orphanages or left to fend for themselves.

Churches and pastors in South Africa have significant influence over how people confront the AIDS epidemic. Some of them understand the severity of the HIV/AIDS epidemic and, through their ministry, collaborate with the HIV/AIDS consciousness, prevention and protection campaigns. These campaigns are to help people understand the importance of protection from infection, as well as the importance of care for the HIV/AIDS patient, together with all the other issues surrounding HIV/AIDS. There are other pastors, however, who deter the campaigns, causing grave consequences for the people by keeping them ignorant of the nature of the illness, as well as spreading fear. One such pastor is a man called Pastor November who leads a huge church in the township. This pastor discourages the use of ARVs because he says that HIV/AIDS does not exist. For his churchgoers who are HIV positive, he lays them on the floor and puts his foot on their chest to will away the virus. Rumor has it that he killed a person some time ago by putting his weight on the person's chest, but what is definitely known is that he has indirectly killed many others by making them throw away their ARVs and not continue their treatment. He is one of the worst foes that the HIV/AIDS education and treatment campaigns have in Bloemfontein.

HIV/AIDS-related illnesses as well as other illnesses and general health require nutritious food on a sustainable basis, which the further I worked and spoke with people throughout the country, the more I realized is quite lacking among the poor and vulnerable.

The stigma of HIV/AIDS

Despite the numerous HIV/AIDS awareness and prevention campaigns, there is still a stigma associated with the disease in the province, and many people prefer not to be open about their condition. Kiki and Ruth's cases are two examples. Esther and Bernard have not told their older children that Kiki is HIV positive, because they are not sure how they will react, based on the stigma associated with the virus. When the children asked why Kiki needs to take tablets every day, Esther explained to them that she needs medication to keep away the ear infection that she had for so long when she first came to live with them, which they remember vividly. This ear infection was a consequence of Kiki's high CD4 count and inadequate care she received from her father, with whom she had been living. So far, the children seemed to accept the explanations and had not been asking many questions, but Esther is preparing herself for the day when she will need to tell them. She said she will ask the doctor to help her with her explanation, but she also realizes that the children are learning about the HIV epidemic in South Africa at school and hopes they will be prepared to understand Kiki's condition.

Ruth's children do not know that she is HIV positive and when they see her drinking the ARVs, they ask her what they are for, and she just laughs and replies, "Let me drink my medicine, do you want me to die?" And they seem to just take it for granted that Mom takes medicine. The two children who live with her are eleven and seven, so they may not realize as yet what the tablets may mean, but her eldest son, who does not live with her, is 16 years old, and he may soon realize it. She says she will handle the conversation when the time comes.

HIV/AIDS is widespread in South Africa, and even though there has been much outreach, educating the people of the country with regard to this public health issue is difficult, for it is still a somewhat taboo subject. People do not necessarily readily disclose their status for fear of rejection and there are still some people who believe that AIDS, further to being spread by infection, can also be brought on by witchcraft. This was what Ruth and her aunts believed happened in the case of her brother. Her 18-year-old brother died of AIDS in 1996, even though his adolescent girlfriend at the time is still alive today, 20 years later. According to Ruth, a self-professed born-again Christian, a deeply religious woman, whose faith is the center of her being, it was her stepmother who did witchcraft on her brother and infected him with AIDS. This is a belief that is hard to argue with within the poor Black population. Ruth explains her belief that this is what happened her brother in the following excerpt from one of our conversations.

> Ya, it was sad, it was sad. Then, once my brother started to get sick, sick and sick and sick. We thought maybe it's cold, but he was . . . I don't know

how can I call it . . . It was a curse; she *(referring to the stepmother)* curse him, and then when he pulls the clothes like this *(she gestures at pulling her blouse and pants off her arm and thigh by lifting them with two fingers)*, they was sticking *(meaning his skin was sticking to his clothes and being pulled off)* . . . sticking, sticking on the skin. Even here *(gesturing to another part of her body)*, he had bad bad spots, smelling bad . . . So some of the people, my neighbors, they were the people . . . who going to support us, because they know how cruel this woman was *(referring to her stepmother)*. And then I call my aunt in Welkom. Luckily, there was a funeral[6] in Botshabelo *(where she and her brother were living)* and then she came. When she came, she cried a lot. She says, "no, no, no, no", and she calls my father. At the very same time, my stepmother took my brother to Lesotho to her witchdoctor . . . You know? That's where she finishes everything to my brother . . .

Ruth explained that after her brother came back from Lesotho, his health deteriorated considerably, and then she and her aunt took him to the doctor, where he was diagnosed as HIV positive: "when he goes to the medical doctors, they say he is HIV positive, because the blood was already the other way round". He was only 18 years old, and the doctor asked him if he had a girlfriend, which he did, but as Ruth pointed out, his girlfriend is still alive 20 years later. Notwithstanding, she had no way of knowing if the girl is HIV positive but well controlled with ARVs, as she is. After Ruth's brother's diagnosis, she decided to do training in AIDS care:

I train in AIDS to do that course, so I can know deeply what is meant by AIDS and all those things. And when I was in the training there, I spoke to one of the social workers. It was something hurting me every time I saw my brother, and then that social worker explains to me the other way around, how AIDS gets to the people and it was that time that the stigma was so high . . . If people have HIV, they not gonna touch what, you not gonna eat with the people, all those things. But I never wanted him to allow that situation to kill him.

Despite Ruth's health training and knowledge of what HIV/AIDS is and how it is transmitted, despite being HIV positive herself, having been infected by her former partner, and deeply believing in God, Ruth still believes that her stepmother did witchcraft on her brother, as is illustrated in the following:

Then after that *(after her brother's diagnosis)* my aunt came, and then she decided to take one of the T-shirts of my brother, go to the doctors in Welkom, so he can be sure what's happening. My aunt went to the five doctors; the witchdoctors, five of them, different, and they told her one same story; that it is my stepmother, she is the one who makes my brother like that.

Ruth's belief system of three intersecting worlds, that of the Christian religious one, the non-Christian spiritual one, and the scientific one is quite common, in

South Africa and in many societies around the world. People who live within these belief systems do not see them as mutually exclusive. To the contrary, these interweaving beliefs help them to make sense of their circumstances, to create spaces of understanding the seemingly incomprehensible. Understanding scientifically that AIDS is a virus, knowing that she needs to take ARVs to control it, learning how to take care of herself, and others, to live with it, coexist with the fact that Ruth still thinks that, in some cases, AIDS can be brought on by witchcraft. This is a complex mindset to work with in South Africa, and other societies where people have similar interweaving comprehensions.

The uneasiness of coexistence and care for 'the other'

The racial 'other' is still an omnipresent reality in South Africa today and very much so in the Free State Province. Its history as an Afrikaner Republic and being a largely farming, Afrikaner-dominated state has left some of the conceptual and economic structures of apartheid in place. Bloemfontein is not cosmopolitan Capetown, nor metropolitan Johannesburg or bustling Durban. It is a small city where Afrikaans is widely spoken, the Afrikaans culture, architecture and societal dynamics are very evident in quotidian life, and Afrikaners still dominate the economy. Racial incidents of Whites against Blacks are still frequent, much to the anger of Blacks and the dismay of progressive Whites. And so are incidents of Blacks against Whites, among the most publicly known are those of Blacks invading White farms and attacking White farmers. The uneasiness of coexistence permeates the air they breathe together. And does this change among the impoverished peoples of the different racial groups, these social constructs that differentiate us?

As can be seen thus far, in the opinion of the unemployed of Phase 9, as well as Abraham, being Black, Colored or White in South Africa today makes no difference when you are poor; they feel that the more affluent treat the impoverished with the same attitude of disdain, regardless of race. Thabo, interestingly, despite denying that there is no such thing as White poverty, agrees with this opinion. In his view, moreover, being Black means nothing today, for he has not benefitted from anything that the New South Africa has promised. He explained that even the Whites are telling Blacks in power today, "You are talking about Black Economic Empowerment, are you not perpetuating racism?" Moreover, even Blacks throughout the country complain that this government only talks about Black Economic Empowerment (BEE), but only a few people have benefitted from it, some of them becoming fabulously rich.

Another interesting point that both Thabo and Tumelo brought up is the issue of solidarity among the Whites as compared to among the Blacks. In their view, Whites have always supported each other and still do so today, stating that "White people look after their people, they support each other", whereas Blacks do not support one another today. They are of the opinion that for Blacks, the issue comes down to money, "whereby if you have money, you have money and they like you, but if you don't have money, they don't". When asked what place Ubuntu has in today's South Africa, they both exclaimed, "Just in paper. Eh, a theoretical thing". And Jack retorted, "Ubuntu? Eh!" in disgust. For them, Ubuntu was very present during apartheid, and Blacks were there for each other, but today, it is every man for himself, for the ever-proclaimed Ubuntu no longer exists.

Working with the poor and vulnerable

The Black staff at the Christian organization know what it is like to be poor and vulnerable, having lived these situations themselves, and they cherish the opportunity to be able to help others. For Ruth, this is very important. Having been poor and vulnerable herself and still living in the township today, working with people who are homeless and/or caught in the vicious cycle of poverty and vice (for many sniff glue, do drugs and drink or are in a life of prostitution) is a responsibility she takes seriously. She wants to be able to help them, but feels that she cannot always do so, for various reasons. With regard specifically to the men who come to the soup kitchen, it makes her very sad to see them in the state they are in. She also wonders why it is only men who come and worries about the women and children some of them have left at home. As she expressed, "they come to eat at least this one meal, but what are their families eating? They are hungry at home . . ."

For Abraham, working with the homeless youth gave him a perspective about their lives, very different to the opinion he had about them before. He explained this as following:

> Before working here, when I walked by, when I passed by the street kids in town, ahhh *(he says in disgust)* actually, I used to annoy, disgust! You understand, disgust me! After doing this couple of street walks with Stephen (the former Youth worker), I realize these are people, human beings, you understand. There's only one thing that should happen, which is to get them to know you better, you know them better, build a trust, build a relationship and everything will be fine.

He also loves working with the older attendees at the organization (whom they call beneficiaries), for they remind him where he comes from. He empathizes with them, the poor and homeless, and understands the circumstances they are living. Talking about his job, he said:

> I found a job here and then I met these wonderful people I am working with, the beneficiaries, whereby they remind me from where I come from, where I come from, where I **am** from, the township, you understand? So when I serve these people, I serve them with a great smile, knowing that I'm also faced with the challenges that they are faced with, despite the fact that at least now, it's not the same as before, but (where) they are from, I am also from there. I don't know how to put this, but when I think about it, not having

both parents on my side fulltime, I would have been a street kid, honestly speaking . . .

Sister Electa, on the other hand, works with the ill and dying; those in their deepest despair of chronic poverty and illness. She is not sentimental about it. Her approach is 'you need to do this. You need to get better for yourself and for your family, and I am here to help you in every way I can, but you need to help yourself'. This is not such a different approach to Abraham's, but the nature of their engagement is different. Sister Electa, Abraham, Ruth, Tumelo and Thabo all live amongst the poor and work with them on a daily basis, but the last four work with the more able bodied people. Sister Electa sees people in dire health conditions and is directly involved in their lives at their worst, on a continual basis, day in and day out. She has dedicated her life and work to the poor, vulnerable and sick of the township, whereas the staff at the Christian organization have not. It is their job, and then they go home to focus on their own personal issues and their families.

Challenges and agency

Many of the people in this book have expressed their agency to confront the challenges they face around food and to alleviate their economic constraints through diverse means. Some of the unemployed women – and a few men – of Phase 9, encouraged by the food initiative of Dr. Meko, have been planting food gardens and their diets have improved. They have been planting vegetables such as spinach, carrots, beans, pumpkins and onions. In this way, they have also become healthier. Esther has also in the past often planted a food garden in the summer, growing some vegetables every year from seeds her uncle in Botshabelo, who plants many vegetables, gives her. I discuss her uncle's garden as his initiative to confront his food insecurity in the section on Botshabelo in Chapter 5. Notwithstanding, in the 2013–2014 summer planting season (summer is approximately November to March in South Africa), she did not plant anything because she is tired of her neighbor's chickens destroying her garden. Further to this, as another manifestation of her agency to improve her life, Esther wants to go to school on the weekends to train as a teacher's aide for kindergarten. This is her dream, and she is saving money to be able to pay for her studies. As I explained above, Ruth is also doing her matric and looking forward to studying nursing at university.

Together with their food gardens, some of the unemployed of Phase 9 look towards self-employment as a means to sustain themselves. The issue of creating self-employment is an important one for them. Some of them have initiative and want to create work for themselves, but explained that the problem is that even if they try to do so, the people in the townships do not have enough money to buy their goods, for they do not have work. One of the women, Emmy, expressed this quite eloquently: "I wants to sell things, probably clothes. I used to sell clothes, but sometimes you wants to sell things but people want to buy on credit and then don't pay. They cannot pay because they don't have money". The group coordinator, Angie, has been thinking of making bread and getting a grant to sell bread to the schools. As she expressed, "everybody buys bread", so she believes it would be a viable option. Another woman, Mariette, is a seamstress who has been trying to bring together a group of women to get some machines and to work together, but she has not been successful in this endeavor. She said that there was no interest on their part. She believes that if five to six women get together, they can create a small business sewing, tailoring and mending clothes. She is willing to teach those who do not know how to sew, but what she finds frustrating is that she has not been able to even get to the point of brainstorming ideas with them, to see what initiatives they can formulate. Moreover, she does not know how they would get the sewing machines, because people do not have money.

Government loans to establish small businesses such as this one are available, but the women do not want to consider them, for they said that the government is too slow. They also said that if you are not working, getting a government loan is difficult. This is their opinion and is one factor that stops them from considering a government loan. The other is that even if they did get a loan, they believe that their potential clientele in the township will not be able to buy what these women would be selling. These women are very frustrated with the situation in which they are living. This group of people wants to do things for themselves. Unfortunately, they do not know of any community efforts to improve their situation, apart from their own.

Tumelo, on his part, is very ambitious and is determined to go to trade school to learn a trade and obtain his certification. He also wants to complete his high school education so that with both achievements, he can get a good job to give himself and his family a better life. He has already done his research on where he can go to academic and trade school part time. What he is lacking is the money to pay for them. With the little income he earns, he manages to survive, but it is not enough to pay for his studies and training, so he looking for a stable job or jobs, so he can do so. Tumelo's determination to succeed is a really good indicator of his initiative; his initiative to overcome his poverty and the challenges to his life, including his food insecurity. When he left school, he began working. When he lost his job, he looked for another and when he could not find another permanent one, he did whatever odd job came along. When he could not find work in Thaba Nchu, he moved to Bloemfontein to look for work and he has survived. He came to the organization initially because he was hungry and had heard that he would be able to get food there every day, but that was not sufficient. As soon as he came to the soup kitchen, he asked if there was any work, if anyone knew of any work, and that is how he got the two part-time jobs to help him get back on his feet. As he is getting back on his feet, he is thinking of how to improve himself and looking for ways to make it happen. Tumelo faces the challenges in his life head on and dreams of a better future for himself. He has agency. When I expressed my admiration about his not being shy to ask for work when he got to the soup kitchen, he responded:

> I was not shy . . . It is my life, there's no people who can help without maybe saying nothing. If I am hungry, I must ask you. If I have a problem, ask you. I should not be ashamed what people are gonna say. It's my life . . . Where I am . . . People are saying "look after your life" . . . Yourself . . . not somebody (else). You must look after you. I'm not afraid of work. I still fight too, until I go under the ground . . .

Abraham is also a man of drive and belief in himself. He has improved his station in life through his hard work and willingness to take advantage of whatever opportunities came his way. He has drive and initiative. Working fulltime, he began to attend university part time, and even though it took him seven years, he finished his studies. He has risen in the ranks of the Christian organization through this drive and initiative. When the Youth worker quit his job, the Managing Director asked Abraham if he was willing to take the chance to take the position and he responded willingly, in his characteristic style of enjoying challenges:

> I said "eh, bring it on!" *(and he laughs)* I'm a chancer, me, you understand? That's one thing I know about myself. You can ask me what is one thing you know about yourself? I take chances, I'm an opportunist. I don't say, this thing I never did it before. If you can do, I believe I can as well. If you can give me a chance and then teach me how to do that thing, I can learn how to do that thing, you understand? And I take that chance.

The latest challenge that he has taken on is creating and coordinating the temporary employment city clean-up program for the men who come for the soup kitchen. Both Tumelo and Thabo are part of this program. The intention is that instead of only giving them food to eat and leave, the organization finds a way to create employment for them. For Abraham and the organization, the clean-up teams represent more than only some money; they also assist the men in maintaining their dignity. As Abraham explained:

> That is how actually we realize that the necessity of the clean-up team; not only for the guys to come here and eat and leave, at least for him, if he can, only for today, even if it's once a week, he can buy for himself a loaf of bread.

Some of the men are regulars on the teams because they have shown commitment, and a number of them have gotten jobs elsewhere now, which is the objective of the program. As Abraham said, "it's not for us to keep them here, but to assist them to prosper".

What Abraham says here is really important, because it highlights the importance of understanding the psychology of the very poor and their dignity. As Abraham explained, for most of them, that is what they want. He said that they tend to feel helpless or hopeless because they are in the position where they have to beg and receive without maybe buying for themselves. So the more they have some money in their pocket, at least they can go out and buy a loaf of bread and some milk for themselves. It's about their dignity.

He has worked hard to make a living for his family, and he is determined to never let himself fall into dire poverty again. He does not earn a lot of money, but what he earns goes toward making his family comfortable, improving his house and making sure they have a roof over their heads. Abraham is a very determined and ambitious man who is not afraid of challenges. He does not blame his past for what he called his "lack of focus and failure during his life", but that his situation of fatherlessness, with a virtually absent mother and two young boys growing up by themselves made him a victim of his circumstances. Notwithstanding, he acknowledges his decisions and shows initiative to overcome the challenges he has faced. After drawing this portrait of structural poverty in the townships, let us now turn to poverty within the city.

Notes

1 RDP houses are the simple brick houses the government has built for the poorer people of the country, but not all the poor have been able to get these houses.
2 Mkhukhus are the zinc houses, held up with pieces of wood, that people build themselves.
3 Pap is one of South Africans' main starches. It is made with cornmeal and is generally made as a hard crumbly cornmeal, a softer cornmeal or a more liquid one, similar to porridge.
4 Similar to hominy.
5 Traffic lights are commonly referred to as 'robots' in South Africa.
6 Funerals are a big event in African culture, which family members come from all over to attend.

References

Africa Check. (2016). *Rape statistics in South Africa: Factsheets and guides*. Retrieved from https://africacheck.org/factsheets/guide-rape-statistics-in-south-africa/

Africa Check. (2014). *South Africa's official crime statistics for 2013/14: Factsheet.* Retrieved from http://africacheck.org/factsheets/factsheet-south-africas-official-crime-statistics-for-201314/

Aliber, M. (2003). Chronic poverty in South Africa: Incidence, causes and policies. *World Development*, 31, 473–490.

Brookfield, S. (2004). Racializing and concretizing Gramsci in contemporary adult education practice. *Interchange*, 35(3), 375–384.

Cameron, T., and Spies, S. B. (Eds.). (1992). *A new illustrated history of South Africa.* Johannesburg: Southern Book Publishers; Cape Town and Johannesburg: Human & Rousseau.

Chase, S. (2005). Narrative inquiry: Multiple lenses, approaches, voices. In Denzin, N. and Lincoln, Y. (Eds.) (2005). *The Sage handbook of qualitative research* (3rd ed.). Thousand Oaks, CA: Sage Publications.

Child, K. (2016, May 10). Government updates HIV policy to allow ARV treatment for all South Africans. *Times Live*. Retrieved from www.timeslive.co.za/local/2016/05/10/ Government-updates-HIV-policy-to allowARV-treatment-for-all-South-Africans

Cooperation (ICCO Cooperation). (2014). *Right to food and nutrition watch 2014. Ten years of the right to food guidelines: Gains, concerns and struggles*. Retrieved from www.rtfnwatch.org/fileadmin/media/rtfn watch.org/ENGLISH/pdf/Watch_2014/Watch_ 2014_PDFs/R_t_F_a_N_Watch_2014_eng.pdf

Department of Agriculture and Rural Development. Free State Province. (2012). *Agricultural land and projects/programme/support profile for effective planning and implementation, Thabo Mofutsanyana*. Retrieved from www.ard.fs.gov.za/files/fs-profile/ Thabo-Mofutsanyana.pdf

Department of Rural Development and Land Reform. Republic of South Africa. (2009). *Free State Comprehensive Rural Development Programme (CRDP)*. Retrieved from www.dla.gov.za/phocadownload/Pilot/free state/proposed_draft_framework_crdp_free_ state_pilot_v1small.pdf

De Schutter, O. (2014, January 24). *The transformative potential of the right to food*. Report of The Special Rapporteur on the Right to Food. United Nations General Assembly, Human Rights Council, Twenty-fifth session. Retrieved from www.srfood.org/images/ stories/pdf/officialreports/20140310_finalreport_en.pdf

Duneier, M. (2011). How not to lie with ethnography. *Sociological Methodology*, 41. doi/ 10.1111/j.1467-9531.2011.01249.x/full

Foley, D. E. (2002). Critical ethnography: The reflexive turn. *International Journal of Qualitative Studies in Education*, 15(4), 469–490. DOI:10.1080/09518390210145534

Hassanein, N. (2012). Practicing food democracy: A pragmatic politics of transformation. In Williams Forson, P., and Counihan, C. (Eds.), *Taking food public: Redefining foodways in a changing world* (pp. 461–474). New York: Routledge.

Hollway, W., and Jefferson, T. (2001). *Doing qualitative research differently: Free association, narrative and the interview method*. London: Sage Publications, Ltd.

Holtz-Gimenez, E. (2012). From food crisis to food sovereignty: The challenge of social movements. In Williams-Forson, P., and Counihan, C. (Eds.), *Taking food public: Redefining foodways in changing world* (pp. 592–602). New York: Routledge.

The Local Government Handbook. A complete guide to municipalities in South Africa. (2014). *Thabo Mofutsanyana District Municipality (DC19)*. Retrieved from www.local-government.co.za/districts/view/10/Thabo-Mofutsanyana-District Municipality

The Local Government Handbook. A complete guide to municipalities in South Africa. (2013). *Free state*. Retrieved from www.localgovernment.co.za/provinces/view/2/free-state

Merriam, S. B., Caffarella, R. S., and Baumgartner, L. M. (2007). *Learning in adulthood: A comprehensive guide* (3rd ed.). San Francisco, CA: Jossey-Bass.Rape in South Africa. (2015). *Rape crisis. Cape Town Trust. Supporting recovery. Seeking justice*. Retrieved from http://rapecrisis.org.za/rape-in-south-africa/

Setena, T. (2016, May 11). Unemployment in FS escalating. *News 24*. Retrieved from www.news24.com/SouthAfrica/Local/Express-News/unemployment-in-fs escalating-20160510

South African Broadcasting Corporation (SABC). (2014, August 20). Labour Act a sign of progression: ANC. *SABC News*. Retrieved from www.sabc.co.za/news/a/8202320045 2b84c58ac29ba5ad025b24/Labour-Act-asign-of progression:-ANC-20142008

South African History Online. Towards a People's History. (SAHO). ((2014). Growth of Informal settlements: Mangaung township. In *Bloemfontein. Bloemfontein, the segregated city*. Retrieved from www.sahistory.org.za/bloemfontein/growthinformal-settlements-manguang township

Statistics South Africa. (2016, November 22). *Quarterly labour force survey*. Retrieved from www.statssa.gov.za/publications/P0211/P02113rdQuarter2016.pdf

Statistics South Africa. (2014a). *Maluti-a-Phofung*. Retrieved from http://beta2.statssa.gov.za/?page_id=993&id=maluti-a-phofung-municipality

Statistics South Africa. (2014b). *Mangaung muncipality: Economy*. Retrieved from www.statssa.gov.za/?page_id=1021&id=mangaung-municipality

Statistics South Africa. (2014c). *Mangaung muncipality: People*. Retrieved from www.statssa.gov.za/?page_id=1021&id=mangaung-municipality

Statistics South Africa. (2012). *Census 2011: Provinces at a glance*. Retrieved from www.statssa.gov.za/Census2011/Products/Provinces%20at%20a%20glance%2016%20Nov%202012%20corrected.pdf

Terreblanche, S. (2012). *Lost in transformation*. Johannesburg, SA: KMM Review Publishing Company (PTY) Ltd.

Terreblanche, S. (2002). *A history of inequality in South Africa 1652–2002*. Scottsville and Johannesburg, South Africa: University of KwaZulu-Natal Press and KMM Review Publishing Company (PTY) Ltd.

4 Poverty and hope in the city

Within the city of Bloemfontein, there is much poverty. One can see many White beggars on the streets, mainly at the robots, with fewer Black beggars, a number of whom are the Black homeless youth. There are also many Black street hawkers at the robots and on the sides of the road, as well as Black, White and Colored car watchers at almost every establishment in the city, be these stores, restaurants, markets or offices – people who are not paid by the establishment, but live off the tips that people give them. In this chapter, I discuss poverty in the city; in the food stores and markets in the wealthier neighborhoods and in the inner city. My focus is on the experiences of two White men, a car watcher at a food market and a homeless man and beggar in the inner city, who is an attendee/beneficiary of the Christian NGO.

The food market

As I began to understand the situation in South Africa better, I came to realize that in some food establishments, such as supermarkets and grocery stores, it is quite common for the lower-wage staff and support workers to be food insecure. Even though they are surrounded by food every day, many of them do not have access to this food because they cannot afford it, and the management of the establishment does not necessarily provide it to them for lower prices or for free. The support workers, such as the people who carry the groceries for the customers and watch the cars, generally live off the tips that the customers give them, and these tips vary in amount according to each person and the state of the economy. The South African economy has been quite troubled for some time; consequently, people are not as generous as they may have been and could be in better economic circumstances.

The Fruit and Vegetable Markets – Fruit and Veg, as they are called – are a popular market chain in South Africa. Piet, one of the participants, is an Afrikaans man who works as a car watcher at a Fruit and Veg on the outskirts of a wealthy suburb in Bloemfontein. Piet prefers the term 'motor guard' to car watcher. He carries the groceries for the customers, retrieves the trolleys (shopping carts) and watches the cars. At the Fruit and Veg where Piet works, there are six motor guards, all white Afrikaans men; there are no Blacks and no women. I found this interesting, and when I asked Piet about it, he told me it was just how it happened, that it was not deliberate. It is telling though, for in the parking lots of other establishments in Bloemfontein, one often sees White and Black car watchers, men and women, working together. There are however, fewer female car watchers than there are male. Moreover, most of the female car watchers I saw were White women. I hardly ever saw Black women car watchers.

The soup kitchen

I have already explained the nature, programs and services of the Christian organization in Chapter 3. Here I will, however, give further description of the beneficiaries of the soup kitchen which is one of its services, for one of the participants whose story I focus on, David, is a beneficiary.

The soup kitchen serves mainly men and boys. In all my time there, I only saw two women on separate rare occasions. Through my conversations with the staff as well as my observations and interactions with the beneficiaries, I realized that these boys and men are in vulnerable life situations. Not having a home, living on the streets, or not being able to work and provide for their families even though they have homes, has undermined their dignity in some ways. But for some of them, living on the streets is their choice, as a consequence of the negative home life that they had. Some of them have families outside of Bloemfontein, some of them in the townships. For those whose families live outside of Bloemfontein, even if they live in the semi-urban areas of Botshabelo or Thaba Nchu, where a number of the Blacks who work in Bloemfontein live, these men cannot afford to travel every day back to their homes because they do not have work. They spend their days looking for jobs in the city, so they happen to sleep on the streets as well and then go back home at the end of the month with some money they acquired from the piece jobs they have found for a day or for a few hours. Piece jobs would include things like cleaning a yard, painting fences, a house, gardening, building something small and so forth. There are certain spots around the city where the men stand, waiting for people to pass by and offer them piece jobs. Much less to say, competition for piece jobs is fierce, and many times, the men stand waiting for days on end without getting a job.

There are yet others, especially older ones, who do have a home and receive a social grant, but either their families take all their money away, or these families neglect them. Some of the older men come to the organization for companionship and a meal. There are also a number of homeless youth who come to the soup kitchen, and Abongile, the Youth worker, works closely with them and with other homeless children. There are a number of reasons why the children are on the streets. Some of them were kicked out of their homes by their parents or guardians, and some ran away. Many come from homes with alcoholic parents and/or parents who do not take care of them; they have no food, they go to school with dirty uniforms or do not go to school at all and, in some cases, their parents have told them they need to start working; some of them are children as young as eight or nine. A vicious cycle in which the older kids exploit the younger ones is created. The children do not use the money they get from begging to buy food, but instead use it to buy glue, to sniff and to use dagga (marijuana). They do not use alcohol frequently, but when they have enough money, they do buy it.

Abongile works with the youth on the street, together with KidsCare Trust, an organization that works with homeless children under the age of 18 to provide them with shelter and send them to school. Some of the youth stay in the shelter, but a number of them do not. They run away and prefer to live on the streets because they do not want to be controlled; they want their freedom. As Abraham explained, "Either it's because of the glue, or either they told themselves that 'I want to do whatever I want to do, at the time it suits me'". This is an interesting point because this issue of control and freedom is also fundamental among the homeless men, as we will see in David's case.

Piet and David

I got to know many of the men as I worked with them, but one with whom I had deeper conversations was David, with whom I established greater rapport. David is a homeless Afrikaans man who comes to the soup kitchen every day and is quite well known and liked by them, except if he becomes bellicose when he is drunk. Then, they are forced to ask him to leave. Table 4.1 succinctly describes some of the characteristics of David and Piet.

Piet

Piet grew up in an orphanage, having lost his parents when he was three years old. He is actually of Italian heritage but grew up Afrikaans and considers himself as such. He is married and has two young children. His wife was in an accident some years ago and cannot work, but receives a disability grant of R500–R 600 per month. This is the equivalent of US$38–$58 (depending on the exchange rate of the day). It is very little money. He has had a difficult life, having been homeless,

Table 4.1 Participants' demographics: The city

Participants	Race and gender	Age	Occupation	Family configuration	Monthly income
Piet	White man	40	Car guard – lives off tips	Disabled wife and two young children	Varied
David	White man	34	Homeless – gets money by begging	No wife and a son he has never seen	Varied

and is now still struggling to make ends meet in his daily life. He and his family live in the poor area of Bainsvlei, in a racially integrated neighborhood not far from the affluent suburb of Langenhoven Park. He walks five kilometers each way to work every day because he cannot afford the daily transportation fee.

After leaving the orphanage, Piet enlisted in the South African Army and was in a support unit there for ten years, from 1991–2001, where he was trained as a welder. Notwithstanding, he does not have the corresponding certification, so he cannot find work as a welder, as this certification is a requirement in the present-day South African economy. He was asked to leave the army to make a place for new people, mainly Blacks, as part of the process of post-apartheid racial retribution and affirmative action. After leaving the army, not having a family to go back to, he was homeless for about two years. He then became a motor guard at several places over the next decade before coming to Fruit and Veg, where he has been working for two years.

David

David is the child of an alcoholic mother and father, and he had a very hard life growing up as such. He and his baby brother were put into foster care when he was six because his parents were not looking after them. He grew up with foster parents who cared for him, but he said he was rebellious. He explained that because his biological parents were not married, the church did not want to baptize him. This is a worry for him, because he wants to be baptized, but he says that getting baptized is a big thing, that "you cannot just get baptized, just like that". As he explained, "there are some things in my life I need to change before getting baptized, like alcohol abuse and other issues, before doing so. I am not deserve be baptized until I makes these changes". This point he makes here about the importance of religion and faith in his life further illustrates something we have seen in the stories in Chapter 3 and will see in those of Chapter 5: that for many people in the Free State, including many poor people, faith is central to their lives.

He comes from a broken home in which both mother and father got married to other partners and formed new families. When he tried to reconnect with his mother and her new husband, he was shunned by them. His stepfather told him that he could not live with his family unless he worked, and he could not find work in the small town where they live. He moved around the country, and has been in Bloemfontein on and off for 11 years, but more permanently for the last three years.

Their lives

Their economic difficulties and survival

Piet is a skilled laborer, and David is an unskilled laborer, but neither of them works as such now. Piet is a motor guard, and David does some odd jobs and is a beggar. After working for several years, he ended up homeless on the streets. In his view, however, he is the only one responsible for the choices he has made, not anyone else, for as he emphasized many times, he has made the wrong choices in his life. Interestingly, David considers himself at present a working man whose job is as a 'traffic light controller'. He explained this, smiling, "Traffic light controller . . . Wow, I stand at the robot and I ask the people for money! . . . I am begging for money at the robot".

For him, being a beggar means more freedom, rather than being on the clean-up team at the organization, for example. His time is his own; no one tells him what to do or when to do it. In this regard, he explained: "If I want to go sit, I go sit, if I want to drink, I drink, if I want to go beg, I beg; my time my own. No one tells me what to do or when to do it". He believes that this sentiment is shared by all beggars but explains the contradiction that this freedom represents:

> It is a sense of freedom, but is also something that swallows you in. It swallows you in because you start to drink, using alcohol and before you realize, you are an alcoholic; you can't be without alcohol. And to beg for money, it does something to your self-esteem and when you drink you don't worry. You just go on. And that's the biggest thing; alcohol. I don't know one hobo who doesn't drink. Everyone does, or uses something.

This contradiction of being imprisoned by alcohol while being free to do what one wants and suffering the indignity of having to beg has shaped David's life and the way he reflects on himself as he narrates his life.

Piet, on the other hand, lives off the tips that the customers of the food market give him. He does not beg, but works hard for his money and depends on people's generosity for his survival. Piet and his workmates earn between R150 to R200 a day, but this amount barely covers their families' living expenses. Piet explained this as follows:

> Yea, you see at Fruit and Veg, you make 150 to 200 rand a day, but from that money, you have to pay your rent, you have to buy electricity, the children need something for school, the books, the bus fees. The school is not supportive. They don't say, we gonna help you with the school fees or we gonna help you with the bus fees, you have to pay it. And after paying all that, you have to see what is over, and from all that, you have to buy food.

Their rent is R2 000 per month, electricity is approximately R240 per week, the school bus fees R100 per month, then toiletries and food and so the list continues. He explained that he needs to make R200 per day just to survive.

In Piet's case, his income varies from day to day, so he and his wife organize their food and other expenses according to his daily earnings. His wife receives a social grant for disability of R500–R600 per month (not the maximum of R1 350), which only helps to cover some expenses. He and his wife could potentially get some more money through social grants for the children, which are R320 per month per child, because they earn less than R6 200 per month. They are hesitant to do so, however, because to be able the apply for the grant, a social worker would need to come to their home to assess their situation. They are afraid that if the social worker sees the empty cupboards, because they buy food on a daily basis and do not have any stored, she will take the children away from them and put them into an orphanage. This is Piet's greatest fear, and it is a valid one, for the social worker could consider that the children are being neglected and that the home is unsafe for them because there is no food in the cupboards and fridge. Nonetheless, he and his wife have been casually chatting with a social worker and that social worker said that in addition to the social grant, Piet and his wife could also receive some money from the state to help pay for the school fees. Neither of these things had happened as yet during the time I knew him because they were still hesitant to begin the proceedings with the South African Social Security Agency (SASSA). Their fear of the possibility of having their children taken away from them was still too high for them to overcome.

Their food situation

Like many of the other working poor in Bloemfontein, for Piet and his family, food is the last item on their list of living expenses, after covering the more pressing responsibilities such as rent, electricity, school fees and clothing, among others, as illustrated in the excerpt above. They eat what they can afford, which is often similar to what the people in the township eat: samp, pap, porridge, bread, potatoes and vegetables. The management of the market gives Piet and the other motor guards lunch every day, mainly porridge and gravy with some meat. This meal helps them get through the day and is one less meal Piet has to worry about for himself. At home, he and his family sometimes eat porridge and milk and at other times only bread and coffee. It all depends on the money he makes that particular day. On his way home, he buys what they will eat that night and the following morning. His children have lunch at school through the school feeding scheme. Moreover, his faith in God helps him to secure food for his family:

> And along with that, we rely on The Lord, because we pray, and every day when you pray to The Lord, he provides. Not so much, but only with enough, the exact amount that you need. Like today; we decided we gonna eat porridge tonight, but with small sugar tonight. I make 60 rand today. That's how much money that we need for a porridge, say coffee, and a milk and a sugar. That's how my life is every, every day. We rely on The Lord and there is not even one day that I can say that me or my children went to sleep hungry. They even get bread to take to school, they don't have to be ashamed before other children, they don't have to be ashamed to say, "my dad is a motor guard", a person who is looking after the cars. Because there are other people

who say, "my dad is a contractor" or "my dad is a police", they lie to protect themselves.

In his explanation, Piet echoes the belief of the group of unemployed men and women in Phase 9 that God gives them what they need, not what they want. Moreover, we can clearly see how he delineates the several issues that shape his food situation: his faith in God; his ability to buy sufficient food for his family for the day as well as some bread for his children to take to school the following day; never having to go to sleep hungry; and his children not having to be ashamed because they are poor and their father is a motor guard. As we have seen throughout people's narratives, these are important issues that underlie poverty in Bloemfontein, irrespective of color.

It was interesting to note, however, that despite Piet's food insecurity, there are some cheap and nutritious foods that he refuses to eat, which his family does not eat either, such as spinach. What is known as spinach in Bloemfontein is kale spinach, and a large bunch of about two pounds would cost between five to eight rand. Spinach and pap is a common meal among poor people in Bloemfontein. Some healthier foods are cheaper in the Free State than other foods are. Vegetables, legumes and fruit – such as kale spinach, pumpkin, squash, potatoes, papaya, bananas and small apples, as well as peas and beans – are plentiful according to season and relatively cheap, and it is what most poor people eat. Meat is more expensive and is considered a luxury. In this region, as happens in many other parts of the world, when people become more affluent, they tend to stop eating as many vegetables and beans and eat much more meat because these vegetables and beans are considered poor people's food. Eating meat is considered a sign of affluence. Notwithstanding, for some people, even these cheap foods are not accessible on a daily basis. Many times, they fill their stomachs with carbohydrates because they are more filling for longer, whereas vegetables are not.

On the other hand, there are some healthy foods that Piet and his family do consume. One of these is milk, when he can afford it. He gets fresh milk directly from the farmers, instead of from the supermarket, for a much lower price. He would get two liters of tap milk (because you take your own bottle to be filled), "fresh and creamy, which be left out all day without spoiling", as he enthusiastically explained, at his neighborhood store for R12, whereas the pasteurized milk which is sold at the supermarket at R18 for two liters "goes sour in just a few hours". His family also eats brown bread instead of white, because brown bread is one to two rand cheaper than white. This was an interesting finding; that different to the U.S., for example, some healthy foods in South Africa, and particularly in the Free State where a lot are grown, are cheap, whereas meats and processed foods are relatively expensive. But meats and processed foods are the sign of affluence. The cleaning women at UFS, for example, told me that one luxury they give themselves once a month when they get paid is to eat Kentucky Fried Chicken. They love this chicken. For many poor men and women, French fries are also very desirable. It's a sign of "I can afford to eat like wealthier people".

In a conversation I had with the Managing Director of the Christian organization, he expressed his frustration at seeing some low-wage construction workers who were working nearby buying fries for lunch every day. He wanted to tell them that they should save their money and buy something more nutritious. He thought they were wasting their money. What I came to realize, however, is that for them, the fact that they were making money made them feel that they could splurge it on a tasty symbol of prosperity, which are fries. In their minds, poor people who cannot afford fries, eat spinach, pumpkin and pap.

"The less you have, the better you work with your money"; this is illustrative of Piet's way of thinking and strategizing to use the little money he has to give his family a home and a life. His pride and dignity are based on his being able to provide for his family. David's food situation is quite different to Piet's. Interestingly, as a homeless man, contrary to what one would initially expect, David's food situation is in no way precarious. David comes every day to the soup kitchen and on Saturdays when it is not open, he goes elsewhere. There are a number of soup kitchens all over Bloemfontein and he can choose which one he wants to go to. With regard to being hungry, he explained that he has never seen someone who sleeps on the street in Bloemfontein who has died of hunger, because of the abundance of soup kitchens where they can go to eat. Moreover, people who he gets to know when begging at the robot sometimes give him leftovers. He also told me with a twinkle in his eye that sometimes he gets so drunk that food is the last thing on his mind.

There are also times when with the money that he gets from begging, he buys himself some meat and pap and at other times, he goes to the supermarket, picks out a few rolls and a tin of beans, for example, and asks someone in the queue for the cashier if they could buy it for him, while he waits for them outside, respectful of their not wanting to be near to him. As a homeless man, he is the subject of rejection and discrimination. It is very interesting to see how self-reflective David is about his life situation and honest about the choices he has made and makes every day. Moreover, he is very honest about what he does with the money he gets from begging; he uses it to buy alcohol. He has no major food concerns, because those are easily taken care of, as we saw from the above, and he has no expenses because he has no home and no family, so his money goes to alcohol. With his brutal honesty and characteristic dry wit, he explained that he does not lie to the people who give him money and ask him what he will do with it. If he is drunk at the robot and begging, and people ask him, "what are you going to do with the money?" He responds honestly and says,

> I am gonna buy myself something to drink. Honesty. Not I'm lying and say, 'no sir, I'm gonna buy myself food', when I'm standing there so drunk *(and he laughs)* It doesn't help . . . He knows I'm gonna buy . . . So rather be honest to tell them. Many people tell me, "thank you that you honest. Yeah, go enjoy it". That's why I say, people are funny, funny.

Through the lives and stories of people all over the province, I came to realize that the difficulties the poor in the Free State face with regard to food is an important manifestation of the structural socioeconomic inequalities and inequities that they are subjected to, irrespective of race. It was interesting to realize that food is not the most important issue for them. The most important issue is their survival; it is having a roof over their heads, being able to clothe their families, send their children to school and pay for their basic living expenses. Food is the last item on the list, because as they continually repeated, they can fill their stomachs with anything cheap and filling, be that porridge, bread, pap, potatoes or anything else that is filling.

David's situation is a different one. As a man with no family and no expenses, and with his need for food and clothing covered by the Christian organization and elsewhere, his preoccupations are more introspective and centered on himself. He worries about the choices he has made in his life. He worries about his soul, about his drinking, about being a good person. He is well aware of his own situation, and expresses his desire to change, but he is not ready yet. About two weeks after our last conversation, David checked himself into rehabilitation, but he only lasted three days there. He left, got drunk, then went back and became belligerent at the rehab center, forcing them to kick him out. It is a sad situation. Those of us who care for him hope that his desire to change will translate into his willingness and finding the strength, together with the resources to do so. It is a long path to carve.

Their perspectives on the food situation in the Free State

In Piet's opinion, food in the province is very expensive, and to explain this, he correlated the prices of petrol and food. He believes this is initially a positive correlation, that is, when petrol prices go up, food prices go up, but then when petrol prices go down, the food prices remain high, thus making food inaccessible. Piet believes that there is more than enough food in the province for everyone, but that there are two major problems with regard to this food. The first is that it is too expensive, as explained above, so poor people cannot afford to buy it, and the second is that the supermarkets and grocery stores waste enormous amounts of food. Their policy is to throw out day-old food and products near their expiration date, rather than to give it to the people in need, which in his opinion is downright awful. He explained this as follows:

> There is more than enough food. Even if you go to the shops, there is some food, there is nothing wrong with it, they don't sell it today, this afternoon, when the shop close, that food is getting thrown away. Why didn't they give it to, for example, I am looking after the cars, or people who don't have? What is the difference to give it to somebody as to throw away that whole set of food? They throw away that lot of food and there is nothing wrong with it. That's every day.

With regard to this, he also said that no one gives food away for free anymore, the way they used to in the 'olden days', when all one had to do was go up to a shop and tell the person you were hungry, and the person would give you food. The olden days that he is referring to are during the time of apartheid, and in his case, specifically 1984, 85 and 86, which is when he was entering his adolescence. He remembers those days with nostalgia and said that the situation was different then. Whereas the Blacks remember that within the oppression of apartheid, they had access to food, Piet thinks about the good times under apartheid.

It is important to place what Piet has expressed above within the context that he is a White Afrikaans man, whose perception of the past comes from growing up as a White Afrikaans teenager under apartheid. As such, he was in a privileged position, even though he was a poor orphan. Also, from 1984–1986, he was 10–12 years old, which is an impressionable age. These were also the years when the apartheid regime was starting to crack. I explain the significance of these changes in the regime as related to White South Africans' recollections of those times in Chapter 6. David shares Piet's opinion that there is enough food in the province and also considers it expensive, but looks upon the situation rather as the consequence of mismanagement on the part of the government.

Their awareness of provincial government food programs and work opportunities

Piet only knows about the government social welfare programs, such as the social grants, and food provided by some churches. He has never heard about the government food policies and programs described in Chapters 1 and 2. He is also not aware of any community initiatives anywhere to help improve the food situation. David, on his part, knows all the soup kitchens in Bloemfontein, but does not know of any government food programs. Most of the people I spoke with were not aware of these. Both David and Piet consider that there are not many work opportunities in the province. David explained that he makes good money begging at the robots, and that he could make even more if he were to do it as a job, from 8 a.m. to noon, take an hour for lunch, and then again from 1 p.m. to 6 p.m. He believes that the employment opportunities in the Free State are few, but that there are more opportunities for self-employment, to "start your own thing and go from there". He referred to the many street vendors in the Free State, especially in a big city like Bloemfontein, who hawk all kinds of goods, as I have explained above. He stated that he could take a day's earnings that he makes at the robot and buy goods to sell, beginning with something as small as cigarettes, then continue onwards to larger items.

This is an expression of how he conceptualizes his potential agency, but has decided not to act on it, at least as yet. He expressed that there are a number of things he can do, in addition to this, such as washing cars, but that it is just easier to beg. He makes good money begging. He explained that he and his friend, who is also homeless and a beggar, write down each week how much money they spend on alcohol, and realized that they spend about R2 440 per week, which is more than a lot of the working poor, in Bloemfontein, such as the cleaning ladies at UFS in Chapter 3, earn in a month from their salaries. Nonetheless, he is conscious that earning his money in this manner is a gamble and is concerned about it but not yet doing anything differently.

Piet expressed that in South Africa today times are tough and that people will do anything to survive. In Bloemfontein, one can see many poor White people, men and women, standing at the robots (the traffic lights) begging. In comparison, there are very few Blacks begging. What many Blacks do at the robots on the streets of Bloemfontein is to sell things from sunglasses, visors, windshield protectors to cushions, ear muffs and stuffed toys, whatever the fancy of the day turns out to be. In Piet's view, White people beg at the robots to survive. In this regard, he expressed that people say, "I will do anything to survive. You don't know that . . . There is no food security, no nothing. You have to pay the rent . . . You must do something, even if it's begging. Even if I have to go out and pitch, but we must do something to eat". Consequently, he said, some people also turn to crime to eat, to provide for their families.

Piet attributes the unemployment in the Free State mainly to two reasons: one economic and one spiritual. He explained the economic reason as there not being enough work, and the spiritual reason as the following:

> People are falling down in their lives; maybe their wives are leaving them, or their children . . . They fall down and they couldn't stand up again. And then they feel sorry for themselves, they feel the world hates them, they don't want to go on anymore and then that's when . . . they feel guilty.

Piet firmly believes that you must stand up on your own two feet and make a life for yourself and your family. His faith in God and in his own capability to get ahead in life keeps him going. The above excerpt illustrates his opinion that people are not as strong as they can be.

Differences in the food situation during times of apartheid and now

"Times are different now . . ." Once again we see this belief, now from the perspective of a White man. In Piet's perspective, in the 'olden days' everything was much better, even the quality of the food. He went even further than people's growing difficulty in being able to afford food; he also questioned the quality of food today. He made the comparison in the taste of food now as compared to then, when people used to grow their own food, and said that it was tastier and longer lasting than it is now. He also believes that the food today is making people sick.

Piet is referring to the times of apartheid with nostalgia through the lens of his own experience, as is understandable. He grew up in the all-White orphanage where he said he was well taken care of. He then entered the Army as a young man three years before democratic elections were held in 1994 and was there during the time of transition. He had a stable and reputable job, a decent income and was able to create a life for himself, which he had always dreamed of. He was building a good life. Then, he was practically thrown out onto the streets in 2001 with no certified training and no social welfare. Since the end of apartheid, poor Whites have felt discriminated against and cannot seem to find their place within society and receive support from the state. They feel they no longer belong in this society, where even poor Whites once had a privileged position with guaranteed jobs, housing and social benefits.

In David's view, racism is still an issue today, even though people do not want to admit it. It is still at the back of our minds, that we are living in the apartheid era. He thinks apartheid is still very present in people's minds, that is, the structures of apartheid. In Chapter 6, I explain the contexts of White privilege during apartheid as well as White poverty then and now in relation to the experiences of the people described here.

Their faith

Piet is a deeply religious man and has great pride in having accomplished things for himself. He explained that because he has had such a hard life, he is close to God. He explained his closeness to God as follows:

> Yes, that's why I'm so close to The Lord, because I start to know the Lord at a very young age and I live a very tough love with him, but that's why I'm close to him. I say tough love, a hard life, a long heavy road, because you get a lot of obstacles. Sometimes it's a very narrow road, you are falling off this side, you are falling off that side and the table is full of obstacle on your course and the obstacles to make you disbelieve. If you don't go on it, there's no way out.

This excerpt demonstrates his faith in God and his trust in Him, despite all the hardships he has faced. He believes that these obstacles are actually in your life to make you disbelieve. This is a common theme I found throughout the multiple narratives and everyday life, that many people who suffer hardships because of their poverty see the obstacles in their path as a test of their faith. In explaining how he faces the struggles in his life, Piet expressed that despite these, he is grateful for what he has, considering them a blessing.

For David, his faith in God is important. He believes that it is God who has kept him alive. He firmly believes that because of the life he has lived, the choices he made in the past to live a life of drugs and violence, he was supposed to be dead many times over, but he is not, so he thinks there must a reason why he is still alive. He has fallen from a height of four floors, been stabbed with knives, been shot, and been in car and bike accidents, among others, so he believes God has a reason to keep him alive. He has thought about this a lot, and he believes that it means that one day he can help people who are in the same situation that he is in at present. In this regard, he said:

> For example, I can talk to someone who is using drugs, because I was there. I can talk to someone who is an alcoholic, because I am there. I can talk to someone living on the streets, because I am there. I can talk to someone that is in jail because I was there. Maybe this life that I am living is settled for me so that maybe one day I can help other people. That's what I think. *(Then smiling, he said)* But that's not an excuse for staying in the way that I am living now.

In my view, this says a lot about who he is as a person, about his strength, his honesty and his integrity as a person.

The problem with being White

In Piet's view, as well as those of other Whites I met in South Africa, being White is a disadvantage in South Africa today. Piet explained this as follows:

> Most of the things changed after 95. For instance, if I go for a job, they will say to me, "your color is not right; we are looking for Black people. We not allowed to take any White people, and I've so much White and so much Black and so much Colored and so much Indian", and that's wrong.

In this excerpt, Piet is referring to the quota system established through affirmative action as retribution to the non-White populations in South Africa, especially the Blacks, who were the most oppressed. Piet firmly believes that both this quota system and the requirement that skilled laborers should be certified have kept him out of the labor force. He believes that one should be employed based on one's skill, not on a certificate. Afrikaners, Whites in general, had job security during apartheid based on race, so not having job security now has hit them hard. He explained that he is unable to become a qualified welder, despite having the knowledge and skills, because the training is about R2 000–R3 000 per semester and is a several-months-long course. He can neither afford to pay for the course, nor can he afford to not work for a long period of time, as his family depends on his income. There might be the possibility of his applying for a government grant to do his training, but then, as he said, "And if I have to go and learn, what the family gonna eat? Who's gonna pay the rent?" He is caught up in the vicious cycle of survival competing with the need for formal training to improve his life.

Sadly, this is the case of many at present. Having the material resources and the opportunity to do something are not always enough for someone to pursue these opportunities. In Piet's case, for him to be able to do his training to open up the possibility of his achieving his dream of working as a welder again, his wife would have to work at least part time to cover some of the expenses, and they would also have to receive the social grant for their children. These are two conditions which are not in the cards for him at present because his wife is disabled and seemingly unable to work, and he is very cautious about initiating the process for his children's social grants, for the reasons explained above. There are other elements of consideration here: Piet's personal pride and social status as breadwinner of the family. While he did not want to speak much about it, one gets the impression that even if he were to get all his family's financial needs covered through stipends and grants, he would not feel comfortable going back to school. He seems to feel a deep sense of pride in being able to provide for his family and dedicate his time to God. On Sundays, for instance, even though the Fruit and Veg Market closes by 2 p.m., and it is the day he makes the least money, generally between R40–R60, depending on people's generosity, he still takes two hours off to go the church in the morning. As he explained, "these two hours are for the Lord. Nothing must interfere with that".

David does not share Piet's views that being White is a disadvantage in contemporary South Africa. His views are circumscribed by his particular circumstances as a White homeless beggar. In his case, he judges himself. He explained that he has realized the mistakes he has made and knows he needs to give his life some direction. Furthermore, he always judges himself, for as he said, "It's difficult not to judge yourself, even when other people may not be judging you". Referring to his days begging at the robots, he explained that when doing so,

> I see many kinds of different people every day. The Black people who see me begging probably don't give me money or treat me badly because of racism, and they say to me, "where were you when my parents were hungry, when they were struggling, when they had to beg?" And sometimes White people are worse. They treat me badly because they are afraid of losing what they have. They only think about themselves and their family, they don't care about you. Maybe they feel ashamed because I am also a White person and I am begging at the robot. Many tell me I am a disgrace to the White people.

The treatment that David is subjected to by Blacks and Whites highlight how vividly the conditions of apartheid remain in the collective psyche of these racial groups. As he illustrates above, for the Blacks, it seems that seeing White beggars makes them feel that they had it coming because of the role they played as oppressors in apartheid and for the Whites, seeing people of their own race begging seemingly shoves their perceived downfall into their faces. These are complex social dynamics that shape people's treatment of each other in the province today, dynamics which I explain further in Chapter 6.

The uneasiness of coexistence and care for "the other"

In Piet's view, people in general are inconsiderate with each other, and he perceives that the same lack of care and consideration has happened within all the races. In this regard, he explained, "All races. It happens between Whites, it happens between Blacks, it even happens between Indians. People don't care. People are scared to reach out to other people". Notwithstanding, he also believes that people of different racial and ethnic groups are living together now, getting along with each other, which is very different to life during apartheid. He also pointed out something important and not often mentioned in the literature on South Africa, which is that during times of apartheid, there was certain integration on the farms, where White, Black and Colored children ate and played together, learning each other's languages. Furthermore, White farm children grew up with Black nannies and the farm workers, who taught them their languages, whereas that did not necessarily happen in the cities. This is quite evident in a number of White people over 40 who grew up on farms in the Free State and who speak Sesotho, Setswana, Xhosa and other African languages.

He is also of the view that, despite the difficulties Afrikaners face in contemporary South Africa, he does see a future for them: "We still got a good future here. Because most people are Afrikaans speaking, even the Coloured are Afrikaans speaking. I still see a future for us. We are getting along good; we are actually getting along good". Two interesting elements of this statement are Piet's optimism and his highlighting his perceived use of Afrikaans as the common language. This illustrates the importance he, as an Afrikaner, gives to his language, being the uniting force. History and contemporary societal dynamics in South Africa contradict his statement. Many English-speaking Whites (known as the English, or Engels, in Afrikaans) in the Western Cape and KwaZulu-Natal, as well as Indians, do not speak Afrikaans and many educated Blacks have fervently resisted learning Afrikaans. Moreover, many of those who have learned it at school, refuse to speak it. It is the poorer Black people who speak it more openly and fluently, especially in the Free State, because they have always worked with mostly Afrikaans-speaking White people. On the other hand, the optimism his statement illustrates characterizes Piet and his approach to life. In all the time I knew him, he was always smiling, working hard as he rolled people's trolleys (shopping carts) back and forth and helping them with their bags, day in and day out, for just a few rand in return. He never gave up hope, and he trusted that God would always give him the strength to go on and the path to follow.

In my interactions with David at the soup kitchen and in church, and during our conversations, I observed that he was often considerate with others. In one of our conversations which took place at Kentucky Fried Chicken where I invited him to eat, he did not eat there, but chose instead to take his chicken to share with his friend who also lives on the street. At the soup kitchen, when I would offer second and third helpings, he would always ask me, "did everyone else have already? Or, no, look, he did not have seconds. I will have after him". As a homeless man, he also lives more closely with Blacks and Coloreds who share his situation of homelessness, so for him, color barriers are more of an impediment than a value. He and his homeless peers of all races have to fight the same battles on the street, and they are all equal in their poverty. He is an impoverished homeless man whose integrity is central to his interpretation of his own life and the meaning he makes of the world.

What poverty means to them

David considers himself a man who lives in poverty because he has nothing to show for his life. As he expressed, "the only time I was rich you know, I was doing my own stuff . . . I got nothing to show . . . Just clothes that I've got on me, that's all I've got . . . And I used to have . . . decent life . . . but the wrong life". He attributes his poverty to himself, to the bad choices he has made. He blames no one but himself. Despite his belief that he is responsible for his own poverty, he thinks that poverty is not an individual condition, but a social one, for, as he elo-quently explained, "there . . . entire communities in the world that are poor, even countries that are poor," giving Ethiopia as an example. This is a very interesting point, for it illustrates David's perception as poverty also as a collective state of being, beyond the individual, with an ensuing collective consciousness, which in turn affects national consciousness. In spite of his attributing his state of poverty to his own decision-making,

Piet also considers poverty a social condition and correlates poverty with peo-ple not caring for each other. This issue of people in Bloemfontein not caring for each other is a heartfelt one for Piet, which he considers directly affects his life, and he attributes this lack of concern as the cause of poverty. He explained this as follows:

> There a lot of poverty here . . . The people don't care about other people here. They only care about themselves; they only looking for their needs, not anyone else's needs. Even the social workers here, they don't care about other people . . . Uhm. Even the churches here, you go to the churches (and ask) "you can help us with a food packet, neh?" So long stories . . . why they cannot give one to you. (They say) "No, you're not a member of this church!" But I told one guy, one pastor at a church, "The Lord didn't ask us, are you part of this church, are you part of that church? The Lord likes everyone. It doesn't say in the Bible, you must only do this for your church, for your church, you do it to everybody". You belong to the church before they reach up and help you. You must . . . It's the same with social workers. (They tell you) "you must first do this and this" and whole lot of papers, papers, before you can get allotment for your children. Because the children is not going to wait a night for that papers, they want bread or something to eat that night. They won't wait two weeks or three weeks.

The point he makes about the churches and the food parcels they distribute is a sadly frequent and interesting one. There are some churches which only distribute food parcels to their church members, even though they may have had enough to distribute to more people. In the case of the Christian organization, these food parcels were given to people after a needs evaluation carried out by one of the program coordinators. They did not force people to attend their church services to get a food parcel. The case for soup kitchens is different. At this organization in Bloemfontein, the food was served daily on a first come first served basis. At the township church in Botshabelo, which I describe in Chapter 5, the soup kitchen on Saturdays and Sundays was for the people they considered the neediest, amongst which the majority were children. There were fewer people served at the township church, and they were all people that the pastor and church leaders knew from the area.

Their agency

Both Piet and David have agency, but Piet has acted upon his in terms of creating employment for himself as a motor guard, whereas David's agency thus far in this chapter of his life has been to beg. As explained above, David has formulated plans for how he can make money, but he had not acted upon them. Piet has. Piet's his first job as a motor guard was through his own initiative. After observing that the motor guards at an establishment were not doing their work adequately, he started looking after the cars and began making a living in this way, while he was still homeless. He finally got off the streets, again through his own initiative, when a school offered him a place to stay on the school grounds, and, in exchange, he maintained the school gardens, as well as being a motor guard. After sleeping on the school grounds for about two years, he went to work as a motor guard at an establishment where he was essentially working for himself, living off the tips he received for watching the cars.

"*Working harder*": This is Piet's attitude in general with regard to his life, and the decisions he makes are expressions of his agency. He firmly believes that with his hard work, his initiative and the Grace of God, he will continue forward. He is a survivor and feels blessed for the little he has, which he feels is just enough for now, but as his economic situation is worsening, he is looking for better opportunities to work, to maintain his family. He is a very hardworking man, who works from Sunday to Sunday at the market, striving to make a living.

David does have initiative, and he has good ideas, as can be seen through his thinking about the possibility of begging on a work schedule and selling small items, but he is aware that he chooses not to follow up on them, to a certain point. Consequently, he has self-unfulfilled agency. With these experiences, I bring to a conclusion the settings of food insecurity within the poor and vulnerable of the townships and city of Bloemfontein and the stories of some of its people. I hope that with these, I have painted a portrait in broad strokes of the lives of these people who face challenges with regard to food within their structural poverty. In Chapter 6, I analyze these themes further as I compare and contrast the experiences of the participants within the settings.

Now I will turn to the University of the Free State to discuss food insecurity among students in the university setting, which is a phenomenon that is little known and recently starting to be studied. Some of these students are from Bloem-fontein and some from other parts of the province, as well as other provinces and countries, especially other African countries.

Food insecurity in the university setting: the No Student Hungry Programme and the Food Insecurity Task Team

Some unexpected places of food insecurity are universities. People often think that if a student, through different means – whether these be parents paying for tuition, bursaries, scholarships and loans, among others – can pay for university tuition, then this student's cost of living is also covered. But this is far from the truth. Many students, even with economic support, can barely afford to go to university, especially in a country like South Africa. Similar to the case of many of their lower income compatriots, for lower-income university students, food is often the last on their list of priorities, and a significant number of them go without food to be able to pay their other living costs such as tuition, housing and books.

In this section, I will briefly explain food insecurity at the University of the Free State and describe two initiatives that have been created to address this issue there. The University of the Free State is a former Afrikaans university in one of the poorest provinces of the country. Today, this formerly exclusively White insti-tution now has a student population that is 65% Black and 60% female, and many of its students come from rural and economically disadvantaged backgrounds. In 2011, the Vice Chancellor and Rector of the University of the Free State, Dr. Jonathan Jansen, who assumed his position in 2009,[1] discovered that many UFS students were going hungry as they pursued their studies, simply because they did not have enough money to spend on food. In an attempt to remedy this situ-ation, at least for some of them, he created the No Student Hungry (NSH) Pro-gramme to provide "the students in need with modest food allowances and daily access to one balanced meal" (University of the Free State: No Student Hungry Programme, 2014). He dedicated the proceeds of his book, *We Need to Talk*, to contribute to the funding of the program.

Under NSH, 100 students on the Bloemfontein campus were selected on the basis of their financial need, academic performance, participation in student life and commitment to giving back to the community. Professor Jansen's wife, Mrs. Grace Jansen, and the Dean of Student Affairs' wife, Dr. Carin Bester, were the sponsors of the program. They also mentored the young women in it, and both Professor Jansen and Dean Rudi Buys mentored the young men. The NSH team works with the students on a regular basis to offer them training, motivation and opportunities for personal growth. As part of their personal and professional development, as well as their contribution to the community, the students are expected to become involved in university or community projects.

Students at UFS, as well as other universities in South Africa, and indeed around the world, are generally too proud to admit that they often go hungry because they do not have enough money to buy food for themselves and their families are too poor to send them money or food. Speaking with them nonetheless, one can begin to understand that they often do without. Student retention analyses at UFS and studies both there and across the country and world also show that student hunger and food insecurity contribute to students' feelings of uncertainty in their academic life, creating, among other things, a lowering of their motivation and level of concentration on their studies. Submerged in the situation of anguish and despair, a number of them end up dropping out of school to earn an income for themselves and to support their families. In this way, these individuals with promise are forced out of their higher education path, which, in turn, leads to great loss for their personal future and that of their country.

The NSH program is an attempt to help some of the most promising students an alternative path, in which they do not have to worry about where their next meal will come from and only concentrate on their studies. The beneficiaries of the program are students with strong academic records, so students who are food insecure but do not have a strong academic record are not eligible for the program. This has constituted a problem for the authorities of the university, because there are many more students who are in need of the program than have been accepted into it.

With the objective of determining approximately how many UFS students were food insecure, professors from the Department of Nutrition and Dietetics and the Department of Biostatistics of the university conducted a study in 2013 which determined that approximately 59% of the student respondents to a food security survey on the Bloemfontein campus faced very low food security (hunger), while 24.5% faced low food insecurity. The respondents represented 4.5% of the student population. The study also showed that undergraduates, men, unmarried, Black and Colored students and those who are recipients of bursaries or loans were more likely to be food insecure than were post-graduate students, women, married, White, Indian and Asian students, as well as those who have their tuition paid by parents or guardians. Furthermore, 21.6% of the students support someone financially, these dependents being mainly their parents, children or siblings. Approximately three fourths, 73.7 %, of the respondents reported that they did not always have enough money to buy food, 70.5% reported to have borrowed money to buy food and 53.3% reported having asked someone for food. Nearly a tenth, 9.2%, of the students reported having sold their belongings to buy food, and 1.6% admitted to having stolen food. The study concluded that university students in developing countries may be a subgroup particularly vulnerable to severe food insecurity (van den Berg and Raubenheimer, 2013).

Further surveys by the authors at the UFS South Campus near the townships in Bloemfontein and the UFS QwaQwa Campus revealed that a number of the students there also face food insecurity. The incidence of food insecurity on the QwaQwa campus, which is a rural campus, was particularly high. Consequently, the NSH program has been extended to these campuses. In April 2013, the program expanded to the QwaQwa campus and in April 2014 to the South Campus of the university. The incidence of food insecurity was particularly high among students who received bursaries or government loans, because the money they receive covers their tuition, board and some books, but there is little left over for food. Some bursaries or loans do not even have provision for food. Some students provide for their families who are not working, with their bursaries or loans. As Dr. Louise van den Berg, Dr. Corinne Walsh and Dr. Lucia Meko from the Department of Nutrition and Dietetics explained to me, the 2013 study, together with conversations that the Dean of Student Life and members of the NSH program team have had with a number of students, determined that many students feel that even though they are in need of food aid, are too ashamed or too scared of being stigmatized to apply for this aid.

As I have explained above, the NSH program, the motto of which is "Nourishing bodies to advance thriving minds" (University of the Free State: No Student Hungry Programme, 2014), only caters to a small number of students, whereas the number of students facing food insecurity is much higher. Consequently, the Student Affairs Management team formed the Food Insecurity Task Team (FITT) with the objective of addressing this problem within the larger population. One of the first concepts that FITT generated is the formation of a UFS Food Club. As described in the working draft document of the FITT Food Club,

> The purpose of the food club is to distribute nutritious food parcels to students who do not currently hold a *No Student Hungry* (NSH) bursary but are severely food insecure. Food parcels will be distributed once per week during the academic term to all students who are UFS Food Club members.

> > (University of the Free State Food Insecurity Task Team:
> > Food Club, 2014)

The administrator of the NSH program is part of the FITT and is also the main evaluator of the applications to the Food Club. Different from the NSH program, the student members of the Food Club pay a membership fee of R50 for the first month, and the membership lasts for three months. The rationale of this membership fee is based on the experience in the NSH program, which has proven that when the students make a contribution to the distribution of the food they receive, their involvement in the initiative is much more meaningful than when the food is distributed freely to them. Students have to reapply for membership in the club every three months.

The NSH program, as well as the FITT, are part of the Human Project of the University of the Free State, working within its framework to enhance the Academic Project (The No Student Hungry Programme, 2014). The mission of the university rests on two pillars: (a) the Academic Project, which fosters the environment and means for academic excellence and (b) the Human Project, which constitutes the human embrace, fostering the environment and means for personal development. The human embrace is a very important dimension of student achievement for the (now former) Dean of Student Affairs, Rudi Buys. For him, students overcoming their food insecurity needs to be simply something operational, not central to their lives, as it has been until now. He worries about how food insecurity has been defining the students' experiences in their academic, personal and social lives and interrelates these experiences with South Africa's history. In conversations with him, he explained this as follows:

> What defines us is not our hunger. Hunger, insecurity does not define you. It's what we do with it that does. In the past, hunger did not define us; it was our struggle for freedom. Hunger today is a symbol of non-achievement, of poverty, to be frowned upon and that's not who we were. What bothered us was change. Young people hide their hunger today; what defines them is to make money.

Through the human embrace, the NSH program wants to reconnect with students' dignity and humanity, which is why Vice Chancellor Jansen and Dean Buys had so much emotionally invested in the program. The students are expected to play a role in the community, to be human and to live with dignity. The program aims to validate people beyond hunger, to help others and to facilitate agency.

As we have seen throughout people's narratives and experiences thus far, food insecurity cannot be understood within a social, political, economic, historical and cultural vacuum. It is a product of the systemic structural inequities and inequalities of the contemporary South African society. And one of the most recent manifestations against these systemic inequities and inequalities has been the student protests of 2015–2016.

We generally think about the student protests in South Africa as being only about protesting against fee increases, but there is much more involved. It is, at its core, a class struggle. What began on October 14, 2015 as a two-hour protest against a projected 10% fee increase at the University of the Witwatersrand by October 19 spread to the University of Capetown, then to other universities across the nation, to protest against the projected national higher education tuition increase. These protests turned into the mass #FeesMustFall movement. The movement was much more than only about fees, however. The protests were intersectional, spanning interrelated sociopolitical, racial and economic issues. As a student protester from Wits explained two weeks into the protests in October 2015,

> Our protest is not just about "one thing", even if that ubiquitous hashtag suggests otherwise . . . It is, firstly, about access to equal and quality education. It is about teasing out the ever-so-confusing intricacies of class relations in post-apartheid South Africa. It is about eradicating the painful exclusions and daily micro aggressions which go hand in hand with institutional racism within these spaces . . .
>
> (Disemelo, 2015)

The cost of university education in South Africa is prohibitive for many Black students and has become a symbol of the inequalities that endure in South Africa more than two decades after the end of apartheid. Many Black students cannot afford university tuition. Moreover, housing, transport and textbooks are expensive. Very poor students are eligible for a bursary, and some may receive one, but these do not necessarily cover all their expenses. On the other hand, students from families that a little better off tend to find themselves caught up in a sustainability gap because they earn too much to qualify for state support but too little to be able to afford tuition, housing, books and other costs.

In South Africa, Blacks are four times less likely to go to university than White students; 60% of them survive the first year, and approximately 15% of these graduate. Thus, structural inequalities along racial and socioeconomic lines continue more than 20 years into their democracy. These student protests express the anger with regard to these inequalities. South Africa today is one of the most unequal societies in the world, with 90–95% of all assets in the hands of 10% of the population (Burke, 2016).

The public education system, which most Black students grow up in, is largely ineffective and prepare students poorly for higher education, creating thus a fundamental barrier to succeeding at university. Most of the students who drove the protests are Black, poor and working class, leaving bare the reality that race and class lie at the heart of opposition to South Africa's existing exclusive university system.

Among the movement's achievements was receiving a one year freeze on fee hikes, and increased state funding in higher education. Most unfortunately, from early on, party politics and power struggles within the movement shaped it. Over time, the movement was fractured, and became more politicized, leading to often violent protests. Most demonstrations have been peaceful, but some have turned violent, where buildings at University of Capetown were set alight and a library at University of KwaZulu-Natal was burned in late 2016. Universities were closed down for days and weeks on end, and students accumulatively lost months of school, many not graduating on time (Chetty and Knauss, 2016; Chute, 2016; Pilane, 2016; McGregor, 2016). The high human toll on students and their families is not often recognized and acknowledged, but they need to be. These protests are ostensibly about systemic concerns and social justice, but unfortunately the involvement of party politics has thwarted the path towards addressing these concerns and building a more socially just society.

At the University of the Free State, registration was free for new students in the 2016 academic year, thus taking one financial burden off the new students, and achieving some calm, but in February 2016, violence erupted at a rugby match at the university when protesters supporting the university workers' strike against outsourcing wanted to get Vice Chancellor's Jansen's attention. They entered the pitch, were singing and the White rugby fans streamed down to beat them up. It was a violent reaction to what the protesters considered their peaceful protest and made headlines across the nation, laying bare once again how the ugly head of racism is still present at this formerly Afrikaans university that is a cradle of the experiment of racial reconciliation, an experiment that has been very difficult and only partially successful. This experiment in racial reconciliation was led by Professor Jansen.

Let us now turn to some other initiatives that have been created to confront the challenges around people's access to food in Bloemfontein. Expanding on those which have been discussed thus far, there are two which are worth describing here. The first is in the townships and the second is situated in the suburbs of Bloemfontein, but connected to the townships.

Some food security initiatives in Bloemfontein

There are several food initiatives around Bloemfontein, as well as in the province, to combat food insecurity, going from household food gardens that some people have planted to school food gardens and community gardens. Some of them are individual initiatives, of people working on their own to grow their own vegetables and legumes, others are community initiatives and yet others are initiatives fostered by organizations, non-governmental or otherwise.

Food gardens in Phase 9

The first initiative I will describe is the one carried out by some of the unemployed women and men of Phase 9 whose perspectives have been described earlier. This initiative is promoted by Dr. Lucia Meko of the Department of Nutrition and Dietetics at UFS, who has been working with the people of this community for several years. They have established a program to improve their eating habits, their access to food and create some community initiatives to improve their health, one of which is to grow household and community gardens. The members of the community are also collaborating with Rekgonne Primary School in the area to create food gardens. Dr. Meko has provided them with seeds to grow their food gardens and some of them have done so successfully. They seemed content with their progress and to have the opportunity for their families to have access to more food. The 2013–2014 year was their first year of planting. They had had good summer crops and were looking forward to planting winter crops, including spinach and cabbage. Some of the women have experience planting, so they knew what kinds of vegetables to plant in each season.

As in every other part of the township, however, and in many places around the Free State, having access to sufficient water is a big problem, and the rains are becoming scarcer and out of season every year in the province. Vegetable seeds are expensive for these people to buy, so they appreciate when Dr. Meko gives them seeds. She has also formed a Health Club to teach them to live a healthy life, and the price of admission to the club is that you plant. There is a coordinator for the group: one of the women, Angie, who monitors their progress. She is a grassroots politician and receives an allowance for being on the local council. She is on the health portfolio of the council.

There are also some government food programs in the semi-urban and rural areas, which are described in the next chapter. I did not learn about any of these within Bloemfontein, but this does not mean that they do not exist in the city or its surrounding areas. The second initiative I will describe is a small social initiative focused on sustainable living, within which food security is one of their primary objectives. This initiative is *Qala Phelang Tala*, which in Sesotho means 'start living green'.

Qala Phelang Tala, start living green

Qala Phelang Tala (QPT) was co-founded in 2012 by two White social justice activists: Thabo Olivier and Anita Venter. Thabo, an Afrikaans man with a Sesotho name and fluent in three African languages, including Sesotho, is a businessman, outspoken ANC politician and former Councilor of Ward 19 in the townships. Anita is a lecturer at the University of the Free State in the Centre for Development Support with a passion for sustainable building methods. In creating QPT, they have brought together their knowledge and determination to help create low-cost sustainable housing, planning and food security to foster local economic development and social development in the Bloemfontein, the Free State and beyond. With these objectives in mind, QPT is

> a South African social initiative focusing on sustainable living environments for the poor. It aims at an appropriate housing technology using recycled products, such as plastic bottles and car tyres, and food gardens. The fundamental concept of this form of housing is that of Michael Reynold's "Earthship" Biotechture. Practically oriented, QPT implements several methods such as recycling, re-using, re-purposing, (rain) water harvesting, or gardening with the so-called "greywater" system with the help of volunteers in local projects. Other products which have been tested through the QPT initiative: solar power, pneumatic products, wind energy, and alternative sanitation options.
>
> (Qala Phelang Tala, "About us", 2014)

I spent some time with both Thabo and Anita at the QPT sites and got to know more about their work and their objectives. They are both activists who live what they profess. This begins with the fact that they themselves have been experimenting with, in their own homes, the low cost housing and the food security that they work towards fostering in the low-income communities. Each of them has been building in their yards with their team of collaborators (employees of QPT and volunteers), experimenting through trial and error, houses, greenhouses and tanks made out of tires, mud, straw, glass and plastic bottles.[2]

Of the two, Anita focuses more on building and Thabo more on food security, even though they work together to achieve their common objectives. Based on this, I spent more time with Thabo, and it is mainly his work on food security that I focused on, always keeping it within the context of QPT as a social, collaborative initiative of a dedicated team of people. Thabo became famous in the Free State as the ANC Municipal Councilor in Mangaung who, during the 2010 World

Cup, frustrated with his government's unfulfilled promises of providing people with decent houses, moved into a mkukhu, with no electricity or running water, in Batho Township for nearly three months (Qala Phelang Tala, 2014; Diodio, 2011). He did so specifically during this period of time in part to attract the attention of the media that was in Bloemfontein for the World Cup, to make public the fact that most families in his very impoverished ward desperately needed decent housing. He had spent years trying to make the provincial government of his own party fulfill its promise to provide housing to the residents, to no avail, so he took this measure. He explained that as a councilor, living this way not only endeared him to his constituents, but also made him understand even further the difficulties they were living.

The premise of the QPT food security initiative is that not only would communities learn to build their own houses using recyclable and easily obtainable, often free materials, but that they would also learn to cultivate their own vegetables, to be employed and to generate an income. Thabo firmly believes that planting does not have to be done on large extensions of land and proves it through his initiatives. He plants in plastic soda bottles, small containers, pipes, tires and blocks, among other objects and small spaces. As Thabo continuously expresses in his multiple talks to people and communities everywhere he goes to help people foster their own development, "Vegetables can grow in anything that has soil. Communities can consume 10% of the vegetables in their homes and 90% for business purposes".

Thabo, Anita and the QPT team do not teach anything that they have not tried out themselves first and have failed at in their first attempts. In this vein, on showing me his garden, Thabo explained, "Everything you see here, for every success, there are three failed attempts behind it". Helping the people in most need to build their own low-cost housing and food gardens for sustainable living is at the core of their social initiative, and to this end, QPT has been working in some of the areas of the townships of Bloemfontein. It has been taking them some time to sow the seeds among the communities, but step by step, they have been working to achieve these objectives. They have had a number of obstacles, including overcoming the culture of dependency that has been created by the ANC government in the last 20 years, together with bureaucratic obstacles such as obtaining permission to work in the townships and helping people to understand the concept of building strong houses with recycled materials, mud, sand and straw. It is a completely foreign concept to them, as it is to many people in general, and it has been taking some time for people to understand it.

As I explained at the beginning of this section, there are several food initiatives in Bloemfontein: individual, community and organizational. I perceived, however, that several of these initiatives are disconnected from each other, not necessarily working together, either through ignorance of the other, because of professional jealousy and competition or for other reasons. This disconnect is, in my view, one of the obstacles that exists towards fostering at least some collective food security, with regard to food gardens, in the city.

With this, I end this chapter on the faces of poverty and hunger in Bloemfontein and the people's initiatives to confront and overcome these. In the next chapter, I will describe these faces in two locations outside of Bloemfontein: the semi-urban area Botshabelo and the rural Thabo Mofutsanyana Municipality in the Eastern Free State.

Notes

1 Dr. Jansen stepped down from his position in August of 2016 after seven years as Vice Chancellor and Rector. He then accepted a fellowship at the Center for Advanced Study in the Behavioral Sciences at Stanford University, where he obtained his Ph.D. in 1991 and received the 2016 Alumni Excellence in Education Award. He is widely considered a public intellectual and transformational leader in education in South Africa and has written a number of books and articles on varying issues in post-apartheid South Africa, including race, education and leadership. An excellent book in which he features and explains his philosophy of life and leadership is Ambrosio, J. (2016) *Educational Leadership for Transformation and Social Justice: Narratives of Change in South Africa.*
2 For further information on QPT and photos of the work they do, see their website: http://startlivinggreen.co.za/wp/.

References

Ambrosio, J. (2016). *Educational leadership for transformation and social justice: Narratives of change in South Africa*. Routledge research in educational leadership series. London: Routledge.

Burke, J. (2016, October 7). South African student leaders vow to continue tuition fee protests. *The Guardian*. Retrieved from www.theguardian.com/world/2016/oct/07/south-africa-tuition-fee protests-student-leaders-universities Bread for the World, FIAN International, & Interchurch Organization for Development

Chase, S. (2005). Narrative inquiry: Multiple lenses, approaches, voices. In Denzin and Lincoln (Eds). *The Sage handbook of qualitative research* (3rd ed.). Thousand Oaks, CA: Sage Publications.

Chetty, R., and Knaus, C. (2016, January 13). Why South Africa's universities are in the grip of a class struggle. *The Conversation*. Retrieved from https://theconversation.com/why-south-africas-universities-are-in-the-grip-of a-class-struggle-50915

Chutel, L. (2016, October 6). Protests on South Africa's university campuses aren't going away anytime soon, not should they. *Quartz Africa*. Retrieved from https://qz.com/801164/students-on-south-african-universities-continue-to protest-for-free-education/

Cooperation (ICCO Cooperation). (2014). *Right to food and nutrition watch 2014: Ten years of the right to food guidelines: Gains, concerns and struggles*. Retrieved from www.rtfnwatch.org/fileadmin/media/rtfnwatch.org/ENGLISH/pdf/Watch_2014/Watch_2014_PDFs/R_t_F_a_N_Watch_2014_eng.pdf

Disemelo, K. (29 October, 2015). *Student protests are about much more than just #FeesMustFall*. Retrieved from https://mg.co.za/article/2015-10-29-student protests-are-about-much-more-than-just-feesmustfall

McGregor, K. (2016, May 21). The human costs of student tumult – an untold story. *University World News*, Issue No. 414. Retrieved from www.universityworldnews.com/article.php?story=20160521140654557

Pilane, P. (2016, January 22). Politics and power struggles define student protests. *Mail & Guardian*. Retrieved from https://mg.co.za/article/2016-01-21-politics and-power-struggles-define-student-protests

Qala Phelang Tala. Start Living Green. (2014). About us. Retrieved from http://www.startli vinggreen.co.za/About-Us/

The Story of the No Student Hungry (NSH) Programme. University of the Free State. (2014). Retrieved from http://giving.ufs.ac.za/dl/Userfiles/Documents/00000/13_eng. pdf

Terreblanche, S. (2012). *Lost in transformation*. Johannesburg, SA: KMM Review Publishing Company (PTY) Ltd.

University of the Free State. (2014). *No student hungry programme (NSH)*. Retrieved from http://giving.ufs.ac.za/dl/Userfiles/Documents/00000/13_eng.pdf

University of the Free State Food Insecurity Task Team (2014): Food Club. Unpublished document.

van den Berg, V. L., and Raubenheimer, J. (2013). *Food insecurity among university students in a developing country*. Department of Nutrition & Dietetics and Department of Biostatistics, Faculty of Health Sciences, University of Free State, Bloemfontein, South Africa. Given to me by authors. Retrieved also from www.thejournalist.org.za/wp con-tent/ . . . /08/UFS-Food-Insecurity-Study-Paper.docx

5 Food insecurity and food initiatives beyond the city

In this chapter, I go beyond the capital city of Bloemfontein, as I explore food insecurity and some initiatives people in different parts of the province have formulated to confront their food challenges. I focus on the semi-urban area of Botshabelo, about 57 km outside of Bloemfontein, and the rural municipality of Thabo Mofutsanyana in the Eastern Free State, particularly the towns of Kestell and Harrismith. In this chapter, I strive to paint a portrait of semi-urban and rural food insecurity in the province, as well as initiatives people have created to confront this challenge, through the experiences and perspectives of people in different areas outside of the main city.

I begin with a concise description of the history of Botshabelo and its state of poverty and food insecurity, then describe some food initiatives there. I then do the same for the Maluti-A-Phofung Local Municipality, where the towns of Kestell and Harrismith are located within the Thabo Mofutsanyana Municipality, as well as the Diyatalawa Agri-Village, which is a model food and community development initiative that the government has fostered to confront structural poverty in the region. To explicate how some people experience food insecurity in Botshabelo, Kestell and Harrismith and the meanings they make of them, I interweave some excerpts of their narratives as I delineate the themes explored throughout this book.

Sites of exploration

Beyond Bloemfontein, my inquiry was focused on: five food initiatives in the semi-urban town of Botshabelo, the HIV/AIDS clinic, a poor Black area, a primary school and a crèche in the rural town of Kestell and the municipal waste dump of the town of Harrismith. I describe the poverty in Botshabelo, Kestell and Harrismith and some food initiatives to confront the challenges around food. In Kestell and Harrismith, I tell the stories of three very impoverished women and one man, whose perspectives illustrate some of their challenges around food within their contexts of dire poverty. I conclude with the experience of a successful food initiative: the Diyatalawa Agri-Village. All of the people whose stories I tell are Black. As I showed in the table of comparative demographics of the Free

State in Chapter 4, 87.6% of the population of the province is Black. In the semi-urban and rural areas, over 97% of the population is Black, as we shall see from the statistics in the following sections.

Botshabelo: initiatives within poverty

The semi-urban town of Botshabelo is one of the major settlements in the Free State Province and has close connections to Bloemfontein. Botshabelo is part of the Manguang Metropolitan Muncipality, together with its sister semi-urban town of Thaba Nchu, the area of Mangaung and the capital city of Bloemfontein. It is about 57 km east of Bloemfontein and was set up under the apartheid government and the then Prime Minister of the QwaQwa homeland approximately in 1979 as a settlement for Blacks, mainly the Southern Sotho- and Xhosa-speaking peoples. They were not allowed to live in Thaba Nchu, eighteen kilometers away from Botshabelo today, which was part of the homeland of Bophutatswana. The governing policy of Bophutatswana dictated that the homeland belonged to the Tswana peoples and the government of the homeland forced out the non-Tswana peoples who had been settling there. The original settlement was on a farm called Onverwatch, and by the 1980s, the settlers began calling their home Botshabelo, which means "place of refuge" in Sesotho.

Botshabelo was incorporated into the QwaQwa homeland in 1987 by the apartheid government, despite the resistance of its inhabitants, who were afraid of

Table 5.1 Comparative Demographics Free State – Mangaung Metropolitan Municipality – Botshabelo

Demographics (in percentage)	Free State Province (pop. 2.7 million)	Mangaung Metropolitan Muncipality (pop. 747,431)	Botshabelo (pop. 181,712)
Black African	87.6	83.3	99.2
White	8.7	11.0	0.1
Colored	3.1	5.0	0.3
Indian/Asian			0.2
Other racial groups	0.4	1.7	0.2
Languages (in percentage)			
Sesotho	64.2	51.9	84.4
Afrikaans	12.7	15.8	1.6
English	2.9	4.2	2.0
isiXhosa	7.5	9.6	7.6
Setswana	5.2	12.3	
Other languages	7.5	6.2	4.3

Source of demographics: South Africa Census, Free State Province, 2011. Table is of my elaboration.

losing their South African citizenship. Nonetheless, this did not happen, because QwaQwa, despite being a homeland, had previously rejected 'independence' from South Africa. The incorporation of Botshabelo into QwaQwa, however, put enormous pressure on the homeland because it doubled its population and stretched its scant resources to their limits (South African History Online: "Botshabelo forced into QwaQwa", 2014/1987). In the section of this chapter on the Thabo Mofutsanyana municipality, I briefly describe the history of QwaQwa and its present-day situation.

The population of Botshabelo fluctuates because there are a number of people who travel back and forth from the Kingdom of Lesotho who make it their temporary or semi-permanent home. As we can see from the table of demographics, the population is overwhelmingly Black African and Sesotho is the most widely spoken language. There used to be some industry in Botshabelo during apartheid, but there has been little in recent years. Unemployment is high and many of those who are employed have jobs in Bloemfontein, a bus ride of almost an hour away. Transportation is expensive and is a significant portion of their paltry salaries or income, so some of these people also stay in Bloemfontein for work during the week and go home on the weekends, the poorer ones going home once a month, or less. As I explained in Chapter 4, this is the case for some of the men who sleep on the streets of Bloemfontein or stay in ramshackle mkhukhus in the informal settlements of the township.

Structural poverty and food insecurity in Botshabelo

Much as in other parts of Mangaung Metropolitan Municipality and the Free State province, there is food insecurity in Botshabelo, in great part because of its underdevelopment, rate of unemployment and poverty. Nonetheless, it has been the site of a number of economic and community development interventions over the last two decades: by the government (Free State mission on rural investment,1997), non-governmental organizations, religious ministries and universities, such as the University of the Free State and the University of the Witwatersrand in Johannesburg, as well as by the some of its inhabitants.

A 2010 Background and Insight Gathering Report by Thabo Community Action Trust on the status of the communities in Botshabelo and Thaba Nchu revealed that some of the biggest challenges Botshabelo faces, as expressed by its people, were: (a) the high youth and overall unemployment and no resources for the youth, such as community centers; (b) lack of communication between the local government and the people on all levels; (c) drug abuse; and (d) the rise of initiation schools. The older adults are concerned about their youth, because they expressed that there is no further education after the youth complete matric and neither is there enough money in the communities. Moreover, the people estimate that approximately 80% of young men do not finish their matric due to initiation school,[1] which they attend in Grade 10. There is also a high level of crime, which they relate to there being no local opportunities for employment. Some people have jobs in Bloemfontein, while others get piecemeal jobs. Most people in the communities subsist on social grants, mainly the child support grant, the older person's grant, the disability grant or the foster child grant.

In their view, the community's biggest needs are finding ways to create their own jobs, community services for the elderly, sick, disabled and children, as well as food security. Some of them believe that creating farming projects would be important for the town. Nonetheless, in this regard, they considered that most people are too lazy to grow their own food. Here we see a recurrence of a theme expressed in Chapter 3, where Black Africans consider other Black Africans today as 'being lazy'. Apparently, the participants knew of only one farming project in Section W of the town. Moreover, they expressed that people have forgotten how to farm. The participants also named several organizations who are doing good work with the community, such as World Vision, Sam Erya (Love Life school projects), some home-based care organizations for the disabled, orphans and the sick and projects in particular sections of Botshabelo (Thabo Community Action Trust, 2010). Six years later, the community is still affected by many of these issues.

These organizations mentioned above are not the only organizations working in Bothshabelo today. There are several others, in addition to government interventions. One of these organizations is the Mosamaria AIDS Ministry which has a number of programs, including HIV/AIDS educational programs and on-site HIV and TB testing (Mosamaria AIDS Ministry, 2016). It also has a well-established food garden project, which was created to help people facing difficulties obtaining food on a sustainable basis because of their economic straits. Seen in this light, Botshabelo is neither an understudied nor an under-intervened area, yet a number of its communities still live within structural poverty. These characteristics are what made it an interesting area to understand environments of food insecurity.

Within these scenarios of structural poverty, there are several initiatives by the town's inhabitants to grow some food for themselves as well as for their communities. Botshabelo is a large, sprawling town, going the gamut from some areas that have nicely built, medium-sized brick houses to many areas where there are firmly built mkhukhus to others where the mkhukhus are merely flimsy zinc huts held together with pieces of wood and rooftops weighed down with stones. It is a barely forested place, but upon closer view, one can observe some household gardens here and there.

Esther, the UFS cleaning woman whose story I described in Chapter 4 was my first point of entry to the town. As I explained there, Esther is from Botshabelo but went to live in Bloemfontein when she got married. I subsequently got to know more about the town and its people through Esther and Dill Borchard, a Namibian *Engels*[2] who is also fluent in Afrikaans and works with some of the people of the community, and the people I met through them. Esther introduced me to her brother, uncle and father, who showed me their food gardens and Tannie[3] Dill introduced me to Mme Maria and Ntate Raphael and their food initiatives at the Modulaqwoha Nursery, their own small farm and their soup kitchen through the Zoe Church Ministry.

Contexts of food initiatives in Botshabelo

Many of the conversations I had with people in Botshabelo took place as they showed me their gardens and/or we participated in activities together. Through our conversations and seeing their gardens, I was able to understand some of their challenges around food and why they decided to plant these gardens. I will first briefly describe the contexts of the people who have planted the food gardens. These people are Thabiso, Ntate Thomas, Mme Fanny and Ntate Simon with their food gardens and Ntate Raphael and Mme Maria with the Modulaqwoha Nursery, their own small farm and their soup kitchen through the Zoe Church Ministry.

Thabiso is Esther's brother, although in the Western conceptualization of family, he is actually Esther's first or second cousin, for his mother and Esther's mother are sisters, or they may be cousins too. Esther was not able to explain this, for the Western conceptualizations of brother and cousin are foreign to the Sesotho culture and language. Thabiso is 31 years old, has a partner and young child and has had difficulty finding employment. He and his family live in a two-bedroom mkhukhu in one of the poorest sections of town. He has been unemployed for quite some time and has decided, with two of his neighbors, to create a community garden as a source of food for themselves, as well as employment for Thabiso and other persons in the community. The two neighbors he has been planting with are an older couple, Ntate[4] Thomas and Mme Fanny, who have experience gardening. Their garden is in their conjoined backyards but is only partially cultivated. They have been struggling to grow crops there.

Ntate Simon lives a little distance away from Thabiso, in one of the older sections of Botshabelo, which is a 'nicer' and more established area of the town. He suffered from a stroke in 2012 and is formally unemployed, but receives the disability social grant and plants his garden in his backyard, the crops of which he sells to supplement his income. Different to Thabiso, Ntate Thomas and Mme Fanny's experience, his garden is thriving. Mme Maria and Ntate Raphael are a husband and wife team who have been working on confronting the challenges of food insecurity in Botshabelo for over 20 years, and today, they have three initiatives that are interrelated: a large nursery, a small farm and a soup kitchen through their church ministry. I will explain these three initiatives together below.

The people of this town face some of the same issues as their counterparts in the city and the themes that exemplify these issues are: their economic difficulties and survival; their food situation; their awareness of government food programs; and their agency.

Food gardens: struggling and thriving

Their economic situation and survival

Thabiso, Ntate Thomas, Mme Fanny and Ntate Simon are all unemployed, but of the four, Thabiso is in the worst economic and living situation. He lives in a mkhukhu with his family, and as a young, able man, neither he nor his wife receive any grants to help them solvent their situation, except for the child support grant of R320 for their little child. His wife does not work, and he works at piece jobs whenever he can. He and his wife rely on the support of their respective families, however little these may able to do so. They face severe difficulty covering their expenses and satisfying their basic needs. As older persons, Ntate Thomas and Mme Fanny receive their older person's grant of $1 350 rand each, which helps to bide them over during the difficult economic situation in the Free State. They also have their own house, a small brick house, which provides them with better shelter than Thabiso's mkhukhu provides him and his family. Ntate Simon and his wife also have a nice, small, brick house, which is fully furnished with the commodities to cover their basic needs and more. He is formally unemployed, but gets a disability grant of R1 350 from the government, and his wife works. He fulfills a large proportion of their food needs with the crops from his garden and complements their income by selling vegetables and fruit from the surplus. They also have a cow, which provides them with milk.

Their food situation: conditions, difficulties and hope . . .

Thabiso is the most food insecure of the four, and Ntate Simon the least food insecure. Thabiso has difficulty making ends meet and ensuring that his family can cover their basic needs, including food. Similar to the poor people in Bloemfontein and throughout the province, they all eat pap and samp, potatoes and other starches, but instead of buying their vegetables to supplement their food, their intention has been to grow them. Thabiso, Ntate Thomas and Mme Fanny have been only partially successful in this endeavor, as they have a struggling garden, whereas Ntate Simon has been very successful, for he has a thriving garden.

Thabiso, Ntate Thomas and Mme Fanny have been planting pumpkins, spinach, corn and a few other vegetables and legumes, but these are growing slowly and the garden is not very lush. There is a severe lack of water in the community and they need water for their households and gardens. The lack of water is in part due to the fact that there has been a drought in the Free State for quite a few years and the rains are scarce and out of season. This has caused an enormous problem for communities and farmers throughout the province. They have a space of about 400 square feet (20 feet by 20 feet) to plant but are only using about half of it. They have not planted the rest because they lack enough viable seed as well as sufficient water. They would like to have a better space for farming with better irrigation. Many homes do not have pipes and taps installed with running water; they get their water currently from a pipe near their yards, and the water doesn't always come out strongly. They would like to have a large extension of more fertile land, nearer to a source of water, to plant more. They know of some such land, which is also unutilized, on the other side of the town. It is government land, however, so they would have to obtain permission to use it. They were uncertain if they would be able to get this permission because of bureaucratic obstacles.

Thabiso would like to expand his knowledge of food gardening and extend it to other people in the community, as well as to create employment as an opportunity within their present situation of unemployment. He said there are other people interested in the project. Further to cultivating food crops, they would also like to do some chicken farming, which requires a different set of skills and conditions, such as chicken coops, sufficient drainage, chicken range and feed, among others. There are several obstacles to this multiple endeavor, however. As I mentioned above, two of these are viable seeds and sufficient water. There are also the problems of money and space. Fortunately, some of the people interested in developing this project do have some knowledge and they would all be willing to learn even more, should there be the opportunity to do so. Thabiso, Ntate Thomas and Mme Fanny having been buying seeds out of their own pocket, seeds which they bought at the small shopping complex in the town, at considerably higher prices than in Bloemfontein and not as good quality.

In another section of the town, Ntate Simon's garden is flourishing. It is smaller than Thabiso's, Ntate Thomas's and Mme Fanny's plots, but much more productive. In his garden, he has many different kinds of flowers, fruit and vegetables, all growing together; the garden is a fine example of intercropping. There were a number of very big pumpkins and squashes, spinach, ripe, juicy, red tomatoes, herbs, peaches, cactus figs, corn, sunflowers and other vegetables and fruit. It is a beautifully bountiful garden. He buys his seeds in Bloemfontein or gets them from a friend who brings them from the adjoining Kingdom of Lesotho, because he says that the seeds sold at the town complex are old and inferior. He sells what he grows to people who come to buy from him. He expressed that he does not make a big profit, but he gets by with what he earns. He does not want to have anything to do with the government. Different to Thabiso's, Ntate Thomas's and Mme Fanny's situations, he does not have a problem with water for his garden. He also does not use fertilizer of any kind or compost for his garden. He has fertile land, and it seems that the intercropping has been beneficial for his garden.

These are two examples of food gardens along the spectrum of small gardens in Botshabelo. Ntate Simon has a very productive garden, whereas Thabiso, Ntate Thomas and Mme Fanny are struggling with theirs. They want to make their garden a productive one, principally for Thabiso's survival as well as to also help Ntate Thomas and Mme Fanny supplement their older person's grant and their food, but the odds have been against them thus far, and they have encountered a number of obstacles to creating sustainable initiatives for their benefit. Their situation is similar to that of many of the people in the rest of the province, who have to face severe challenges to their initiatives to overcoming their structural poverty. Thabiso's situation as a young unemployed man with a family who is looking for ways to create employment for himself, as well as for others, faces grave obstacles in his endeavors, which has led to his losing hope in his future. Not having grown up under apartheid, he did not live the struggles of the past, but faces the struggles of his generation, of poverty within freedom. Ntate Simon's case is different. He has created his own initiative, on his own terms, and is content with this.

Their awareness of government programs

Thabiso, Ntate Thomas and Mme Fanny did not know about the *Re Kgaba Ka Diratswana* programme, which is the food security program in the Free State, but they were aware of some government aid to family and small farmers. They also know some people who had received seeds from the government (they were not sure if it was through a program or not), but these people said the seeds were not good, so they did not continue using them. Instead, they just continued with their personal gardening initiatives for food by buying their own seed at the town complex. Ntate Simon had heard of some government programs, but wanted nothing to do with them. In general, people do not really trust the government to always fulfill their promises. Despite Thabiso's reservations about government help, however, he said that he wanted to ask the government if they could supply his community with Jojos (water tanks), for that would benefit them greatly with both their household and gardening needs.

Their agency

For these four people, their food gardens express their agency and the manifestation of their desire to overcome the challenges of poverty that they face. These gardens represent their will to confront these challenges with the resources that they have, but these resources are unequal. Ntate Simon has not only had a better economic situation to start with, for he used to work and he was in a more economically advantageous situation than Thabiso, Ntate Thomas and Mme Fanny, but his wife is still working and he has more fertile land, better seed and running water than the other three do.

Thabiso's, Ntate Thomas's and Mme Fanny's gardening plots are an example of a food initiative that is struggling to survive and become successful. It does help them to solvent their food insecurity in part, but not much, because of all the problems they have encountered. Their agency is also expressed in the fact that they have created this food garden of their own initiative, as partners, who want to help themselves as well as their community. Thomas and Fanny as older people receiving grants, and living in their own brick home, are in a better economic situation than Thabiso is, so they are not as interested in creating more initiatives. They are, however, happy to share their knowledge with other people who wish to learn from them. Thabiso's agency is expressed in his thinking about more than he has, about creating more sustainable means of income for himself and others.

Other gardens

In Thabiso, Mme Fanny and Ntate Thomas's section as well as other sections of Botshabelo, there are a number of small household gardens amidst the bare lands. Quite a few of these had corn, pumpkins, butternut squash, morogko (a spinach-like plant) and kale spinach, among other edible plants and some flowers and herbs. Most of the gardens were not prolific, however; it was evident that people were coaxing whichever plants they could out of the ground.

There are also some community gardens, some more productive than others. One of them is a school garden in front of Ntate Simon's house, which he collaborated on with the school and other members of the community in cultivating. In another section of town, where one of Esther's cousins lives, the community came together to create a garden. There are also small backyard gardens dotted in different areas of the town. These are all initiatives that individuals and groups have formulated to overcome their own food insecurity, and to some extent, that of their communities. This last point is not as simple as it seems, for while there are a number of both individual and small community/neighborhood initiatives, these seem not to have extended throughout the town as a whole, for there are still a number of people in the town who face food insecurity.

In another part of town, there are three interrelated initiatives of Mme Maria and Ntate Raphael: Modulaqhowa Nursery, their small farm, and Zoe Church Ministry. As I explained above, Mme Maria and Ntate Rapahel are a husband and wife team who have created food initiatives to help the people of their community to solvent their food challenges. Through these initiatives, they express their agency.

Modulaqhowa nursery, the family farm and Zoe Church Ministry

Among the garden initiatives in Botshabelo, Modulaqhowa Nursery in Block B stands out. The nursery began in 1992, as the apartheid system was being dismantled, through the initiative of two African men, Petrus and Raphael, with the support of the Department of Forestry at that time. They created this initiative as self-employment and a source of sustainable development for their community. Ntate Raphael's wife, Mme Maria, helped them to build the initiative and then Bishop Ananias joined them later. In 1995, the University of the Witwatersrand (Wits University) in Johannesburg began supporting it, and today, the university provides the nursery with seeds and is the purchaser of most of the plants that are grown there. Other nurseries and people from the province and neighboring provinces also go there to buy their seedlings and plants. In the springtime, the local schools also come to buy plants. The nursery is run today by Mme Maria and Bishop Ananias.

Further to decorative plants and trees, the nursery also sells fruit, herb and vegetable seedlings at moderate prices and they also teach people how to plant these in the best ways. Notwithstanding its availability to the community, Mme Maria, Bishop Ananias and their associates have been unable to motivate many people in the community to grow their own plants. They have found resistance to do so. The nursery sells starter kits of 240–300 seedlings much below the market price in Bloemfontein, but even so, they have not been able to involve the community in planting, as much as they would like to. They also have problems with the authorities in the area, who seem to feel threatened by the success of the nursery and deliberately hamper some of their efforts. I found it interesting that as successful and well-known as the nursery is in other areas of the province and in other provinces, there are people in the town of Botshabelo who had not heard of it.

Ntate Raphael is no longer directly involved in the nursery, but left it several years ago in his wife's hands so as to begin a new initiative to confront the food insecurity in their town; a small farm in which he has been trying to involve the people of the surrounding community. This small farm of about 15 hectares is in another section of Botshabelo, where Ntate Raphael and Mme Maria grow vegetables and raise some chickens. The land is not theirs, for they lease it. They have been unable to cultivate all the land because they lack machinery and good irrigation. Nonetheless, they grow a number of crops on the land that they do cultivate. They strive to involve people of the surrounding community to work with them on the farm. They cannot afford to pay the people, but when harvest time comes, people can take home as many vegetables that they have collaborated in cultivating as they can carry. Unfortunately, not many people take up this opportunity to confront their shortage of food, much to Raphael and Maria's despair.

One of those who does take advantage of this opportunity is a young woman who has been working with them for about ten years. She has been unable to find a job for a number of years and loves working the land. She lives with her mother and siblings in a mkhukhu nearby and they struggle to survive. The vegetables and chickens that she takes home for her family constitutes the greater part of their daily meals. Even though she receives no pay, being part of the farm and being able to meaningfully contribute to her family's food are very important to her. She would love to be able to have a farm of her own and make it productive but does not have the means to do so as yet.

Ntate Raphael and Mme Maria are also devout Christians and consider it their duty to God to help the people who are in need. This belief is what underlies their initiatives. In this way, beyond being a farmer, Ntate Raphael is also the pastor of Zoe Church Ministries, a neighborhood church which they built together with their congregation. It is a two-room mkhukhu of zinc, brick and wood, with one large room for the service and a small room that serves as the kitchen. All the cooking is done on a small three-burner range. The mission of the ministries is not only to preach the Word of God, but also to help the communities of Botshabelo in their struggles. As part of their mission, they have a soup kitchen every Saturday to provide a hot meal to the most vulnerable members of the community. The children are always served first, then the adults.

The above are just a few of the initiatives that people in Botshabelo have created to confront their own food insecurity and that of their neighbors, as well as to foster collaboration amongst them to work together towards this end. Underlying these initiatives is not only overcoming the challenges of food insecurity, but also the objective of creating sources of employment through unity of labor. These endeavors have only been partially successful, especially in the aspect of unity, but Thabiso, Ntate Thomas, Mme Fanny, Ntate Simon, Ntate Raphael, Mme Maria and Bishop Ananias continue with their labor. The meanings that they have made of their own food insecurity and that of their communities have led them to becoming agents of their own initiatives, as well as attempting to bring together their communities to achieve the collective benefit of overcoming their food insecurity. Their struggles are ongoing. Explaining scenarios of food insecurity and some initiatives in the province would be incomplete without going into the rural areas. To this end, my focus turned to two areas in the rural Thabo Mofutsanyana Municipality in the Eastern Free State.

Structural poverty and food insecurity in Thabo Mofutsanyana Municipality

The focus in the Eastern Free State was in two towns of the Maluti-A-Phofung Local Municipality within the Thabo Mofutsanyana Municipality: Kestell and Harrismith. Some of the areas in this municipality were formerly part of the homeland of QwaQwa and had benefitted under the Regional Industrial Development Programme of the apartheid government, but after the subsidies were no longer given, the socioeconomic situation of the area became critical (Department of Rural Development and Land Reform: Free State CRDP, 2009). Maluti-A-Phofung was declared a nodal area in 2001, one of the 22 nodal areas of the country at that time. As I explained in Chapter Two, a nodal area is a severely impoverished area to which the successive ANC governments directed *The Urban Renewal and Integrated Sustainable Rural Development Programme. War on Poverty Programme* and then the *Comprehensive Rural Development Programme* to address underdevelopment in the area. The homeland of QwaQwa was a rocky infertile land which could not sustain the thousands of Black Africans forced to live on it. Maluti-A-Phofung is the third most densely populated area in the province and has a high rate of poverty and unemployment. The majority of the population lives in the rural areas. The key nodal challenges of the municipality are:

> Poverty, Inadequate provision and maintenance of basic infrastructure, Informal housing and insecurity of tenure, Inadequate public transport, Lack of economic opportunities, High illiteracy and innumeracy, Non-payment of services, Droughts, HIV/AIDS, Unemployment and Crime.
>
> (Department of Agriculture and Rural Development.
> Free State Province: "Agricultural land", 2012, p. 3)

As we can see from the demographics in Table 5.2, similar to Botshabelo, the overwhelming majority of the population is African. There is a striking difference to other areas of the province, however, in that a tenth of the population is Zulu speaking. This is because of the municipality's proximity to KwaZulu-Natal Province, historically the region of the isiZulu peoples. People from that region have migrated to the Free State in search of work. The municipality has a population

Table 5.2 Comparative Demographics Free State – Maluti-a-Phofung Municipality

Demographics (in percentage)	Free State Province (pop. 2.7 million)	Maluti-a-Phofung Muncipality (pop. 335 784)
Black African	87.6	98.2
White	8.7	1.3
Colored	3.1	0.2
Indian/Asian		0.2
Other racial groups	0.4	0.1
Languages (in percentage)		
Sesotho	64.2	81.7
Afrikaans	12.7	2
English	2.9	1.5
isiXhosa	7.5	0.6
isiZulu		10.7
Setswana	5.2	0.3
Other languages	7.5	3.2

Source of demographics: South Africa Census, Maluti-a-Phofung Municipality, 2011.Table is of my elaboration.

of 335,784, 62% of whom are of working age (15–64 years). The unemployment rate is 41.8%, and the youth unemployment rate is 53%. Only 31.9% have piped water inside their dwelling. The majority of the population depends on subsistence farming and household gardens as their source of food and some income. Nonetheless, in recent years, the support and service sectors have been expanding and there is more production in arts and crafts, pottery, traditional beadwork, sculpting, cultural heritage projects, conservation products and guesthouses, such as bed and breakfasts (B&Bs), which provide other sources of income (Statistics South Africa: Maluti a Phofung, 2014). Let us begin with the town of Kestell.

Kestell: food initiatives within poverty

Kestell is a small town and serves as a center for the predominantly agricultural area of the municipality. My point of entry to the community of Kestell was Busi, the Food Security Coordinator in charge of the Thabo Mofutsanyana District for the Department of Agriculture and Rural Development of the Free State Province. Through her work, Busi has been creating and implementing the household and school food garden program in the municipality under the *Re Kgaba Ka Diratswana* program, which I explained in Chapter 2.

Article 27 of the Constitution of the Republic of South Africa establishes that everyone has the right to health care, food, water and social security, and, to ensure these, "The state must take reasonable legislative and other measures, within its available resources, to achieve the progressive realisation of each of these rights"

(Constitution of the Republic of South Africa. No.108, Article 27, No. 2, 1996). Following this mandate, a number of the government departments have each formulated food security policies and programs. All government departments are supposed to have a food security program under the government Food and Nutrition Strategy, which is a national policy, but not all do.

To implement the *Re Kgaba Ka Diratswana* program in the Free State, the MEC (Minister) of the Department of Agriculture and Rural Development of the Free State Province identified three towns in five municipalities. The objective is to have 100 gardens per town, with the goal of 2 000 household gardens per year for the whole district. The 100 garden per town objective had been achieved by 2014 in some towns, but in 2015, the 2 000 target still had not. The MEC chose these towns because they are very impoverished and the land is rocky, so it considered that the tire garden concept would be appropriate for them. The Department assists people with garden tools and seeds. 'Re Kgaba Ka Diratswana' (which is Sesotho) can be roughly translated as "we are grateful for what we receive from the soil".

The Department of Agriculture and Rural Development of the Free State lacks resources. The people who work there expressed that there is corruption at the administrative and government level and believe that the money allocated to the Department goes to the people in power. As Food Security Coordinator, Busi has been unable to do her job properly because of the lack of resources. One example of this is that her office had not had electricity, computers, telephone or fax service for about two years until 2015. Moreover, she pays for her own travel expenses, as she drives around the region to do her job and goes to monthly meetings in Bloemfontein, two hours away. As part of her work, she checks all the schools, clinics, churches and crèches within each ward of the municipality, based on the inquiry, *how many church gardens, school gardens, crèche gardens do we have? And what state are they in*? Based on her findings, she endeavors to help them to create or improve their gardens. She also asks the other departments, such as the Department of Social Development, to ask their food 'champions' (people who have successfully created food gardens, food centers or other food access initiatives) to identify their friends and people who are suffering from food insecurity. The Department of Agriculture and Rural Development and the Department of Social Development in the province, which is creating a food distribution center and soup kitchens in QwaQwa, have a political arrangement to unite their forces to foster greater food security in the region. One of the many issues that Busi works with the Department of Social Development on is whether that department will accommodate people who do not know about the soup kitchens.

Busi has been motivating people all around the municipality to grow food gardens to help them ensure their food security and to beautify their gardens by mixing vegetables and flowers in them. The project began in 2010 in Cornelia, a town in the northern part of the province and then was brought to this municipality. Rolling out the project in the municipality has not been easy, nonetheless, because it has been hard for her to motivate people to plant their gardens. She continually expressed the opinion that "Our people are lazy. I must say they are lazy. So if you don't come to them so often, they just leave it like that. They want you to come every day". Here, again, we can observe the repeated theme of people's perceived laziness in people's narratives in other parts of the province, as explained earlier.

In the homelands during apartheid, people did a lot of farming and many of the homelands achieved food self-sustainability, but the case of QwaQwa was different because the lands were difficult to plant. Despite this difficulty, in the past, the older generation used to plant their food and they survived on it, but the younger generation, the post-apartheid generation, has not been doing the same. Some of the older people are still farming, but not all have the energy to do so. Notwithstanding, the older generation would like to teach the younger generation to farm, but many of these are just not interested. In Busi's view, this is an expression of the laziness of the younger generation.

The department has held town competitions, district competitions and provincial competitions for the best gardens in an effort to get people to participate. The accountability of the program is supposed to be held through forums at three successive levels, with each local food security forum reporting to the district food security forum, which in turn is supposed to report to the provincial food security forum. The provincial forum is inter-organizational, where different government departments, municipalities and NGOs, who each have a food security program, meet. The Department of Agriculture and Rural Development, the Department of Social Development and the Department of Education meet with local municipalities and NGOs like Save the Children. The forum is supposed to be held monthly, but this does not necessarily happen.

As I explained briefly above, there has been some interdepartmental collaboration to combat food insecurity in the province. One recent collaborative program between the Department of Agriculture and Rural Development and the Department of Social Development in the municipality and QwaQwa region is the Food Bank Distribution Programme, which is an initiative of the Department of Social Development. This department also wants to assist in improving the food gardens, the program of the Department of Agriculture and Rural Development. QwaQwa has been declared a food insecure area, which is why the Departments of Social Development and Agriculture have placed the Food Distribution Centre there. The Centre is for people throughout the province, but the pilot is in QwaQwa.

In Kestell I visited four food gardens, three promoted by the Department of Agriculture and Rural Development and one by the Department of Basic Education. The first is a tire garden at the HIV clinic, the second is at an impoverished family's home, the third is at a primary school, which has a school feeding scheme and food garden, and the fourth is at a crèche. I also visited and spoke with persons in a poor area of the town where many people face food insecurity, and met with patients at the HIV clinic. In the following section, I will describe some contexts of food insecurity in the town, as well as some food initiatives.

Contexts of food insecurity and food initiatives in Kestell

It is the mandate of the national food policies in South Africa that every clinic should have a food garden to confront the challenge of food insecurity. Nonetheless, in reality, not many clinics and schools in this municipality follow this mandate for a number of reasons, among which are: lack of resources; scarcity of water; lack of knowledge about how to plant efficiently; and lack of interest on the part of the community to upkeep the garden. Notwithstanding, in Kestell, there is a clinic and some schools that have followed the mandate, mainly through Busi's determination and persistence. In the following, I describe several food initiatives, beginning with one at an HIV clinic, another at a primary school, a third at a crèche and the last a household food garden created under the Re Kgaba Ka Diratswana programme of the Department of Agriculture and Rural Development.

The HIV clinic tire garden

The HIV Clinic in Kestell is focused on serving the lower-income HIV-positive patients, providing them with ARVs and primary health care. Many of these people are very impoverished and face varying degrees of food insecurity. Despite the national mandate, few clinics have food gardens. The clinics provide the patients with nutritional supplements, but they do not cultivate the gardens. It is often left up to the Department of Agriculture and Rural Development in this municipality to create these gardens, but its employees do not have the necessary resources. Consequently, they struggle to help the clinics cultivate their gardens.

At the HIV clinic in Kestell, Busi has motivated and taught a group of five women to create a tire garden on the premises of the clinic to combat their food insecurity. Busi introduced the concept of tire gardening to the women so that they would not have to dig into the ground. As food insecure HIV/AIDS patients, they are rather weak and get tired easily, so cultivating gardens in tires lying on the ground and filled with soil is more physically comfortable for them to work with. They have been growing vegetables in the garden and in this way have been able to improve their nutrition, which is essential in their state of health. Notwithstanding, not all the women have continued planting. Only one has continued to do so: Mme Lily, who told me her story. The second initiative is at Dipelaneng Primary School.

Dipelaneng primary school

Dipelaneng Primary School in Thlolong location in Kestell has a school food garden, mandated by the Department of Basic Education. As is the case of primary schools with lower-income students, this school has a school feeding scheme, through which its students eat lunch at school every day. The majority of the pupils at the school have unemployed or underemployed parents, and for a number of them, the lunch at the school is their only meal of the day. As I explained in

Chapter 2, the National School Nutrition Programme, or school feeding scheme, as it is popularly known, is an initiative of the Department of Basic Education, and implemented throughout the country in collaboration with the Provincial Departments, District Offices and other partners.

In the case of the primary school, the Department of Basic Education provides the school with a budget of R1,90 (approximately US0.19) per pupil for the feeding scheme, which is very little and barely covers the food expenses. The school has 1 387 pupils, and they have very little varied food. Their school lunch, which is cooked on the premises in a small classroom converted into a kitchen, consists mainly of porridge, samp, beans, tinned fish, pumpkin and cabbage. The department gives the school a weekly menu and tells them what to cook, based on the availability of items. One weekly menu was the following (1 spoon is the measurement of a cooking spoon):

Monday: 1 spoon of samp, 1 spoon of beans, two spoons of cabbage
Tuesday: I spoon of pap, two spoons of pumpkin,
Wednesday: 1 spoon of soya, 1 spoon of beans, two spoons of cabbage
Thursday: I spoon of samp, 1 spoon of beans, two spoons of pumpkin
Friday: 1 spoon of pap, 1 spoon of cabbage, ½ spoon of tinned fish

The school also has a food garden, and some of the produce from the food garden goes to the school kitchen, but most of the food used in the school meal is bought from department-approved sellers, who are not necessarily people from the community. This is contrary to the objective of achieving economic sustainability for the community, but it is the reality. The school has a gardener who takes care of the school food garden, which is quite large and on the school grounds, but enclosed in a metal structure. Neither the teachers nor the students are involved in cultivating the garden or using it as an out of classroom learning space. Moreover, in the principal's opinion, the idea of using the school food garden as a learning space is a ludicrous one, for as he explained to me sharply, visibly annoyed at my question in this regard, having the children help to cultivate the garden would be more of a burden for the teachers and himself, rather than a benefit for the children.

Despite following the national mandate of creating a school food garden, this school was not using its food garden to fulfill the objective of alleviating the food insecurity of its students and staff. The school was using it merely to demonstrate to the department that it was complying with the mandate. There are several reasons why the school garden was not fulfilling the objective; three of the main ones being the lack of interest on the part of the principal and most of the teachers, their lack of knowledge of planting and the scarcity of water. It is also a school with a large student population, so the garden would have to grow abundant vegetables and legumes to feed these students, which it was not doing.

The Crèche

School food gardens include those at crèches, and my visit to a crèche in Kestell showed a very different situation to that at the primary school. In this crèche, there was a flourishing food garden which was well laid out and colorfully decorated, creating an inviting environment for the children for learning and for recreation. The school gardener is a community member and the produce goes to the school 'feeding pot', which is the term that is commonly used to refer to the food that is prepared for the children. These children are also from low-income families with unemployed and underemployed parents, and, for some of them, the school meal may be their only meal. This crèche had a much smaller student body, so it was easier for them to feed the children almost exclusively with vegetables grown in the garden. In this way, it was fulfilling the objective of alleviating its students' and staff's food insecurity.

Household food gardens

As part of the *Re Kgaba Ka Diratswana Programme* of the Department of Agriculture and Rural Development, Busi has helped a number of people in the poor areas of the town to cultivate household food gardens. Some of these have been flourishing, while others have not, mainly because of lack of interest. I visited one of these gardens with Busi. The grandmother of the family is the gardener, with the teenage grandchildren not showing any particular interest in planting the vegetables and beans. The houses surrounding the garden which has been planted are mkhukhus, made of zinc. The families living there are very poor and have been food insecure, so planting the garden has helped them to considerably alleviate their food insecurity. Within these contexts of food insecurity and initiatives are people's stories, two of which I will convey here: those of Mme. Lily and Eugenia.

Mme Lily and Eugenia

Mme Lily is a very poor 62-year-old widow who lives in Kestell. She is HIV positive and unemployed. She lives in a small RDP house with her young grandchild, who has been in her care since his father, Mme Lily's son, died of AIDS. The child's mother abandoned him, but the child is not HIV positive. She is illiterate and was a domestic worker all her life until some years ago. She was fired from her job in Bethlehem, which is a large town about 45 minutes away from Kestell, when her employer found out she was HIV positive, and she has not been able to find a job since. It has been several years since she has had a job.

Eugenia is a poor 42-year-old woman, married with three children: a son and two nephews she is looking after, the children of her sisters who have passed away. This is common in South African homes, where one family member looks after their nieces, nephews, cousins, grandchildren and other members of their extended families. Many of the children are HIV/AIDS orphans. Eugenia and her husband receive a student care grant of R320 for each of their nephews, but have been unable to get the full foster care amount of R830 because they have been unable to find the children's fathers to give them permission to do so. Eugenia's husband is the only one who works and he only earns R1 500 per month, so they struggle to cover their basic needs.

As I have been explaining throughout this book, the reality is that food insecurity, and especially the kinds of food insecurity experienced by the participants of this study, is never only about food. It is much more than whether you have food or not. Within the realities of structural poverty these people live are intertwined the issues of social and economic inequity and inequality, among other pressing issues, such as the public health issue of HIV/AIDS. Some of these issues are expressed in the same themes as in earlier chapters: their economic difficulties and survival; their food situation; their awareness of government food programs and non-governmental programs; work opportunities in the area; differences in the food situation during times of apartheid and now; their faith; what poverty means to them; and their agency.

Their economic difficulties and survival

Mme Lily is very poor and survives mainly on her older person's grant of R1 350, which she receives from the government. With this, she supports herself and her young grandson. They live in a small RDP house, so fortunately, she does not have to pay rent. Nonetheless, her social grant barely covers their living expenses. She comes to the HIV clinic in Kestell for her ARVs, and she has been participating in the food garden at the clinic. On her part, Eugenia does not work and neither does her 21-year-old son because they have found no sources of employment. Her husband is the only person who works in the household, and he only earns R1 500 rand per month. Together with the child support grant, the family of five consequently lives on an income below R3 000 per month, which is very insufficient. Eugenia inherited her mother's house, which she and her family now live in, after her mother passed away, so, like Mme Lily, at least they do not have the expense of rent. With the little income they have, they pay for electricity, other utilities, clothes, toiletries and then food. As is the case of many of the poor, food is always last on the list, after taking care of their other obligations.

Their food situation

Both Mme Lily and Eugenia have been food insecure for a long time, Mme Lily much more than Eugenia. Mme Lily is very poor, and the food she is growing in the tire garden at the clinic is helping to supplement her diet. She has been very food insecure and is very fragile. When she was working, she was able to have greater access to food, but in recent years, since she has been unemployed, she has sometimes struggled to get food. Her neighbor has occasionally helped her by giving her mealies (corn), which she then supplements with the vegetables from the food garden. Mme Lily's food situation had improved somewhat since she began planting the food gardens outside the clinic, but in the winter, there are fewer crops. Her health has also improved now that she is on her ARVs and being able to eat the vegetables she grows on a continuous basis has helped her to be healthier than she used to be. She is one of five women who originally planted the tire food gardens, and she is the only one who is cultivating the gardens now, because one of the women got a job and the other four are apparently no longer interested in planting the gardens. This decision by the women only served to strengthen Busi's view that in her experience, "people are very lazy and want things given to them without working". This is an interesting point which I analyze in Chapter 6 for, as I explained earlier, it is an observation I heard frequently during my research, that some people are lazy and have become dependent on the state and charity to help them.

Eugenia's family faces food insecurity on a daily basis, for their income does not allow them to live comfortably and eat properly. Nonetheless, they do their best not to go to bed hungry. They eat food which is cheap, some of which is healthy, such as beans and pumpkin, and on occasion, they eat some meat. Like most impoverished people, they also eat a lot of pap and complete their meals with carbohydrates to keep them full. As is the case of many mothers, Eugenia tends to feed her children first when they are at home. During the school week, they also have lunch at school through the school feeding scheme. She gives them breakfast and dinner from Monday to Friday and then all three meals on Saturday and Sunday and during the holidays when they are not at school. The holidays are the most difficult for Eugenia with regard to feeding her family, for she is obliged to provide them with all three meals, seven days a week, on the same income. Unlike Mme Lily, Eugenia receives food parcels from her church on a monthly basis, in which she gets some basic staples such as milk, mealie meal and some vegetables, which assist her in alleviating her economic constraints and her food insecurity.

As is the case with all the people who face food insecurity, in both Mme Lily and Eugenia's cases, by improving their economic situation, their families' food situation would also improve. As I have emphasized time and again, food insecurity is one manifestation of the economic challenges that poor people face in the Free State. Being able to pay for living expenses is the primary concern and food is last on the list. In Eugenia's case, she wants to work to be able to make sufficient money to make her family's economic situation less precarious.

Their awareness of provincial government food programs

Both of these women are aware of some government food programs, such as the school feeding scheme at the crèche and the primary school and the food garden projects at clinics, homes and schools, these last of which are Busi's programs. Eugenia believes that the school feeding scheme is good, because her children are able have one meal at school, which helps her considerably, for it is one less meal she has to worry about. This further confirmed my perception that for poorer parents, the school feeding scheme is good because it takes the pressure off them to provide more food for their children. They know that their children have at least one meal a day at school. The principal of the primary school with whom I spoke also explained that a large number of his students struggle to eat for the rest of the day and on the weekends, as well as during school holidays, which was confirmed by what Eugenia expressed with regard to her own struggle to feed her children during these times. With regard to non-governmental food programs, Eugenia receives a monthly food parcel and knows of several churches that provide food parcels to their members. Mme Lily had heard of some but had not received any.

Work opportunities in the area

Both women were of the opinion that there is little work in the area. Moreover, for Mme Lily, obtaining employment was difficult, because of her fragile health and HIV status. In Eugenia's case, she has never worked and has tried looking for jobs, but has not been successful. Notwithstanding, she would like to work, but explained that in Kestell, there is a lack of employment and no facility to make things. She gave as an example that she and other women could come together and sew, but that they do not have either machines or material. Nonetheless, she thinks there is the possibility that there are people who are in the community who would think of doing so. She says they would "have to strategize", and she is willing to do so. She explained a strategy she has formulated as the following:

> I not sell on credit. People like credit in the community and that is a problem. But there is not much money in the community. One strategy not force people to give money, but to make a deposit, then I can do the work, then they pay me the rest.

In her explanation, Eugenia describes two of the problems her community faces, which may be interrelated: that people do not have much money and that they like to buy on credit. Nonetheless, she also formulates a strategy to overcome this problem, for the benefit of all the parts involved. In my view, this is an expression of her agency.

Times are different now . . .

Mme Lily grew up during apartheid and believes that the situation is a little better now, because during the apartheid era there was no means of Blacks working and getting a house, which she has now. Moreover, the White people (referring particularly to the police) used to chase Blacks and demand their IDs and passes. Consequently, in her opinion, life is better now than it was during the apartheid era because she now has a house (an RDP house), whereas, as she explained, during those times, if a woman did not have a husband, she did not qualify for a house.

　　She grew up without parents, so she had to work from an early age. She was a maid and her employers gave her food, but what they normally did was give her the food outside. Her cup was a jam jar, and they would pour the coffee in and give her food on an enamel plate, which she would then eat in the yard. She used to clean the house, but she was not allowed to bring her belongings inside the house. Her employers would give her one meal at work, sometimes pap and tea, sometimes bread and tea, but otherwise they would give her money to buy her other meals at home. In her view, despite her dire poverty, life in South Africa today is better than during times of apartheid, because even if she is sick, she can get ARVs for free and moreover, through the food security program of growing vegetables, she can grow spinach or morogko and take them home.

Eugenia's view of life during the apartheid era is considerably different to Mme Lily's. Eugenia was in her early twenties when the democratic era began in South Africa and expressed that in her view, times now are tougher than they were during apartheid. During apartheid, her mother, who was a teacher, was working, and Eugenia was living a better life economically, albeit not with equality in social recognition. At that time, she did not experience the difficulties that she is experiencing now. She and her family have a more difficult life now. Her husband is working at a low-wage job, she cannot find work, and their son, who is now 21, cannot get a job in Kestell because there is no employment there. He has completed his matric and wants to go to FET college (similar to a community college) but is unable to do so because he cannot afford the taxi fare to go to Bethlehem, where the FET is. Their lives, like those of so many others in their situation, have become entrapped in a vicious cycle of structural poverty. In her view, times now are tougher because people do not have jobs, whereas during times of apartheid, they did. She also said that those jobs were good jobs, which allowed people to feed their families as compared to today.

We can see from these two drastically different perspectives that each woman's view is dependent on the kind of life they lived under apartheid, as compared to their lives now. As the daughter of a teacher, Eugenia was living in a more privileged situation than Mme Lily was as a domestic worker, and now she misses the comfort of the life she had then. For her, not having rights is not as important as living comfortably. For Mme Lily, who had neither rights nor lived comfortably and was treated as an inferior being, life now is better, despite her dire poverty, because she has a house, which she did not have before. I will discuss this important issue of the difference of perspectives of life under apartheid as compared to life in the democratic South Africa in further detail in Chapter 6.

Their faith and their poverty

As is the case of so many other poor South Africans, Eugenia is a deeply religious woman. Her faith in God has helped her to understand her circumstances and she deeply believes that God protects her and guides her life. Her faith keeps her going and gives her life meaning. Mme Lily is also a devout woman, but she asks God why she has so many problems in her life. When talking about her problems, the pain and anguish of her life were very evident, and she burst into tears during one of our conversations. This is a woman who has had a very hard life.

For Mme Lily, poverty is deeply painful. Despite feeling that she has more benefits now than she had during times of apartheid, talking about her poverty now is very painful for her. For Eugenia, poverty means "not being able to do some of the things you want to do and have some of the things you want to have". For her, it also means powerlessness, because in her view, it is the people who are in power who benefit from the programs which are supposed to benefit the people of the country, referring to the corruption which is endemic in the South African government ministries and programs.

She also believes that despite the South African Constitution which lays the groundwork for South African democracy, there is great inequality in the country today because of money. As she expressed, "If you don't have money, you can't even get a funeral policy. And people look at you and you have to go to the loan office, you cannot get loans". This point illustrates cultural and personal pride and the embarrassment that a Black South African faces at not being able to pay for one's own funeral or that of a loved one. Funerals are important and expensive events in Black South African cultures. She also explained that the government can bury the people whose families cannot to have funerals for them, but that this would mean that they (the government) can take the dead wherever they choose to take them and bury them on any land they want to, which could mean that the deceased's family will not be able to see them. In her view, this would deeply disrupt funeral rites and traditions of putting one's loved one to rest, which is a sacred matter in African cultures.

Their agency

In my view, cultivating the garden as a means to improve her food situation constitutes Mme Lily's agency. It was Busi's initiative, as Food Security Officer, to create the program and motivate people to cultivate food gardens, but it was up to the people to continue with these gardens. Busi started them off by teaching them how to grow the food gardens, in the case of those who didn't know how to do so, and provided them with the seeds. Then she supervised their progress and supported them along the way. The fact that Mme Lily is the only one of the five women who is still cultivating the food garden to help herself is an important expression of her agency. In Eugenia's case, the fact that she is reflecting on her situation and that of her community and trying to conceptualize strategies to confront the employment challenges that they face is, in my view, a manifestation of her potential agency. With this, I end my discussion on structural poverty and food insecurity in Kestell and turn to these same issues in the town of Harrismith.

Poverty in Harrismith: the Wastepickers

Harrismith is a much larger and more urban town than Kestell is and is at the crossroads between the Free State, Gauteng and KwaZulu-Natal Provinces. It is the center of one of the five wool-producing districts in Southern Africa and is near a number of tourist attractions.

It is interesting to note from Table 5.3 that the demographic composition of Harrismith is different from those of the township in Bloemfontein, Botshabelo

Table 5.3 Comparative Demographics Free State – Maluti-A-Phofung Municipality – Harrismith

Demographics (in percentage)	Free State Province (pop. 2.7 million)	Maluti-A-Phofung Muncipality (pop. 335 784)	Harrismith (pop. 27 869)
Black African	87.6	98.2	87.06
White	8.7	1.3	10.72
Colored	3.1	0.2	0.76
Indian/Asian		0.2	1.28
Other racial groups	0.4	0.1	0.17
Languages (in percentage)			
Sesotho	64.2	81.7	32.62
Afrikaans	12.7	2	10.35
English	2.9	1.5	3.74
isiXhosa	7.5	0.6	0.83
isiZulu		10.7	49.44
Setswana	5.2	0.3	0.79
Other languages	7.5	3.2	2.33

Source of demographics: South Africa Census, 2011, Maluti-A-Phofung Municipality. Table is of my elaboration.

and Kestell. While its population is still overwhelmingly Black African, a tenth of its population is White, and almost half of the Black population is isiZulu. Different to these other places, only a third of the population is Sesotho. This has to do with the town's proximity to KwaZulu-Natal Province. As a relatively urban town in a rural region, Harrismith is affected by the structural poverty of the municipality it is a part of, which, as I explained at the beginning of this section on the Maluti-A-Phofung Municipality, constitutes a nodal area of development. In view of this, it has a high unemployment rate and very poor people. In this town, I got to know some of the poorest of the poor; the waste pickers from the municipal waste dump. My point of entry to Harrismith and to the waste dump was Dr. Dipane Hlalele, a professor of the University of the Free State QwaQwa campus who lives in Harrismith. He takes his garbage every week to the municipal dump, and when he told me about the site and the people there, we both thought it would be an important place for me to understand, at least in part, the lives and opinions of some of the people who live at the lowest rungs of society.

The Harrismith municipal waste dump

The municipal waste dump is on a hill on the outskirts of town, where all the waste of the municipality, recyclable and non-recyclable, is taken. A few plump cows walk among the small mounds of garbage everywhere, nuzzling the bags of waste as the waste pickers work around them, rummaging through the bags in their quest for pickings they can sell or take. Seeing cows walking is commonplace in the Free State Province. Throughout the province, from the townships of Bloemfontein to the semi-urban areas, urban and rural areas, there are cows grazing everywhere, even in the impoverished areas and among the garbage.

Around election time, the national and regional TV stations come to the municipal dump and film the waste pickers, creating segments where they always show surprise that there is such poverty in the area. A waste picker is one of the terms used in English in South Africa for a person who salvages recyclable materials from garbage for resale and/or personal use. At the municipal waste dump in Harrismith, there are about 30 waste pickers, all Black. For many of them, waste picking is their main means of survival. I spent some time with them and spoke at length with two of them: Boitumelo, a 23-year-old man and Katlego, a 24-year-old woman. During our conversations, we sat on two rocks in a small clearing in the waste dump, with the large piles of garbage all around us, the nearest about 20 feet away. Our conversations were periodically interrupted by trucks coming to the dump bringing garbage and leftover food from the restaurants in town. Whenever a truck came rumbling up, all the waste pickers, including Boitumelo and Katlego, would run off to climb onto the trucks to get the garbage and food.

Boitumelo and Katlego

Boitumelo is a 23-year-old man, married with a wife and two small children. He lives in one of the poorest areas of the township, in his grandmother's home with his grandmother, wife, children and other family members. He has been a waste picker for three years and stated that before that period of time, he was in his mother's home. It seemed, nonetheless, that he had been in jail for a period of time, because of some tattoos that he has on his arms. He did not speak about this, but Dr. Hlalele, who was accompanying me and served as my translator, explained to me that Boitumelo's tattoos are typical of a person who has been in jail. Boitumelo is a quiet, intense young man, with years of poverty and anguish etched in his face, aging him beyond his years.

Katlego is a 24-year-old woman, a single mother of a seven-year-old daughter. Katlego was born in Harrismith and dropped out of school when she was in Grade 10 because she got pregnant and had to support herself and her baby with income from piece jobs. She, her daughter and her younger sister, who is 11, live with her grandmother in the poor area of the township. Her daughter's father left them. Like Boitumelo, Katlego is a quiet, and rather shy young woman, but quite open to telling me about her life once she felt comfortable with me.

As I have explained throughout this book, the reality is that food insecurity, and especially the kinds of food insecurity experienced by the participants of this study, is never only about food (Dréze, Sen and Hussain, 1995). As I will describe below, within the realities of structural poverty of Boitumelo and Katlego, are intertwined the issues of social and economic inequity and inequality, among other pressing issues explained throughout the narratives of the people of this book. Similar to those stories, in these two, I delineated the themes of: their economic difficulties and survival; their food situation; their awareness of government food programs; work opportunities in the province; differences in the food situation during times of apartheid and now; what poverty means to them; and their agency.

Their economic difficulties and survival

Boitumelo and Katlego are waste pickers. They go to the municipal dump every day to sort through the garbage to see what can be salvaged to resell, mostly recyclables, and to look out for the truck that brings them leftovers from the restaurants for them to eat. They are not begging on the street, but prefer to work for their money. Boitumelo has been a waste picker for three years and Katlego for about two; they both earn R120 every two weeks from the waste they collect for recycling. Boitumelo and his wife also receive the monthly child social grant of R350 per child, which amounts to R700 for their two children. Together with his income from recycling, that gives them about R940 rand per month, which is very little for the needs of a family of four. Boitumelo also does some piece jobs now and again when he has the opportunity, through which he supplements his income to maintain his family of four. The piece jobs offer him probably R30 a day but are not constant. Fortunately, he does not pay rent and his grandmother pays the electricity, but he still has to feed and clothe himself and his family. He explained that the money he gets covers food, soap and some minimal toiletries, but not shoes and clothes. He gets shoes that people discard at the dump. His grandmother collects the older person's social grant, which amounts to R1 350. His wife does not work, but is unfortunately an alcoholic and she often takes the money from the children's social grants to spend it on alcohol. This worsens his family's possibility of survival. He depends heavily on his grandmother's economic and emotional support.

During the farming season, Katlego works plowing in the fields, but in the off -season, she is a waste picker. Like Boitumelo and the other waste pickers, what she mainly does is separate the recyclables from the rest of the garbage and packs them in large bags of about 50 kilos each, that they are paid R1.20 per kilo, making about R120 per two bags. They all get left over food, clothes and shoes at the municipal dump. Katlego gets a social grant of R350 per month for her child. Unlike other older adults, however, her grandmother does not get the old age pension that she is eligible for, because she does not have an ID. In this way, Katlego's economic situation is more difficult than Boitumelo's. Every two weeks a White man, whose name they do not know, nor do they know where he comes from, comes and picks up the huge bags of recyclables to take them to the recycling plant. He pays the waste pickers R120 for two bags which, as I explained above, generally takes each person two weeks to fill the bags.

Their food situation

In principle, these waste pickers are food insecure because they and their families do not have sustainable access to food and a stable income. Notwithstanding, they do not starve, for they get some leftover food every day from a truck that passes by the restaurants in Harrismith, picks up the leftovers and brings them to the municipal dump. When Boitumelo, Katlego and the other waste pickers see the truck coming, they fly off to jump on it to get whatever food they could. They take whatever food they can home to their families and use some of the little money they get to buy more food. At home, they supplement the meals with what they buy. They would generally eat pap, morogko (pronounced *morroho*, different varieties of green leafy vegetables and a dish of the same name), cabbage, potatoes, tamphu, beans and such. Katlego explained that they eat every day; that her family does not generally go hungry. Her little sister and her daughter also eat at school every day, through the school feeding scheme. Boitumelo's children, who are two and four years old, eat at their crèche every day. There is also a food program for the poor children of the town. Some meat sellers put aside meat for the children, then they take them to a particular place and cook them in big pots and often once a week the children go to get the meal.

Government food programs and work opportunities

Boitumelo is not aware of any government food programs, and Katlego is aware that there are some government programs but believes they are not regular. In her experience, they are mostly rolled out around election time. Near election time, government officials go around to the houses and register the people. They also get some parcels perhaps twice or thrice a year. These parcels include food such as tinned fish, mealie meal and flour and commodities such as candles and a blanket (the winters are very cold in the Free State). Both Boitumelo and Katlego believe that there are not enough jobs for everyone in the Harrismith area. In Boitumelo's opinion, to get a job, you need to know someone and moreover, you need to give them a bribe. This was an observation I heard from almost everyone I spoke with, including the participants in the township of Bloemfontein; you get jobs through contacts and if you do not have contacts, your job opportunities are minimal. In Katlego's opinion, the economic situation in the Free State, and hers, are what they are because of a lack of job opportunities and unemployment. These are both young people, who were mere toddlers when South Africa entered its democratic era. Nonetheless, in Boitumelo's view, life is better now than it was during apartheid because now Blacks can participate in society.

What poverty means to them

For Boitumelo, poverty means "Being insufficient, like not having food, meats, also money. Everything is not enough, or basic needs. No money". He also believes that poverty exists in South Africa today because there are many people who are born poor. He perceives this poverty is an intergenerational one. He also said that there are people who come to the municipal dump to pick the garbage, but they are not poor; they have money. They come for the recyclables, which cuts into the waste pickers' income. For Katlego, poverty is "the lack of power, of the ability to get things for oneself". She conceptualizes this power as more than having money. She thinks of it in the light of *Amandla*, the Xhosa and Zulu word which was the rallying cry of power and resistance for Blacks during times of apartheid. In her view, through this power, the government will be working for the people and there will be job opportunities. She also thinks of poverty as inequality and that there is inequality in South Africa today. In her view, she is a victim of this inequality, for people laugh at her because she is so poor. This affects her deeply and makes her want to better herself, so as not to be the victim of people's disdain.

Their agency

In my view, their working at the dump site is one manifestation of their agency to combat the challenges of poverty and food insecurity that they face. They earn very little, but they prefer to do this, rather than do nothing. They would both like to go beyond their present sources of income through piece jobs and waste picking, and improve their lives. Boitumelo would like to improve his economic situation, and consequently his food situation, by having his own store. He would like to open his own store where he would sell vegetables and fruit. He is aware that there are some government grants available which can help him set his store up. He knows someone at the government agency who can help him get the grant. Nonetheless, the problem is that he needs seed money to set up the store and he does not have it. He would need R350 as the down payment for the government to provide him with the initial stock. But the problem is that his wife drinks heavily. Apparently she takes the money they have (e.g., from the child grants) and she goes drinking, so he has not been able to save any. Female alcoholism is a problem amongst poor people in the Free State, which I discuss further in Chapter 6. Katlego also really wants to improve her life and to do this, she wants to go to the Adult Basic Education Centres, which are now the Adult Education and Training Centres, to do one or more of their programs to learn a trade and get a job or create her own employment.

Katlego and Boitumelo's stories of severe economic constraints and food insecurity are those of two people who live at the bottom rungs of society, but have hope that they can change their lives for the better. Despite their very difficult circumstances, they dream of a better life for themselves and their families. To end this chapter on food insecurity and food initiatives, I will describe a model food community in the QwaQwa region, of which the Maluti-A-Phofung Local Municipality is part, as well as some other food initiatives in the province.

Diyatalawa Agri-Village: a food community

Diyatalawa Agri-Village is a model settlement deep in the farmlands of the QwaQwa region, approximately 20 km from Kestell, between Kestell and Harrismith (Department of Rural Development and Land Reform: Free State CRDP,

2009). It is one of the three villages in the Maluti-A- Phofung Local Municipality that were selected to be part of the Free State Comprehensive Rural Development Programme (CRDP), which has the objective of improving the lives of people in these areas. The other two villages are Makgolokeong and TSHIAME I and II. This objective of improvement is formulated as: "The CDRP is focused on enabling rural people to take control of their destiny, with the support from the government, and thereby dealing effectively with rural poverty through the optimal use and management of natural resources" (Department of Rural Development and Land Reform: Free State CRDP, 2009, p. 5). To achieve this objective, the Department established a three-pronged strategy (p. 5):

(i)   **Agrarian Transformation** includes increasing all types of agricultural production; optimal and sustainable use of natural resources; the use of appropriate technologies; food security; and improving the quality of life for each rural household.
(ii) **Rural Development** includes improving economic and social infrastructure.
(iii) **Land Reform** includes restitution, redistribution and land tenure reform.

Through the CDRP, the government of President Jacob Zuma has created similar villages in other provinces. Diyatalawa used to be an old rural settlement and then the government relocated the people and built them a new settlement; a nicely built village with new houses and all the basic services such as water, electricity and indoor plumbing, with some solar power panels on the streets. It also has a new rural boarding primary school where the children from the village as well as the neighboring farms are placed, and a new football court for sports and recreation.

My informant on the history and evolution of the agri-village was Mme Dimekatso, an older Black woman who has been in Diyatalawa since its inception, and has lived through the different phases of its development. I triangulated her narratives with written sources. The original settlement was created in 1996 with the Diyatalawa Apple project, as it is famously known. People from different places were moved to this region to begin apple orchards. Originally, each family was given a hectare to cultivate an apple orchard. AgriEco, a public-private corporation (parastatal) established by the former QwaQwa government and the private sector, assisted the people of Diyatalawa in this endeavor, to uplift the poor in the rural areas. AgriEco plowed the fields for the people, the government trained the people in apple farming and they were given a monthly stipend of R2 000. The intention of the second phase of the project was to export the apples to Australia and Chile, among other countries. Due to poor management of the project on the part of AgriEco, it began failing. The apple farmers were well trained, but there were insufficient resources to maintain the apple farms. One example of this was that the government gave the people the apple trees, but then AgriEco failed to give them nets to protect the trees. AgriEco was liquidated in 1998 and the farmers were given a severance package, but the people of the community were left jobless and had to fend for themselves. The government then intervened again and created a program in which White commercial farmers would collaborate with new Black farmers, among other things, to train them in farming techniques and to create a productive relationship for all (Mkhize, 2013)

In a twist on this story, from around 1997 to 2000, the government paid the people of Diyatawala to train a White commercial farmer in apple farming, so that this farmer would then collaborate with the people with his knowledge to further develop their apple orchards and build up their businesses. In this manner, the objective was that it would be a mutually beneficial relationship for the people of Diyatalawa and the White farmer. After receiving the training from the apple farmers, however, this farmer went off on his own and cultivated his own apple farm, with his own employees. Since then, he has had a thriving business but has never employed anyone from the village.

After this disappointment, the people of the village were left with struggling orchards and a big competitor. Then to make the situation worse, in the early 2000s, somebody set fire to the apple orchards and the people lost their livelihood. In the face of this situation, they then went to the fields to grow other things on their own. This is important as an expression of their agency. Over the years, on their own, they have been planting maize, beans, cabbage and other vegetables. It is important to point out here that the people of Diyatalawa do not actually own the land they cultivate. It is state land, but they are trustees of the land; they can enjoy the usufruct of the land.

Through the CRDP, in 2009, the government began to once again assist the people, advising them to create cooperatives and training them in other kinds of farming, helping to develop what is now the Diyatalawa Agri-Village. The new village was built in 2010. The government has told the community that they will give them a collective title deed for the farms and the houses, so that people can own them together. They work as cooperatives, but everyone has her own house.

This settlement is a partial success story, but the people of the area believe that even this partial success is an indication that the government is taking matters seriously, which is hopeful within the context of disappointments based on promises made and not fulfilled by the government since 1994. There are approximately 50 households in the agri-village, and, at present, there are several cooperatives which farm apples, beans and wheat, as well as a hen layer and broiler cooperative and a broiler plant. They also have a dairy collective and used to sell the milk to Nestlé, but now sell it to Mountainview, which has fewer regulations and pays better than Nestlé. Both the cows and the farm are owned collectively. In addition to the milk cow cooperative, there is also a beef cooperative, a 'rocks' (sandstone quarry) cooperative and a vegetable cooperative. They are also planting green beans, beetroot, squash and one hectare for pumpkin.

It is interesting to note that the government is not directly helping the people with the cooperatives; they are doing it on their own. They have taken ownership of their process, which is in the spirit of the CDRP, and in the community's own opinion, they are doing very well. Together, these villagers are working towards their food sustainability. The older people, the original settlers, are the farmers. Their children are going to school and are occupied in other things. Unemployment in the village is low, and those who are unemployed are waiting for jobs. The government has bought them some paving machines, which they take to mean that if there are roads to be paved, then they could potentially get the contract. There are opportunities for work within the village itself. There is a crèche, for example, where some people work, as well as at the school. Local men and women are employed at the school in different capacities, such as serving as the drivers, doing the laundry, the cleaning and maintaining the premises, among other essential tasks.

Different to many other villages in the Free State, Diyatalawa is doing quite well. In the opinion of the inhabitants, they are not as yet at the stage where they want to be, but they are progressing. They have a mobile clinic in the village and are building a police station. Their children go to the crèche and primary schools in the village and then for high school, they go to a boarding school in QwaQwa. The majority of the community is food secure because they grow and raise most of their food, and have an income, but the few people who are unemployed are less food secure. Nonetheless, there is no hunger.

Mme Dimakatso is an example of how the people in the community are doing quite well. She provides employment for 29 people during planting and harvesting, and she was able to pay back a government loan she had taken out to start her business. With that money, she was able to put her children through university. One has a diploma and the other one is working, while another is involved in tendering (granting contracts). Moreover, beyond her income from farming, both she and her husband receive the older persons grant. Near their home they also have some small plots where they plant vegetables for home consumption. She is creating jobs, but she believes she needs some assistance from the government to create more jobs. She wants to build a greenhouse, to plant throughout the year and explains that she needs a loan from the government for this. She has applied to the Independent Development Trust (IDT), which is a government agency, for this loan and is awaiting their answer.

Other food initiatives in the province

There are other food initiatives throughout the province, including community and household food gardens as part of the ReKgaba Ka Diratswana program led by the Free State Department of Agriculture and Rural Development, which I described in Thabo Mofutsanyana Municipality. One example is in Zone 14 of Meloding township in Virginia. This area was infamous for its high rate of rape and gangster activities (known in South Africa as gangsterism), but through the work of the people of the community in collaboration with the Department, the area was targeted to become a "Place of Hope". The Department identified 45 households and helped them to establish household food gardens in their backyards, as well as using an open space where criminal activity had been extensive in the past, into a community garden (Department of Agriculture and Rural Development, Free State Province: "Community garden", 2014).

Another example of food security initiatives in recent years has been that a number of school food gardens have been established throughout the province, as well as other provinces, following the mandate of the National Department of Basic Education, as we saw in the case of the primary school and crèche. In some cases, the department has carried out its initiatives in collaboration with the private sector. Notwithstanding, the department had not evaluated the progress and impact of these gardens, so in 2014, it decided that it was time to do so in three provinces; Free State, KwaZulu-Natal and Limpopo. The Faculty of Education of the University of the Free State was chosen to carry out this evaluation in the Fezile Dabi and Lejweleputswa Municipalities of the province, and I was invited to be part of the project.

The objectives of the evaluation were to conduct an expert assessment of the state of the school food gardens through a diagnostic survey and the potential these gardens have or can have to contribute to the holistic learning experience through an opportunities evaluation. These two assessments were based on the need that the department has expressed for these school food gardens to be a holistic educational resource, contribute regularly to the school kitchen as part of the nutritional feeding scheme and beautify the environment, both school and surrounding community. This initiative illustrates that there is some government interest in making food security initiatives in the country work in a holistic and sustainable manner. Further to the above two, we also delineated activities that will build school food gardens as holistic learning environments and sites of school and surrounding community beautification. We collaboratively constructed the university – government department – private sector sustainable working model as a systemic approach to re-shaping existing school food gardens as the center of community engagement and ownership for community, regional and national sustainability, within the framework of water as a critical problem. This model focuses on school-community self-envisioned and self-directed capacity building, developing leadership skills among the participants, together with stakeholders' mobilization and public awareness.

With these initiatives, I will end this chapter. In the next chapter, I will do a deeper level of analysis of the themes I have delineated throughout the preceding chapters. I bring the narratives into critical dialogue, explicating this dialogue as one of power, critical consciousness and survival, of which food insecurity is only one manifestation.

Notes

1 For tribal initiation, the rite of passage as a boy enters manhood. Initiation schools are becoming a huge problem in South Africa as many of them are expensive and poorer families enter into debt to send their sons there. Moreover, in some rites of initiation, the boys are circumcised, and the number of botched circumcisions has increased over the years at the hands of inept individuals, killing some boys and destroying the genitalia of

others, scarring them physically and emotionally for life. In other cases, boys are kidnapped off the street and taken to Initiation School against their parents' will and knowledge; then, the school sends the parents the expensive bill that they are forced to pay.
2 A native English-speaking Namibian or South African, in Afrikaans.
3 Tannie means 'aunt' in Afrikaans and is used as a term of respect when referring to Afrikaans women.
4 Ntate is a term of respect in Sesotho that is used when referring to men.

References

Constitution of the Republic of South Africa. No. 108. (1996). *Statutes of the Republic of South Africa – constitutional law*. Retrieved from www.gov.za/documents/constitution/1996/a108-96.pdf

Department of Agriculture and Rural Development. Free State Province. (2014, December 15). *Community garden a beacon of hope*. Retrieved from www.ard.fs.gov.za/?p=1873

Department of Agriculture and Rural Development. Free State Province. (2013; 2014). Retrieved from www.ard.fs.gov.za/

Department of Agriculture and Rural Development. Free State Province. (2013, March 27). *Qabathe bolster farmer support programmes*. Retrieved from www.ard.fs.gov.za/?p=1631

Department of Agriculture and Rural Development. Free State Province. (2012). *Agricultural land and projects/programme/support profile for effective planning and implementation, Thabo Mofutsanyana*. Retrieved from www.ard.fs.gov.za/files/fs-profile/Thabo-Mofutsanyana.pdf

Department of Rural Development and Land Reform. Republic of South Africa. (2009). *Free State Comprehensive Rural Development Programme (CRDP)*. Retrieved from www.dla.gov.za/phocadownload/Pilot/free state/proposed_draft_framework_crdp_free_state_pilot_v1small.pdf

Dréze, J., Sen, A., and Hussain, A. (Eds.). (1995). *The political economy of hunger: Selected essays*. WIDER studies in development economics. Oxford: Clarendon Press.

Free State mission on rural investment. (1997). *Action programme for the creation of the sustainable livelihoods in the rural and peri-urban economy (1996–1999)*. Prepared by a joint task team of the Department of Agriculture, The Rural Strategy Unity and the World Bank. Free State Province: Rural Strategy Unit.

Friedman, I., and Bhengu, L. (2008). *Fifteen year review of income poverty alleviation programmes in the social and related sectors*. Report produced on behalf of the Policy and Advisory Services Unit of the Presidency, Government of South Africa. Durban, South Africa: Health Systems Trust. Food and Agriculture Organization of the United Nations (FAO). Retrieved from www.fao.org/home/en/

Hassanein, N. (2012). Practicing food democracy: A pragmatic politics of transformation. In Williams Forson, P., and Counihan, C. (Eds.), *Taking food public: Redefining foodways in a changing world* (pp. 461–474). New York: Routledge.

Hollway, W., and Jefferson, T. (2001). *Doing qualitative research differently: Free association, narrative and the interview method*. London: Sage Publications, Ltd.

The Local Government Handbook. A complete guide to municipalities in South Africa. (2014). *Thabo Mofutsanyana District Municipality (DC19)*. Retrieved from http://www.localgovernment.co.za/districts/view/10/Thabo-Mofutsanyana-District Municipality

The Local Government Handbook. A complete guide to municipalities in South Africa. (2013). *Free State*. Retrieved from www.localgovernment.co.za/provinces/view/2/ free state

Mkhize, N. (2013, April). Govt projects give hope to Diyatalawa residents. *Vukuzenzele,* section on rural development. Retrieved from www.vukuzenzele.gov.za/Pages/ RuralDevelopment/413RD1.htm

Mosamaria AIDS Ministry. (2016). Retrieved from http://mosamaria.co.za/ovc-project/

The Nordic Africa Institute. Nordiska Afrikainstitutet. (2014). *Rural and agrarian change: Property and resources research cluster*. Retrieved from www.nai.uu.se/research/ agrarian_change/

South African History Online. Towards a People's History. (SAHO). (2014). Botshabelo forced into QwaQwa. 3 December, 1987. *Timelines, this day in history*. Retrieved from www.sahistory.org.za/dated event/botshabelo-forced-qwa-qwa

Statistics South Africa. (2014). *Maluti-a-Phofung*. Retrieved from http://beta2.statssa.gov. za/?page_id=993&id=maluti-a-phofung-municipality

Thabo Community Action Trust. (2010). *Background and insight gathering report*. Retrieved from www.thabotrust.com/about-thabo-trust/insights-into-botshabelo andthabanchu/ 116backgrounds-and-insight-gathering-report

6   It is never only about food

Power, critical consciousness and
survival within poverty

The stories of the co-creators in this book have vividly shown us that food insecurity is never only about food. In our contemporary world, food insecurity is
a consequence of deep social injustice, gross inequalities and inequities and
manipulation of power, creating what Nelson Mandela aptly called 'the prison of
poverty' in his 2005 speech at the Campaign to Make Poverty History in London
(BBC News, 2005).

Throughout the chapters, we have seen how persons who face food insecurity
in the Free State Province, South Africa, make meaning of their food circumstances within the sociocultural, political and economic contexts they are living
in post-apartheid South Africa, as well as their views of the government's food
security policies and programs. Within this meaning-making, we have been able
to discern some forms of agency they have been constructing to confront their
food insecurity. Moreover, we have also been able to perceive non formal educational processes within this agency expressed by them with regard to the structural
issues of inequities and inequalities they may be facing to resolve their struggles
with food. In this chapter, I bring together their stories in critical dialogue with
each other to further analyze the overarching themes that unite them, as well as
their points of divergence. We will begin this dialogue by delineating the complexity of the societal dynamics in South Africa.

The complexity of societal dynamics in South Africa

We have seen through the preceding chapters that the complexity of the societal
dynamics in South Africa today is deeply enmeshed in the constructs of race,
class, power and culture, as well as the political and economic policies based on
these. These constructs were particularly as shaped during the twentieth century,
before and during the apartheid regime and in the 23 years since South Africa
elected its first Black president in 1994. To this end, examining these constructs
is essential to understanding the dynamics of the contemporary South African
society in the Free State Province and the meanings poor people make of their
poverty and food insecurity.

As I explained in Chapter 2, Blacks, Coloreds and Indians were historically
oppressed politically, racially, culturally and economically in South Africa, with

Blacks suffering from further indignities than the other two groups. For example, millions were forcibly removed to live in Bantustans where in some, such as QwaQwa in the present day Free State Province, they were subjected to eking an existence out of arid lands and little industry. These dynamics, particularly between Blacks and Whites, are still quite evident in the Free State Province. Furthermore, in light of the sociocultural, political, economic and historical contexts of South Africa carving its path towards democracy, it is essential that we also understand the significance of how the policies that the Mandela, Mbeki and Zuma governments have implemented since 1994 are interrelated with the meanings that poor people make of poverty and freedom as associated with food security and insecurity. The themes that emerge from the narratives delineate the importance of these interrelationships.

In this chapter, I analyze these themes at a deeper level by engaging the findings in critical dialogue, to create a portrait of the province. Through this, we can begin to understand impoverished people's meaning-making of their situations of poverty as one of their quest for power over their own lives, their critical consciousness of their own situations and the reasons underlying these situations (i.e. what their situations are and why they are this way), their desire for social and economic justice and the means they have created for their survival. Food insecurity is only one manifestation of what they conceptualize as their lack of power and the social and economic injustices of which they are victims. The narratives of Blacks, Whites and Coloreds reveal that they tend to perceive these injustices differently, even though they agree that people treat them as the poor with equal disdain. As we have seen through these narratives, the reality is that food insecurity, and especially the kinds of food insecurity experienced by the people of this book, is never only about food. It is about their poverty and their opportunities, or lack thereof, to create better lives for themselves, within the political freedom that Black South Africans have achieved in the post-apartheid South Africa and the political downfall that many poor Whites feel imprisoned by.

Within the structural poverty that poor people live are the issues of social and economic inequities and inequalities, power imbalance in their social and economic positions as the poor, attitudes towards race (in this case, of Blacks' perspectives of other Blacks, of Whites, and Coloreds, and Whites' perspectives of other Whites, as well as of Blacks and Coloreds), their agency and food insecurity at different levels. There are also public health issues such as HIV/AIDS, TB, alcoholism, drug abuse, teenage and multiple pregnancies, as well as social violence such as domestic abuse, child prostitution and rape. The themes through which they expressed their views are: their economic difficulties and survival; their food situation; their perspectives of the food situation in the Free State; their awareness of government food programs and non-governmental programs; their perception of work opportunities in the province; their perspectives of the government; their conceptualizations of people's desire to work; the value of education; differences in the food situation during times of apartheid and now; their faith; what poverty means to them; White poverty from the Black perspective; HIV/AIDS, poverty and food security; about racial differences with regard to people caring for each other; working with the poor and vulnerable; the problem with being White (from the White perspective) and their agency. Through these themes, we have been able to understand the meanings the poor make of their social, cultural, political and economic contexts, which have shaped their lives and influenced their perspectives of food insecurity, as well as their agency to confront their challenges.

Food insecurity within poverty

The research on which this book is based has been focused on the meanings that those persons facing food insecurity make of their food insecurity within their social, cultural, political and economic contexts. To understand how food insecurity is related to their meaning making, however, it is important to restate how food security has been defined in the democratic South Africa. We saw that under the RDP in 1994, food security was encompassed in the core objective of the people's right to be free from hunger (ANC, 1994; RDP White Paper, 1994). In the 1996 Constitution of the Republic of South Africa, which established the legal guidelines for societal transformation, food security became a fundamental right, for every citizen of the nation has the right to have access to sufficient food and water; further, the state will ensure the realization of this right (Constitution of the Republic of South Africa, "Statutes", 1996, Provision 27). Under the Growth, Employment and Redistribution strategy in 1996, a Food Security Policy was formulated which stated that South Africa become "a country where everyone has access to adequate, safe and nutritious food", declaring furthermore that "such a policy should address in a comprehensive manner, the **availability**, **accessibility** and **utilization** of food at a macro and a micro level"(Food Security Working Group, 1997, pt.1.1). (The emphasis is in the original statement.)

Building on these, in 2002, the government developed the IFSS, which "defines food security as the physical, social and economic access by all households at all times to adequate, safe and nutritious food and clean water to meet their dietary and food preferences for a healthy and productive life" (Department: Agriculture. "The Integrated Food Security Strategy -South Africa", 2002, p. 6). Moreover, in the Department of Social Development's 2009–2013 Strategic Development Plan, one of the core objectives is *Food For All*, and the IMC on Food Security has been "tasked with delivering an integrated, intersectorial food security programme based on the Brazilian 'Fome Zero' (Zero Hunger) programme which has played a key role in addressing citizen's rights to food" (Department of Social Development, 2012, p. 13, pt 3.4.1). This paradigm continues in the successive Strategic Plans. In the Free State Province, one of the most recent policies specifically directed to the poor and vulnerable has been *ReKgaba Ka Diratswana*, which is "a household food production programme that promotes the establishment of food gardens for personal consumption in addressing food insecurity and poverty alleviation" (Department of Agriculture and Rural Development, "Qabathe bolster", 2013, para.12). Looking at the situations and experiences of food insecurity across the different areas of research as based on these definitions, we can understand its complexity.

The food insecurity of the poor

Multidimensional poverty, with its structural socioeconomic inequities and injustices, and food insecurity are undeniably linked in the Free State. Poor people are food insecure in some of the ways that food insecurity has been defined in South Africa, but not in all. Understanding people's experiences living in poverty leads us to realizing that alleviating food insecurity must be carried out within the context of confronting this multidimensional poverty

These definitions have drawn upon how food security has been universally defined, based on the four pillars of food availability, food access, food utilization and food stability (World Food Program: Food Security Analysis, 2012; FAO, IFAD and WFP: The State of Food Insecurity in the World, 2014). As I explained in Chapter 2, the government identified that in the province in 2013, 8.0% of the households had severely inadequate access to food and 14.7 had inadequate access, and by 2015, the percentage of the inhabitants that have severely inadequate access to food decreased to 5.4%, but the percentage with inadequate access increased to 21.1% (DAFF, "Fetsa Tlala integrated", 2013; Statistics South Africa: "General household survey 2015", 2016; Statistics South Africa: Free State community survey, 2016). This indicates that the number of people who face hunger per se has decreased, which may in part be the result of the implementation of government food policies and non-government initiatives. However, these statistics also indicate that the root causes of food insecurity have not been adequately addressed, for from 2013 to 2015, approximately one-fourth of the population still has inadequate access to food. But what does this inadequate access mean?

With regard to the 1994 precept that people have the right to be free from hunger, almost all the participants in this study stated that they and their families do not go to bed hungry, that they have 'at least something' in their stomachs. This 'something' can be bread and tea, as Piet, the White motor guard in Bloemfontein, and the unemployed mothers of Phase 9 explained. Even the waste pickers, those who earn the least of all the participants, have some food on a daily basis, from the leftovers that they receive from restaurants in the town. With regard to those who can be perceived as the most vulnerable, those living on the streets, David, the homeless participant, explained that he knows of no person who is living on the streets of Bloemfontein who has died of hunger, mainly because there are a number of soup kitchens that they can go to; they can buy food with the money they get from begging, or they get leftovers people give them. These statements in no way mean that there is no hunger in the Free State Province, for there is. As I explained in the case of Mme Lily, she has gone hungry on occasion in recent times, and her hunger has been alleviated with the food garden she has been planting, together with some food aid from her neighbor on occasion. Further to this, there are undoubtedly people with whom I did not become acquainted who are facing hunger. What their statements mean is that hunger for these participants, as in the lack of food on a regular basis, is not the problem. The problem is more multidimensional than this.

When we analyze the more encompassing South African constitutional and food policy precepts that *every citizen of the nation has the right to have access to sufficient food and water*, that *the state will ensure the realization of this right* and that food security *is the physical, social and economic access by all households at all times to adequate, safe and nutritious food and clean water to meet their dietary and food preferences for a healthy and productive life*, we can perceive where the varying levels of food insecurity of the participants whose stories are told in this book lie.

The first evidence of this food insecurity is that for all of the participants, a greater part of their food is often pap, samp, bread or other carbohydrates, together with some vegetables, and legumes at times. Animal protein, fruit and nuts, as well as dairy products, which are considered healthy foods, some of which are also important components of their cultural foods, are more lacking in their diets. An interesting finding with regard to this has been that, different to the US, for example, vegetables and legumes in the Free State Province are relatively inexpensive and it is what poorest people consume, together with the carbohydrates; but the greater part of their diets consists of carbohydrates. In this way, they do not have economic access to adequate and nutritious food on a sustainable basis. The second point where their food insecurity is evident is that they do not all have sustainable access to clean water, for as they explained, the majority of them suffer from severe water shortage. The state has not ensured the realization of this right, as has been legislated since the beginning of the democratic era in South Africa. Notwithstanding, one also has to take into account that the severe water shortage has also been the consequence of the droughts that the province has been facing in recent years. In view of this, any good intention on the part of the government to ensure the right to clean water is at least in part compromised. The third point is that the foods that they eat do not necessarily meet their dietary and food preferences for a healthy and productive life. The excessive consumption of carbohydrates is unhealthy.

There is a twist in this situation, however, and it has to with their food preferences, as compared to their dietary needs for a healthy and productive life. Even though vegetables are relatively cheap and they could also grow them, albeit in some cases with difficulty, as we saw in the cases of Thabiso, Ntate Thomas and Mme Fanny and their struggling gardens, for some people, these foods are not what they value or really want. In their eyes, these foods are 'poor people's foods', so for them, meats and processed foods are the sign of luxury, and meat – beef, pork, lamb, wors (sausages) – are the foods they want. These would be their food preferences, some of which in excess are not conducive to having a healthy and productive life.

Food security programs within the context of poverty

As we have seen, there are a number of food security initiatives in place in the Free State Province, both governmental and non-governmental. Both the government, on an irregular basis, and the NGOs and numerous churches, on a more regular basis, provide people with food aid to alleviate their hunger. These give out food parcels, and there are soup kitchens that operate on a daily basis to feed the hungry. The government has also given out seeds, hosepipes, wheelbarrow and spades to some people to help them plant their gardens, among other initiatives. It is ironic, nonetheless, that not many people are aware of how many government food security programs there are, nor are they particularly interested in these, because they do not perceive these programs as benefitting them. There are some exceptions, obviously, such as *ReKgaba Ka Diratswana*, the household food garden program which Busi, the Free State Department of Agriculture and Rural Development Food Security Officer, carried out in the Thabo Mofutsanyana Municipality. But it seemed that the beneficiaries of this program attributed the program to Busi, rather than to the government. They were aware that it is a government program, but in their eyes, it is Busi who is helping them, more than the government. This is very telling of the influence that one person can make, more so in a context of heightened political divisions and economic difficulties.

In the democratic South Africa, the government dictates what the food security policies are going to be and how they are going to be implemented. All of this is decided without necessarily considering the particular circumstances of the people in the different regions of the different provinces. So the question arises: Are these policies and programs really addressing the needs of the people, their communities and regions in the most appropriate ways for their development? Let us take the example of the *Fetsa Tlala Integrated Food Production Initiative*, "which seeks to afford smallholder farmers, communities and households the ability to increase production of basic food, and increase access and availability of it to attain basic food security at household and local levels" (DAFF, "Securing access", p. 3). As I explained in Chapter 2, through this intervention, the government is motivating and supporting people in rural and urban areas to grow food for their households and their communities so that they could have sustainable access to food.

As we have seen through people's experiences, however, there are a number of problems that have hampered this initiative. Three of these are: arable land, water availability and fostering the educational process of developing sustainability for the individuals and the community. The government has been giving people seed and equipment and the know-how, as we saw in Kestell, for example, but what about the severe shortage of water? Has the government improved people's access to water? We saw that in the township surrounding Bloemfontein and in parts of Botshabelo and Maluti-A-Phofung, there is a severe shortage of water that impedes the progress of these gardens. However, the most important question is: Does this initiative address the core problem of the people, which is their poverty?

As I explained in Chapter 3, for the cleaning women at the University of the Free State, a fiery issue of discussion was the difficulties they experienced in their daily lives and what they see in society. They acknowledge that they live in a land of plenty, but the question that these women asked over and over again however was: *Of what use is living within plenty if you cannot really access it?* This is a fundamental question in their lives and how they understand the struggles they endure, among which is their food insecurity. This question is at the core of the meaning they make of their difficult circumstances.

We also saw that the issue of growing vegetables was a polemic one for the cleaning women. As Valentine said, quite eloquently, "You may have food in the garden, but if you don't have paraffin or electricity to cook it, then what do you do with the food? You can go and buy R.10 in electricity, but it is still too little". As I had explained, this is a very interesting point, for it elucidates how growing your own food is not the solution per se to food insecurity, for it needs to be accompanied comparatively with the means to prepare this food on a sustainable basis. People need to cook the food they prepare, and electricity and paraffin are expensive. Growing food is only half of the equation to alleviating food insecurity.

Toward this end, the government's objective of achieving household food security through household food gardens would need to be attained not only through giving them seeds, equipment and knowhow, but also sufficient water, and economic means such as creating more and better paid employment or fostering self-employment. Alleviating food insecurity must be carried out within the context of confronting structural poverty, and what *kinds* of food insecurity are being addressed, as well as *where* they are being addressed, in *which* situations of poverty, are of fundamental importance. Poverty in the urban, semi-urban and rural areas certainly share some characteristics, but there are also some differences. Each area has its particular kinds of poverty and the people have their own kinds of food insecurity. Within the context of this analysis, let us look at poverty in the QwaQwa region, of which Kestell and Harrismith are part.

Dr. Hlalele, the professor of rural learning ecologies who was my point of entry to Harrismith and Diyatalawa Agri-Village, has lived in the QwaQwa region all his life, experiencing the trials and tribulations of its people since it was a homeland and throughout these 20 years of democracy. His experience and research has led him to conclude that food security/insecurity is a concept defined by a framework that is external and foreign to the farmers of the province and cannot be applied as is to the situations of the South African people. Herein we see, from the viewpoint of a South African who has lived and studied his people's ways of living and learning, the affirmation of the importance of understanding people's meaning making of their situations as shaped through their cultural and historical epistemologies.

In his view, the high level of food insecurity in the QwaQwa region today is a consequence of the deterioration of the economic situation during the twenty years of democracy. During apartheid, the Black Homeland government played a greater role in terms of job opportunities. There were many industries in the homeland and they employed many people. With the advent of democracy, however, industry in the former homeland became highly unionized, so the minimum wage became a vexing issue and many of the employers left. The employers at the time were mainly South African Indian and Chinese, who were not receptive to the union demands for higher wages for their employees. They did not agree to the terms that there should be a minimum wage, minimum hours and certain numbers of hours for the workday. So they left and created a void in sources of employment that has not been filled. When these employers moved away, many cooperatives were formed, but a number of the people were in the cooperatives for their individual interests. If their needs were not met, they did not collaborate with the others in the cooperative. Dr. Hlalele believes that the conceptualization and management of the cooperatives were not promoted properly, because the promoters were not able to identify the problems when they appeared, and to this I would add, address them appropriately. He pointed out, moreover, that people waiting for help from outside in rural (and other) communities often got "a raw deal", for help is offered to them but often not given.

In this way, we can see a separation between the government policies and their implementation. As this research has shown, especially in Kestell and Harrismith, there have been times when the government policies have been implemented as proposed, but the results have not been completely as expected because of the problems they have encountered. The only initiative that has been relatively successful has been the Diyatalawa Agri-Village, which has been based on government intervention, together with people's initiatives. Pointing out these problems leads us to the important issue of the culture of dependency in South Africa today.

One of the main issues that underlie the problems of building much needed sustainability in South Africa is the culture of dependency that has been created, that many people, including the co-creators of this book, have pointed to. The phrases that I repeatedly heard from Blacks – *People are lazy; Black people are lazy; Our people are lazy; People want you to do everything for them* – emphasize their belief in this culture. Whether the roots of this culture were planted before 1994 or since is an important issue to understand and address in future policy formulation in South Africa. But it is not one I focus on here in depth. What I do focus on here, however, is the fact that the underlying causes of this culture have to be understood and addressed, for poverty in the country, as well as food insecurity, to be eradicated, as has been the expressed objective of the government since 1994. The latest iteration of this is through the NDP 2030 National Development Plan, which has the objective of eliminating poverty and reducing inequality by 2030 (National Planning Commission: National Development Plan 2030, 2013).

People taking ownership of their own development – from the identification of their needs, through the formulation of their strategies and means to achieve their objectives, to implementing the same, as well as monitoring and evaluating their progress – is essential for their success. In this vein, Dr. Hlalele expressed that "Our way of doing things in Africa; if we do it for ourselves, we are better. If we conceptualize the project, the prospect of living, this cohesion, is better". From his perspective, people would work better if they did not get handouts. He is of the opinion that if people were to have to fend for themselves, they would have more initiative. Moreover, he highlights that the contemporary education system, in his opinion as a scholar-practitioner of rural learning ecologies, is not helping to prepare the people to benefit in their own environment. In this regard, he expressed,

> In rural ecologies, the problem is with our education system, even though it looks like we are preparing everybody for when heaven comes next. It's like if you become an engineer, nobody thinks about becoming an agricultural engineer, or a farming engineer. I think that is what we need to reverse and say *how can this education we are offering in rural areas help with the development of the rural areas?*

What he explains here points directly to one aspect of how education is valued today in this particular rural area of the Free State Province. People who were starved for education or young people whose parents were denied an education under the apartheid regime now have the opportunity to have an education, and many want to escape from the rural areas. The conceptualization of 'rural is backward' is still pervasive. Further to this, the higher education system is preparing people for professions that are indeed needed in South Africa, but not necessarily needed in the rural areas. So the professionals that QwaQwa needs are not there. The brain drain from the region continues, and consequently so does the poverty. Poverty, in its multiple forms in the urban, semi-urban and rural areas is the main issue with which the people who face food insecurity have to contend.

The problem is poverty: poverty is the new apartheid

The research on which this book is based has revealed that people who face food insecurity in the Free State Province make meaning of their food circumstances within the sociocultural, political and economic contexts that they are living in post-apartheid South Africa. The context that has the most influence in their opinion is the economic one. They live in poverty, and their poverty shapes the meaning they make of their circumstances. As I explained in Chapter 2, the province has a poverty rate of 61.9%, which is higher than the national poverty level of 56.8% (Statistics South Africa: Poverty, 2014). In their eyes, this poverty within democracy that they are living is a completely unexpected situation, for it was not within the promises of freedom that Nelson Mandela, the ANC and other freedom fighters had promised. It is a situation of new oppression for them, which has been testing their capacity to confront these socioeconomic adversities. This economic oppression is reflected on a national basis in South Africa today based on the fact that,

> 21.7% of South Africans live in extreme poverty, not being able to pay for basic nutritional requirements; 37% of people don't have enough money to purchase both adequate food items and non-food items so they have to sacrifice food to pay for things like transport and airtime; 53.8% of people can

afford enough food and non-food items but fall under the widest definition of poverty in SA, surviving on under R779 per month.

(Nicolson, 2015)

These statistics come from the *Methodological report on rebasing of national poverty lines and development of pilot provincial poverty lines*, based on research carried out by Statistics South Africa, which updates these two poverty lines, establishing the minimum socially acceptable standard to distinguish the non-poor from the poor in the country. These measures use three lines of poverty: the food poverty line (FPL); the lower bound poverty line (LBPL); and the upper bound poverty line (UBPL). The FPL sets the rand value below which you cannot purchase enough food to meet a minimum energy intake of about 2 100 calories per day. In 2014, this value was R400 per month.

This state of poverty, considered one of the country's triple threats, together with unemployment and inequality, is an important issue of discussion in South Africa. At the government level, however, the proposed solutions do not necessarily address the roots of the problem, despite years of research and discussion on these roots that have been done at and among governmental, academic and non-governmental institutions and civil society actors. One recent example of this is the government-proposed national minimum wage; a policy which is more common in developed economies. In late 2016, a government panel recommended a minimum wage of approximately U.S. $260 per month, about $1.50 per hour. This is a small amount in South Africa, and is barely a living wage, but it is close to the median income in this country with an official unemployment rate of 27 percent, and nearly half the population lives in poverty. In February 2017, Deputy President Cyril Ramaphosa endorsed the panel's recommendation, vowing, moreover, that this minimum wage would be in effect by May 2018. But what would be the effect of this policy on the sluggish South African economy? Opponents say that it will kill jobs, whereas supporters counter that implementing a minimum wage would definitely reduce poverty in this society where, despite over 20 years of majority Black government rule, the structures of the apartheid era system which was created to provide cheap Black labor for an economy dominated by a White minority still exist.

The discussion of what to do with this state of poverty is alive at universities, research centers and NGOs, as well as government departments, in terms of analyzing this poverty within the democratic South Africa, understanding its complex nature, and formulating strategies to confront it. The underlying question to this discussion is: Why has so little changed in South Africa today with regard to the poverty that exists, despite all the policies formulated and measures taken with the best intention by the new democratic government? In Chapter 2 I describe work done at some of these institutions. Together with these, one of the many spaces in which this discussion has been taking place was at the 2012 *"Towards Carnegie 3": Strategies to Overcome Poverty & Inequality* Conference, hosted by the Southern Africa Labour & Development Research Unit (SALDRU) at the

University of Cape Town, South Africa.[1] It is important to succinctly describe the nature, content and tone of this conference, because it encompassed some core elements of the post-apartheid South African society.

This five-day conference brought together government officials, academics, civil society organizations and individual practitioners to share ideas and models for effective action in keeping with the goals delineated in the National Development Plan. The main goal was to create a platform of discussion and debate amongst the participants to learn about, and from, existing effective, practical strategies that have been conducive to addressing the current levels of poverty, inequality and injustice in different places of the country, rethink some of the strategies and policies and formulate new ones to create keys of change at a local, regional and national level. As Wilson and Cornell (2012) explain, "It served as a platform for many working on the issues of poverty and inequality to share and cross-pollinate ideas" (p. 9). Salient in the discussions was that the approach to understanding the multiple dimensions of poverty and its manifestations, and formulating policies to confront and eventually eliminate it in the country has to change. Through the multiple presentations, it became evident that there are many successful initiatives throughout the country at local and regional levels and much will to understand how to expand upon these, not in a one size fits all. We can interpret this as understanding the need to focus on the significance of place and characteristics of the population. The presentations and discussions were grouped in nine themes: the role of law; unemployment; using the land; urban and environmental challenges; investing in people: nurture, education and training; health; government policy; job creators; and community mobilization.

Great emphasis was made on the importance of critically reflecting on the reasons underlying the state of poverty and inequality in the country and in "thinking creatively about effective action to move the society towards the goals spelt out in the National Development Plan (NDP), notably *the elimination of poverty and the significant reduction of the current levels of inequality*" (Wilson and Cornell, 2012, p. v). (Italics in the original.)

In their paper, *Tuberculosis and Structural Poverty: What can be done?*, underscoring the vital relationship between this scourge of public health in South Africa and the state of poverty in the country, Benatar and Upshur (2012) postulate that the approach to understanding poverty and formulating policies to eliminate it in the country has to change. They state that critical reflection is required on how current economic policies can be changed. Moreover, they affirm that the use of new metaphors to reshape thinking and action should include a shift from the idea of sustainable development to the more credible notion of developing sustainability. These propositions definitely make sense in the light of what the narratives of the people of the Free State Province have revealed, for developing sustainability indicates educational processes for transformative conceptualization and formulation of initiatives on the part of the impoverished. Their theorizations of their own realities underlie their agency.

A number of cases of successful small-scale initiatives striving toward achieving household food security in different areas of the country were presented.

Together with the successes, the difficulties inherent in them were also explained. The discussions around food security reflected concern about how it is defined and measured, for this definition and measurement are the shaping forces of the strategies and policies adopted. As Wilson and Cornell (2012) eloquently explain in their summary of the conference, "the way we define and measure reflects the underlying ideology and shapes the approaches and solutions we adopt" (p. 40).

Meaning making: the food insecure are theorists of their own realities

In Chapter 3, Thabo, one of the part-time workers at the Christian NGO, framed his narrative of what poverty means to him by quoting former President Nelson Mandela "Where there is poverty, there is no freedom". The findings of this inquiry have substantiated this statement. The participants – Black, White and Coloured – appreciate the fact that there is political freedom in South Africa today. They are, however, mainly bewildered and to some extent angered by this freedom, because the promises of this freedom have not materialized in the ways they have expected. In the view of the Black participants, life has improved to some extent, in the sense that some of them have houses today, they have the freedom to choose their government and have the possibility of getting an education. Nevertheless, they are also struggling in ways that they felt they did not struggle under apartheid. During that time, they were oppressed, and they had no civil liberties or rights, but they feel that their basic needs of food and clothing were met. For all of them, the poverty they are living today is struggle and for some, such as Mme Lily in Kestell, poverty is painful. Thabo further elaborated on his above statement by calling poverty "a rawness". For these people, the economic situation that they are living today is a new form of oppression. As Mariette, one of the unemployed women of Phase 9, expressed angrily, "it is the new apartheid".

The female waste picker, Katlego, has a broader view of poverty. In her view, poverty encompasses three important elements the other participants pointed to in separate ways: the lack of power; the inability to get things for oneself; and social and economic inequality. Black people have the vote today, but they have no real power to make decisions about their own lives. Some White people feel that their opportunities are no longer there. In some ways, they feel that they do not know what their place is in this new South Africa. The opportunities for all to improve their lives are there, but in some ways there is a chasm between opportunities and their being able to benefit from them. They just do not have the money to do so. It all comes down to money in their lives today. The basic question of their lives is: Do I have the money to cover my family's basic expenses? And the answer to that question tends to be for them that they barely do. The end of the month is a struggle; their lives are a struggle. For poor Whites, there is an additional dimension to their struggle, which is that they feel that because of affirmative action, they are being kept out of the workplace. They may have the skills, but no longer have the opportunity to use their skills because the work they used to do has now been given to a Black or Colored person.

Together with the fact that during apartheid, the poorer Black and Colored South Africans were subjected to inferior education and victims of job reservation of skilled labor for Whites, there are at least two generations of Blacks who are caught in the vise of low-wage labor, with few possibilities of breaking this vicious cycle. These limited possibilities are not because the opportunities do not exist, but because these people are so focused on surviving, with few economic resources, that they cannot take advantage of the opportunities. Moreover, there are poor Whites who have the skills, but not the certification or opportunities, so they are also forced to survive. We saw this in the case of Piet, the White car watcher who would like to go to trade school to obtain his certification as a welder, a trade in which he has already been trained, although he does not have the appropriate certification to demonstrate it. He cannot afford to go back to school because he does not have enough money, and even if he were to get it, through a government or non-government loan, who would look after his family? The vicious cycle of poverty and the struggle to survive are perpetuated.

There is the persistent rumor in South Africa that many women in the townships become pregnant so that they can live off the social grants the state provides to their children. While in some cases this may be true, none of the women I knew in the townships and in other poor areas indicated that they would prefer to live on grants rather than work. They were willing, even desperate, to work, but could not find jobs or any other sustainable source of employment. Understanding the structural economic difficulties of people's lives, one comes to realize that a social grant of R350 per month is not sufficient to raise a growing child. The social grants provide a little alleviation of the poverty in the province and in South Africa but do not address the structural problems underlying this poverty.

The narratives show that the Black participants consider themselves people who were 'made to struggle', as the unemployed of Phase 9 stated. The Blacks who are working and are barely making ends meet, as well as those who are unemployed but want to work, conceptualize their lives as an endless struggle, regardless of who is in government. They express that they know what it means to struggle because they have been struggling for so long; they are accustomed to having a hard life. In my conversations with other poor Blacks, I heard the same theme again and again: *We know what it's like to have a hard life* . . . So for them, being poor and having to struggle is not the problem. The problem is the *kind* of poverty that they are living in and the *kind* of struggle that they are being forced to engage in; it is poverty and struggle within the first freedom and the first democracy they have ever had as South Africans. They have rights, but they do not have a life with dignity.

The situation with the Whites seems to be somewhat different. They do not share the same history of struggle, even though there have always been poor Whites in South Africa, including in the Free State Province, despite widespread belief both outside and inside the country to the contrary. There are just many more poor Whites now, and those who are much more visible. Their experiences of poverty, with regard to the lack of economic resources, are similar to those of the Blacks and Coloreds today; they are all poor. How they live their poverty and the measures they take to confront it seem to be different. As I explained in Chapter 4, there are a number of White beggars on the streets of Bloemfontein, whereas there are much fewer Black and Colored beggars. Blacks on the streets tend to be street hawkers. Their forms of agency seem to be different.

It is important to note that in the view of most of the participants, people treat them as the poor with equal disdain, whether they are Black, Colored or White in South Africa today. Nonetheless, we saw through David's experience that more affluent Whites consider him, as a White beggar, an embarrassment to Whites. The shadow cast by apartheid with regard to the pride of the Whites in this Black-governed South Africa has reached through the 20 years of democracy in many ways.

The new democracy: times are different now

There are multiple facets to the statement *times are different now* in the minds of the poor and vulnerable people of the Free State. What democracy means to them and how times have changed are viewed in different ways by different groups of people and the reasoning underlying these views are very interesting. As we have seen, for most of the Blacks, democracy has given them rights: the right to vote, the right to better education, the right to work, the right to food, the right to land and to own property among others and to live a dignified life in accordance with their human condition as free beings in a democracy (Constitution of the Republic of South Africa, 1996). They certainly cherish these rights, but many of them wonder what the democracy that is so touted by the government has really brought them. They have the right to work, but there is little work to be found. They have the right to a better education, but the public education system is deeply unequal and, among other fundamental educational issues, many teachers in impoverished areas are ill-prepared. A number of poor parents, such as Esther and Bernard, make sacrifices to send their children to private school, but not all can, nor should they have to, if the constitutional mandate of quality education for all were fulfilled. Parents cannot afford to pay even the most basic school fees for their children if they do not have work. If they do, and their children pass matric and qualify for university, these young people cannot afford to go to university unless they get a bursary, which not everyone who qualifies for one necessarily gets. Moreover, some of them cannot afford to go to university full time because they cannot afford to not work.

We saw this in Abraham's story in Chapter 3. We also saw the cases of food insecure university students who do go to university with bursaries, but these are insufficient to cover the costs of their food. Consequently, some of them are forced to leave school and to work to maintain their families. Non-Whites now have the right to land and to own property; some have received RDP houses from the government (many of which are poorly constructed) for which they are grateful, but then how do they upkeep the houses if they have no work? They are grateful for the social grants that they receive, for at least it is some money for their living costs, but as we have seen, this is not enough. A number of them would prefer to work for their money. These rights all underlie the right to a dignified life, but with all these circumstances under which they are living, are they really living a dignified life? As we saw through their narratives, many do not think so.

This leads some of them to favorably think about – for maybe 'yearn' is too strong a sentiment, particularly within their historical context – the times of apartheid when they had no rights, but they had employment and food. But are they really not yearning up to certain point for some conditions of those times? They were terribly oppressed and treated as much inferior beings, there is no doubt about that. But they consider that three of their basic needs for survival – food and water, clothing and shelter – were covered. In modern times, we have included needs beyond these, such as sanitation, education and health care. The 1996 Constitution, which creates the legal framework for the building of a democratic South Africa, includes the rights to all of these, and more. So all South Africans have the rights to have all these needs covered, but how these constitutional rights have played out in reality is a different story.

I spoke about education above. Now let us talk about health care, which is an essential right in democracy. There is a free medical care system in South Africa today which has greatly benefitted many poor and vulnerable South Africans, the access to free ARVs being one of the major accomplishments. Nonetheless, this medical system is also fraught with maladministration and corruption, for there are regions, including areas in the Free State, where the Provincial Department of Health uses the allotted resources for personal benefit or does not distribute the medications to the people. Sanitation is a basic need, but many poor people in the Free State lack basic sanitation infrastructure. Water, together with healthy food, is severely lacking. Many homes in the townships and in rural areas do not having running water in their homes, but only a tap in their yards. Such was Jenny's case. Or, there are community taps, as I described in Botshabelo in Thabiso's case, where a number of families share one tap. The bottom line for people today is that they live with political freedoms, and there is availability of food. But they are often unable to buy this food in adequate quantities, because they do not have sustainable economic access to it. The new poverty in the democratic South Africa is weighing them down. In their view, it is a new oppression within freedom.

Meanings the food insecure make of their lives: some central themes

Their conceptualizations of people's desire to work

"Our people are lazy . . .". I heard this statement so many times in my conversations with Black South Africans, which was repeated by many of the participants. While listening to them, as well as on further reflection, I have wondered, is this really true? Or has it just become imprinted on the collective psyche? My interest in this statement is not with regard to its veracity, but rather to whether because people believe it and say it so much, it has become an obstacle to people coming together to formulate and strengthen their collective agency. Some of the people I spoke with seemed to think, *why bother trying to get together to do something if people are lazy anyway?* But then, there were those who, despite complaining about this, still tried to get people to come together, such as Mariette in Phase 9 and her sewing collective and Eugenia in Kestell. Democratic agency does not have to be only individual, for it is through people working together that democracy is created and strengthened. The Constitution of 1996 was drawn up to lay the foundation of a democratic society, and many people have come to think of it as a democracy, as compared to the autocracy of apartheid. The word *democracy* is now a familiar and much used term, but is the perception that "our people are lazy" in any way creating an obstacle in the need for democratic agency to strengthen this democracy?

The central role of religion

People's narratives clearly show that religion, Christianity in particular, plays a central role in the lives of the people of the province. In South Africa, 85.6% of people regard themselves as Christians, whereas only 5% subscribed to religions that were described as ancestral, tribal, animist or other traditional African beliefs. In the Free State, 96.9% of the people consider themselves Christians, whereas 2.0% subscribed to traditional African beliefs (Statistics South Africa: Free State community survey, 2017). Notwithstanding, as is common in many parts of the world, in South Africa, Christianity is imbued with ancestral beliefs. Their narratives reveal that many people, and in the particular case of many of those who face food insecurity, embrace their religious beliefs as central to their existence. This means that they believe that God has a reason for why their lives are the way they are. Most of the participants are devout Christians and attend churches in their respective areas. Working at the Christian organization, Ruth attends both the services there as well as at her home church. Many of the women dedicate a lot of time on the weekends to church activities and families spend a greater part of their Sunday in church. Moreover, Ntate Raphael is the pastor at the Zoe Church Ministries in Botshabelo, which he and Mme Maria and their congregation have built together, both the physical church with their own hands and expanding the congregation.

Most of the people I spent time with expressed that they put their faith in God and that He is leading the way. The unemployed of Phase 9, for example, expressed that God gives them what they *need*, not necessarily what they *want*. In many ways, some of them feel that despite their socioeconomic situation, "things are not as bad as they could be without God". They gave as an example that even though they do not have much food, they do not go to bed without eating. They consider that they are never hungry, for as long as there is a little mealie meal and spinach, or even bread and tea, there is food. Piet, on his part, believes that God gives him and his family the amount of money every day for exactly the amount of food they need. Whether this belief helps or hinders their agency is an interesting issue of consideration. On the one hand, their faith keeps their hope alive, and through it, they give meaning to their circumstances. On the other hand, I cannot help but wonder if it also hinders their agency to a certain degree, for they believe that God knows why he is making them experience their trials and tribulations. Most of the participants expressed their agency to confront their challenges, but I wonder. Some of them have implemented their initiatives, whereas others have not. There are a number of reasons why they have not done so, and some of these are beyond their control.

David's story is a little different because he believes that God has a plan for him and this helps him to conceptualize his potential agency as being able to eventually help others who are in the same situation as he is or has been in. Abraham and Tumelo also believe in God, but they also believe that they have to help themselves, while God is helping them. In their case, their faith helps them in realizing their agency. In Mme Maria and Ntate Raphael's cases, their faith helps them to create food security initiatives to help themselves and others.

When I first conceptualized my research, I had not considered the issue of people's belief in God as part of it. As I got to know poor people in the province better, I realized how central their faith is to the meanings they make of their lives and their situations of food insecurity, and this helped me to reframe my inquiry in a beneficial way. It is an essential issue without which I would not have been able to understand people's meaning-making with regard to their lives and the food insecurity they experience.

HIV/AIDS, poverty and food security

Another essential issue to understand is the interrelationship between HIV/AIDS, poverty and food insecurity. HIV/AIDS is pandemic in South Africa, with approximately 12.7 % of the population, 7.03 million people living with HIV. This percentage is higher in the population aged 15–49 years, in which an estimated 18.9 % of the population is HIV positive (Statistics South Africa: Mid-year population estimates, 2016). Despite all the interventions that there have been in South Africa from 2002 with regard to HIV prevention and treatment, the percentage of HIV prevalence has increased from 10.3% to 12.7%. We do need to consider this, however, within the context that the population of South Africa has also increased over the same period of years. I am certain that many people I met and interacted with are HIV positive, but only two of them, with whom I subsequently did in depth interviews, told me that they are: Ruth and Mme Lily. I witnessed the ravages of AIDS through spending time with Sister Electa and her patients. In my time with her and her patients, as well as with Ruth, Lily and Esther's little girl, Kiki, I saw firsthand the importance of good nutrition in keeping the HIV positive patient in good health. HIV/AIDS is also still a polemic issue amongst some people, for they believe that AIDS can also be brought about by witchcraft, as we saw in Chapter 3, where Ruth told the story about her brother.

The South African HIV/AIDS response program was dealt a severe blow during the Thabo Mbeki government (1999–2008), under the then Minister of Health, Minister Manto Tshabalala-Msimang. She was called the beetroot and potato minister, among other derogatory names, because of her negative views of ARVs in the treatment of AIDS, advocating instead beetroot, lemon, garlic and African potatoes to protect people from the disease. Interestingly enough, she and other so-called AIDS dissidents, who questioned the link between HIV and AIDS, stated that the cause of the disease was because of nutritional deficiencies (Mail & Guardian, "Manto Tshabalala – Msimang dies", 2009). It was an ironic twist to focusing on the importance of food security as related to HIV/AIDS and health.

Sister Electa's vast experience working with the poor people of South Africa for over 40 years has made her realize that health and food are very interconnected. The unemployed women and men of Phase 9 are also being educated by the UFS Nutrition and Dietetics team on the importance of good nutrition and exercise to overcome non-communicable illnesses, such as diabetes and high blood pressure, as they are being encouraged to plant their food gardens. Ruth and Mme Lily as HIV-positive women are also aware of how important it is for them to have good nutrition as well as Esther, with her little daughter, Kiki. The scourge of TB as a critical public health issue in South Africa today, interrelated with the AIDS epidemic, brings forth the importance of good nutrition to assist in fighting the epidemic. TB is actually the greatest killer in the country today. South Africa has free medical care, and poor people can go to the clinics and get medication for their illnesses. But these medications can only work well in tandem with good nutrition. Medicine goes only so far in a weakened, malnourished body.

Alcohol abuse, dependence and food insecurity

In Chapters 4 and 5, I mentioned the high rate of alcohol abuse and dependence – male and female – in poor communities in the Free State. People generally refer to high levels of alcohol use as alcoholism, but psychologically and medically, excessive alcohol use is not a homogeneous condition. Within it, we can find the differentiated conditions of alcohol abuse and alcohol dependence. Alcohol abuse "means having unhealthy or dangerous drinking habits, such as drinking every day or drinking too much at a time . . . When you abuse alcohol, you continue to drink even though you know your drinking is causing problems" (Substance Abuse and Addiction Health Center, 2014, para.2). Alcohol dependence, on the other hand, which is also called alcoholism, is an addiction, for the person is "physically or mentally addicted to alcohol". He/she has a strong need, or craving, to drink and feels he/she must drink just to get by (para. 3).

In the preceding chapters, I briefly mentioned two cases in which alcohol abuse has interfered with people's use of their paltry sums of money to cover their basic needs, which includes ensuring their food security: Jenny's son, who spent most of his money on alcohol, and Boitumelo's wife, who wastes her children's grant money on alcohol. These are not isolated cases. Mesea, a Black social worker who has spent the last ten years working with poor families in the township of

Bloemfontein, has seen the ravages that the high rate of alcoholism has wreaked on families. In her experience, the alcoholism of the parent(s) lead(s) to their children becoming vulnerable, for they do not provide them with the money and care to cover their basic needs, food in particular. In some instances, children then look for money by engaging in activities such as prostitution to ensure their food security. Mesea carries her analysis of the children's food insecurity further than only alcoholism, however. In her view, in many poor families today, there is no longer any family responsibility. She has seen time and again homes where one will find the children looking for food for themselves because the parents do not take the responsibility to take care of their children.

Alcohol abuse and/or alcoholism in poor communities of South Africa is a very important point, for the excessive use of alcohol is destroying the family and social fabric through parents neglecting and/or abusing their children physically, psychologically and emotionally, spouses neglecting their families and relatives hurting family members (Seggie, 2012; Ojo et al., 2010). Moreover, it disrupts the societal dynamics of healing and progress that are supposed to be strengthening South Africa's path to a democratic society. There are certainly instances where alcoholics neither affect their family situation nor are food insecure, such as in David's, the homeless participant's, case. In his case, he has no shortage of soup kitchens he can attend, or he uses the money he makes by begging to buy some food for himself. His vulnerability lies instead in the precariousness of his living situation and the ravages of alcoholism in his health and life.

There is also a cultural component to the use of home brewed alcohol among Black women, a type of beer they refer to as 'traditional beer'. Among some women, there is the belief that there are benefits to drinking this beer during pregnancy, because "it makes you and the baby strong", as the women in the sewing group at the Christian NGO explained. How high the alcohol content of this beer is, how much of it is consumed during pregnancy, and what detrimental effects it has on the mother, child and family, are issues of consideration when determining if this consumption is alcohol abuse or not.

The central role of multigenerational households

It is quite common in South African society for households to be multigenerational. This is especially true among the people of the lower socioeconomic strata in the Free State Province, and it is a central feature of their lives. What has generally brought them together in contemporary times are poverty and the HIV/AIDS epidemic. Being poor and/or being unemployed means that some nuclear families, single mothers, young couples or grown children cannot live on their own, but instead depend on the social grant and/or home of their parent(s)/grandparent(s). This was the case of Boitumelo and Katlego, the waste pickers of Harrismith, who both live with their respective grandmother, partner, children and siblings. Tumelo, the part-time worker from the Christian NGO, also grew up with his grandparents after his mother abandoned him. When he was narrating his story to me, he only referred to his grandmother. This is common in the Black South African culture. The grandmother is the matriarch and moral center of the family. Many times, she is also the economic center and sole or main financial supporter of the extended family. Many children grow up with their grandmothers in a woman-centered home, with physically and/or financially and emotionally absent men. In Tumelo's case, his grandfather was physically present, but Tumelo's grandmother was his moral and emotional center.

As I have explained in the prior chapters, the HIV/AID epidemic has left thousands of children orphans, a number of whom live with their grandparent(s), aunts, uncles and cousins. This was true for Esther with Kiki, her cousin's child. In these situations, having extra family members stretches the already limited resources of the poor. Moreover, as I explained in the section above on HIV/AIDS and food security, it is essential that HIV-positive persons have sustainable access to healthy foods, not merely foods that fill them. For this group of people, food security in its full definition is essential.

The meaning making of the food insecure as democratic agency

In this qualitative inquiry, it was essential to understand the meanings people made of their food insecurity through the economic, historical, sociocultural and political circumstances which have shaped their lives, and have created their challenges and opportunities. In their meaning-making, these persons have questioned and critiqued the societal dynamics, social structures and institutions of the society in which they live. The participants in this study, as well as many poor people in the province, critique their difficult economic circumstances, but give different reasons for these circumstances. Further to how they make meaning of their circumstances, another of my objectives through my critical inquiry has been to analyze any forms of agency they may have been constructing to confront their food insecurity, and possible educational processes within this agency expressed with regard to the structural issues of inequities and inequalities they may be facing to resolve their struggles with food. To this end, I asked, does their meaning-making lead to agency in their own lives and that of their communities?

Conceptualization of agency

In a general sense, agency is defined as the capacity that people demonstrate to not merely react to their circumstances on a superficial level and repeat given practices, but to take action to confront or change these circumstances for their benefit. Building on this, agency can also be seen as people acting in authoritative and accountable ways "to initiate purposeful action that implies will, autonomy, freedom and choice within the affordances of the worlds that they inhabit" (Kangas et al., 2014, p. 34). It entails their taking control of their lives, in whichever ways they can find, through their own initiative or uniting with the initiatives of others, to improve their social and material worlds for their benefit. This was what I was interested in understanding in my research; whether the participants' meaning-making fostered any initiatives to confront their challenges around food which is mainly based on their constrained economic access to food, because of their structural poverty.

The core of the kinds of agency that the participants exercise is in their thinking about which actions would be the best ones for them to take in their circumstances, and in some of their cases, actually implementing these actions through the initiatives they have created. These might be food gardens, soup kitchens, a sewing collective, buying and selling clothes, creating a small business, going back to school to learn a trade or further their education, all initiatives the participants had. The main point I want to make is that it is important to understand that thinking is strategizing, it is meaning-making, it is knowledge building and it comprehends their agency. Benatar and Upshur (2012) highlight the importance of agency as related to poverty when they postulate that as severe poverty is the result of human agency, we can choose to use agency to improve the circumstances that have been created.

Democratic agency and its underlying educational processes

Democratic agency is considered the core element of a democratic project, and post-apartheid South Africa has legislatively been attempting to shape itself as a democracy over the last 20 years. The kind of democratic agency which I explore here is with regard to the initiatives that people who face food insecurity have thought about, as well as those they have actually implemented. Among the participants, we saw both types of initiatives. The fundamental question we need to ask is: Why would it be important for the food insecure to express democratic agency? Essentially, because they need to be able to directly create the space in which to advance their strategies to confront their challenges around poverty, and within these, those with regard to their economic access to food.

In his discussion of hunger and people's lack of representation within our food systems, Korthals (2012) refers to democracy as citizens having a voice and participating in the decision making process, not merely electing people to speaking for them, as is customary in our political democracies. It is in this vein that I delineate democratic agency; one which we can consider participatory democratic agency. We need to take this conceptualization further. Underlying achieving food security as part of a democratic project is the concept of equity. This is fundamental, for without equity, food security cannot be constructed. Korthals (2012) also states that "the social forces that determine what crops should be produced and eaten do not represent the farming and food preferences of local inhabitants; rather, social forces suppress those preferences, which are then not represented" (p. 107).

The social forces that he is referring to here are mainly those that have thus far shaped the food systems of the South African people, directly affecting the poor and vulnerable of the country, including those of the Free State Province. In this regard, Patel (2011) states, "A truly democratic food system will need to rewrite the rules of the financial system" (p. 17). In the case of South Africa, and in particular in the Free State Province, I would carry this further than only the financial system, for it is the rules of the larger economic system which need to be rewritten for the participants of this study to enjoy economic justice. In turn, this could potentially lead to constructing their more equitable participation in the economic system, which would directly relate to their achieving better economic access to food, which in their opinion is their main problem.

Most of the participants have a clear sense of who and what are oppressing them. They are theorists of their own realities and some are educating themselves to be catalysts of change in their own lives. They understand the sources of their oppression and those of the people in situations similar to theirs, or worse, and some of them are working to further their individual and collective causes. In this way, they are organic intellectuals of their own realities.

As I have explained throughout the chapters, the South African government has formulated a number of poverty alleviation and food security strategies and programs targeted at the poor and vulnerable. We have also seen that the participants of this study were not always aware of what these programs were, nor did they seem particularly interested in finding out, because they looked upon the government with suspicion. Nonetheless, these programs exist and they are being implemented in some regions, such as in Thabo Mofutsanyana Municipality. In light of this, it is important that we ask certain critical questions with regard to their effect on the poor and vulnerable of the Free State Province. Some of these questions are: Will these people, who are being motivated to produce their own food at household, community and local levels, be motivated by the government to exercise democratic agency through their actions? Will their production and entrepreneurial actions be sidelined to being only household and community food sufficient within their own communities or will the government foster inter-community and interregional networks? Moreover, will the government create avenues to integrate the small farmers into the national market in equitable ways? Or will they have to compete with the corporate farms at the national level, in an unequal playing field? Overall, how will these initiatives contribute to achieving structural economic improvement, lifting these food insecure South Africans out of poverty, as well as achieving social equity, equality and environmental sustainability in a land that has been ravaged by endemic racism, poverty and land degradation, among other social ills? These are important questions that need to be asked.

The political and economic significance of democratic agency as fostering the means for people to achieve economic equity, justice, food security and the dignity of a life where their needs are satisfied is an important issue of consideration. Among other things, it may possibly go against political and corporate interests both within and outside the country. There is a big difference between helping the people of the nation to *grow their own food*, for household and local consumption, as well as forming cooperatives and helping them in some ways to *gain control over their food systems.* Having control means having power and being in interrelationships with other actors means forming new power relationships and sharing power. Will the other actors in the food systems be willing to share this power for the common good? This is left to be seen. One of the main actors, the South African government, is known for being corrupt and President Jacob Zuma in 2014 once again won national elections, despite widespread complaints about his governance. Notwithstanding, his support among the people has considerably decreased in recent years, and in the 2016 municipal elections, the ANC lost important areas throughout the country.

Educational processes within their agency

With regard to exploring the possibility of educational processes within the participants' agency, it is important to understand the kinds of agency that they have manifested, within their contexts, as learning processes. In this regard, Kangas et al. (2014) explain that "In a socioculturally oriented research field, agency is conceptualized as an ongoing process of learning that is contextually and historically situated" (p. 34). This is indeed the research field of this inquiry.

The kinds of learning that the participants of this study engaged in is adult learning in its non-formal and informal modalities. Some questions underlying this learning are: How have the food insecure in the Free State learned to cope with the challenges they face with regard to their limited access to food? Are these coping strategies interrelated to their history of segregation and apartheid? And if they are, what is the nature of this interrelation? Moreover, how are they interconnected with the contemporary societal dynamics, including racial, economic and political dynamics, of the post-apartheid Free State Province? Most of these questions have been answered. The narratives of the food insecure reveal them as theorists in their own right and of their own socioeconomic, political and cultural circumstances.

Some, but not all, of the people who face food insecurity tend to be among the poor and vulnerable groups, marginalized in different ways within their own societies, so it was important to understand that these people theorize their food security within their marginal spaces. Furthermore, their meaning-making through narratives may possibly elucidate the critical awareness that is necessary for the democratic transformation of society, which is one of the declared main goals of the post-1994 South Africa. It is important, then, that these people can manage to carve out the political space that is needed for their voices to be heard and taken into account. Carving out this space may be complicated, for their narratives have revealed that the potential of their critical awareness to improve their collective economic constraints through collective democratic agency is possibly being restricted by the urgency of their survival.

The critical consciousness and initiative of the food insecure in this study can be understood through their epistemologies and ways of being in the world. The theoretical delineations of the capabilities approach also allow us to interpret this critical consciousness and initiative. If we are to look at food insecurity from the capability approach, through its means-end distinction, we would ask whether people are able to have sustainable access to healthy food and whether the means or conditions for the realization of this capability are being met. Among the basic means and conditions would be sufficient food supplies and food entitlements, but then we need to ask further, are these supplies of healthy food? Is the economic access to food sustainable? Do people have jobs or other income (e.g., social grants) that allow them to have continuous access to this food, without wondering what they will have to feed their families that day, or how much of this food they will be having?

We see through people's stories here that the answers to these questions are not that simple. The participant one might consider the most economically bereft at first glance, David, who is homeless, actually has access to healthy food on a sustainable basis through the soup kitchens he goes to and the food he occasionally buys with the money he gets through begging. He chooses to buy alcohol instead of food, he chooses to beg instead of looking for a job because he can earn more this way, and he chooses to live on the street. These are his choices. But David is ironically one of the more fortunate persons in this book with regard to basic needs. By living outside what are considered the desirable parameters of living a good life (i.e. having employment/income and other societal measures that allows you to cover your multidimensional needs), he has his basic needs covered, if he chooses to take advantage of them. He has food, through begging, and going to soup kitchens, he has temporary shelter at the homeless shelters (which he refuses to go to unless it is extremely bad weather out, because he considers that the rules of the shelter constrain his freedom) and he has clothing from the Christian organization and other clothing giveaways.

As I have explained, the majority of the people in this book have access to food, but not necessarily healthy food. Nor do the means or conditions exist at present for them to realize their human capabilities to their full extent. As Sen (2002) explains, people differ in their ability to convert means into valuable opportunities (capabilities) or outcomes (functionings). Furthermore, the more relevant question is whether "a person is being put in the conditions on which she can pursue her ultimate ends" (Sen, 2002). Moreover, he further explains,

> The concentration on distinct capabilities entails, by its very nature, (a) pluralist approach. Indeed, it points to the necessity of seeing development as a combination of distinct processes rather than as the expansion of some apparently homogeneous magnitude such as real income or utility . . . the valuable capabilities vary from such elementary freedoms as being free from hunger and undernourishment to such complex abilities as achieving self-respect and social participation.
>
> (Sen, 2002, p. 54)

As we have seen throughout people's narratives, they are developing their capabilities through their elementary freedoms, but it is the complex abilities of achieving self-respect and social participation that are not.

The theorizations of Mayo (1999) also serve as another prism of interpretation. He brings together the Gramscian conception of seeing education and the cultural formation of adults as central to counter-hegemonic action for social transformation, with the Freirean conception of education for critical consciousness, with the adult as educator–educatee and critical agent committed to social transformation. Through this, he delineates the importance of subordinated social groups to engage in the transformation of their circumstances of subordination. Following his theorizations, some of the participants of this study can be understood as people who engage critically and dialectically within the system to work collectively for change by being "concerned with engaging in educational *processes* that are not meant to consolidate 'what is' but are driven by a vision of 'what should and can be'" (p. 5). In the theoretical framework for transformative adult education that he delineates, he explicates the importance of commitment and agency for social transformation, especially on the part of those he denominates the subordinated. In this case, these subordinated groups are the food insecure.

Most of the people whose stories are told here are critically aware of their situations and some have created paths to confront the challenges that they face. Some of them, like Mme Maria, Ntate Raphael and their collaborators are educators–educatees in the Freirean sense, as they teach and learn together through and with their critical consciousness of their situations, and as they also foster and strengthen their democratic agency. They, as well as Busi and Thabo Olivier, teach others systematically how to create sustainable food gardens. Busi has a university degree in agriculture, and she teaches others much of what she has learned at university. In Thabo's case, he learned off the internet, talked to other people inside and outside the country and learned through trial and error. Everything that he has learned, he has learned through his own efforts, making many mistakes along the way, to achieve success.

The fundamental point here is with regard to how the democratic agency discerned in the participants in any way constitutes critical educational processes. The analysis reveals that it does, particularly as non-formal and informal educational processes. It leads us to understanding that the participants manifest critical consciousness and are organic intellectuals in their own quiet way, not necessarily as part of influential groups or social movements. They are not visible participants in the struggle against food insecurity in the Free State; they are quiet critical agents, fighting for their own survival. But when you actually sit down and talk with them, listen to them, ask them about their lives and their opinions, they are very conscious of their own situations and to some degree the challenges surrounding food in the Free State and in South Africa. In these ways, they are theorists of their own reality and agents in building their own democratic spaces. The stories here have revealed that some 20 years after the end of apartheid, structural poverty in the Free State Province has led to there being food insecurity for a number of the poor and vulnerable, mainly because they do not have economic access to food. This is despite the implementation of national policies to right the wrongs done to the sectors of the population which had historically been socially, economically and politically oppressed. This included numerous legislations, policies and programs that have been formulated and implemented in an attempt to create paths for people to have sustainable access to nutritious food and clean water, as established in the food security policies of the country.

The people's narratives show that this food insecurity is not necessarily the *lack* of food, that is, that people go hungry day after day because there is not enough food in the province. Instead, the fundamental problem is their tenuous *economic access* to food, i.e. that there is food, but poor people cannot have a sustainable access to it through their own means because they are too poor. People perceive their main problem as being their poverty. Starting under South Africa's first Black president, Nelson Mandela, was the desire to create a more socially, economically and politically just nation inclusive of all its peoples. Despite his efforts, the ANC governments over the last 23 years have not alleviated the suffering of the poor and vulnerable of South Africa.

Moreover, the findings reveal that because of this poverty that they live, some of them compare their present-day situation to the apartheid era, casting a favorable light on that era in terms of people having food and employment, two of the issues that are their gravest concerns.

The main objective of the research that led to this book was not to determine only whether people have enough food or not and whether the government food policies and programs are really addressing their food insecurity. These were two smaller objectives that helped carve the path towards the larger objective. The first dimension of the main objective was to understand the meanings people make of their situation of food insecurity and what these meanings reflect about their lives as individuals and as communities within the contemporary socioeconomic, political, cultural, racial and historical contexts of the Free State Province. The second dimension was to understand what initiatives they have taken to confront their challenges. The third was to discern whether these initiatives, and their perspectives in any way constituted democratic agency on their part and whether there were any educational processes underlying this agency.

Through my inquiry with my co-creators of this book, I explored how it is that they, the people who are facing food insecurity, and some of those who are around them, make meaning of their situation. I based my inquiry on questions such as: Do they think they are food insecure? What does their food insecurity mean to them? Why do they think they are food insecure? Why do others think of them as food insecure? We saw in the case of David, the homeless man, that he does not consider himself or any other homeless person for that matter, as food insecure. Let us remember his statement: "I don't know of any person living on the street who dies of hunger".

The reasoning underlying the inquiry was based on a fundamental question: Why do I as a researcher think that the meanings people make of their own food insecurity and that of others are important? The answer to this question is that it is because I believe that this meaning making fundamentally shapes how they see the world in which they live and how they respond to the challenges that they confront. I believe that their worldview and their responses are a crucial element that we as researchers, policy makers, program and project coordinators and government agencies, among other actors and agents of food security policies and programs need to take into account for these to effectively address the multidimensional nature of poverty and food insecurity in the Free State Province. Some of my analysis may also be useful for other provinces in South Africa and may ultimately contribute in a meaningful manner to the ongoing dialogue about food insecurity in Africa and other parts of the world. My main objective, however, is that it meaningfully contributes to this dialogue, policies and programs in the Free State Province.

The voices of the food insecure with regard to how they conceptualize their food insecurity are not generally heard. Through this qualitative inquiry, I make the case for how important it is that their voices be heard, and furthermore, that they need to be included in the policy making processes. Moreover, the findings reveal, and my analysis of these postulate, that it is imperative that we understand the food insecurity that many people in the Free State are experiencing within the racial, cultural and socioeconomic dynamics of the province, which are somewhat different to those of other provinces of South Africa. The separateness of those who have economic and social access to food and those who do not is evident in the narratives, and deepened by the structural socioeconomic inequities and inequalities within which the people of this book live.

The dearth of qualitative food security studies about South Africa, and the Free State Province, that examine the issue of food insecurity through the prism of what meanings the people make of their circumstances within the socioeconomic, political and cultural contexts of post-apartheid South Africa and in particular within the Free State is what motivated me to conduct this inquiry. Through it, I have clearly demonstrated that food security is an issue of social and economic justice and that the food insecure in the Free State are victims who are entrapped in the vise of structural poverty. Their stories of food insecurity and unsustainability have been shaped by many factors, including: structural poverty, socioeconomic inequity and inequality; racism; historically discriminatory government policies, which increased significantly during apartheid; poorly conceptualized and implemented government policies since 1994; trauma and attempts or non-attempts at reconciliation at an individual and societal level during and after apartheid; public health issues such as HIV/AIDS; and environmental circumstances, such as increasing drought and wildfires.

This research mainly focused on poor Black men and women in the city of Bloemfontein, the semi-urban area of Botshabelo and two towns in Thabo Mofutsanyana Municipality. For future research, it is important that more poor White men be included, as well as White women, more Coloured men and women, and

Indians.. Further to this, I think it is important to understand, through qualitative analysis, the meanings the poor and vulnerable people make of their food insecurity in other large and small towns in the Thabo Mofutsanyana Municipality, where there are more White-owned farms, industry and settled Whites, as well in as the other three municipalities of the province that I did not study. These provinces have their own socioeconomic realities, based on their economy and state of development.

There is much still to be learned about the states of poverty and food insecurity in the Free State Province. I also believe that to get a fuller picture of the reasons underlying food insecurity in the province from the dimension of food production, it would be interesting to understand the perspectives of White and Black farmers. Within this framework of food production, it is also important to do deeper research on the influence of environmental factors on poverty in the province and poor people's access to food and clean water.

With this I conclude. My journey with the poor and vulnerable people of the Free State Province carried me to unexpected places of inquiry of some of the multiple dimensions of food insecurity. It has been a rich and fruitful journey.

Note

1 This conference is the third major study on poverty in South Africa sponsored by the Carnegie Corporation. Together, these three studies provide an interesting longitudinal view of poverty in South Africa over a period of 80 years. The first was the Carnegie Commission, a 1928–1930 inquiry into White poverty. The findings of this inquiry helped to create strategies and policies to lift poor Whites out of poverty with the vehicle of the National Party. The second one, the Carnegie Inquiry into Poverty and Development in Southern Africa, was carried out in different stages from 1980–1988, at a difficult time in South African history, when the apartheid regime was fracturing. Very importantly, it was an inquiry that strove to "have a black center of gravity" (Wilson, 1988), involving Black activists, academics and students, to listen to the unheard voices to the dispossessed Black majority, which was a difficult endeavor to carry out while the apartheid regime was still in place.

References

African National Congress (ANC). (1994). *The reconstruction and development programme (RDP)*. Johannesburg: Aloe Communications.

BBC News. (2005, February 3). *In full: Mandela's poverty speech*. Retrieved from http://news.bbc.co.uk/2/hi/uk_news/politics/4232603.stm

Benatar, S. R., and Upshur, R. (2012). *Tuberculosis and structural poverty: What can be done?* Paper presented at the C 2 Conference on Strategies to Overcome Poverty & Inequality. University of Cape Town, September 3–7.

Constitution of the Republic of South Africa. No. 108. (1996). *Statutes of the Republic of South Africa – constitutional law*. Retrieved from www.gov.za/documents/constitution/1996/a108-96.pdf

Cooperation (ICCO Cooperation). (2014). *Right to food and nutrition watch 2014: Ten years of the right to food guidelines: Gains, concerns and struggles*. Retrieved from

www.rtfnwatch.org/fileadmin/media/rtfnwatch.org/ENGLISH/pdf/Watch_2014/
Watch_2014_PDFs/R_t_F_a_N_Watch_2014_eng.pdf

Department: Agriculture, Forestry and Fisheries (DAFF). Republic of South Africa.
(2013). *Fetsa Tlala integrated food production initiative 2013/2014: An overview*.
Retrieved from http://lgbn.co.za/home/attachments/article/71/FETSA%20TLALA%20
%20INTERGRATED%20FOOD%20PRODUCTION%20INITIATIEV-%2012%20
NOVEMBER%202013.pdf

Department: Agriculture. Republic of South Africa. (2002, July 17). *The integrated food
security strategy for South Africa*. Retrieved from www.nda.agric.za/doaDev/sideMenu/
foodSecurity/policies.pdf

Department of Agriculture and Rural Development. Free State Province. (2013, March
27). *Qabathe bolster farmer support programmes*. Retrieved from www.ard.fs.gov.
za/?p=1631

Department: Social Development. Republic of South Africa. (2012). *Strategic plan
2012 – 2015*. Retrieved from www.dsd.gov.za/index2.php?option=com_docman&task=
doc_view&gid=283&Itemid=39

Food and Agriculture Organization of the United Nations (FAO). (2014). *The state of food
and agriculture 2014. Innovation in family farming*. Retrieved from www.fao.org/3/a-
i4040e.pdf

Food and Agriculture Organization of the United Nations (FAO), International Fund for
Agricultural Development (IFAD), and World Food Programme (WFO). (2014). *The
state of food insecurity in the world 2014. Strengthening the enabling environment for
food security and nutrition*. Retrieved from www.fao.org/3/a-i4030e.pdf

Food Security Working Group (Agricultural Policy Unit). (1997, November). *Food secu-
rity policy for South Africa. A discussion document*. By the Food Security Working
Group (Agricultural Policy Unit) for the Department of Agriculture and Land Affairs.
Retrieved from www.nda.agric.za/docs/Foodsecurity/foodsecurity.htm

Holtz-Gimenez, E. (2012). From food crisis to food sovereignty: The challenge of social
movements. In Williams-Forson, P., and Counihan, C. (Eds.), *Taking food public: Redefining foodways in changing world* (pp. 592–602). New York: Routledge.

International Food Policy Research Institute. (2014). *Sustainable solutions for ending hunger and poverty*. Retrieved from www.ifpri.org/ourwork

Joubert, L. (2011). Environment and sustainability. In Du Preez, M. (Ed.), *Opinion pieces
by South African thought leaders* (pp. 85–106). Johannesburg: Penguin Books.

Kangas, M., Vesterinen, O., Lipponen, L., Kopisto, K., Salo, L., and Krokfors, L. (2014).
Students' agency in an out-of-classroom setting: Acting accountably in a gardening project. *Learning, Culture and Social Interaction*, 3, 34–42.

Korthals, M. (2012). Two evils in food country: Hunger and lack of representation. In
Kaplan, D. (Ed.), *The philosophy of food*. Berkeley and Los Angeles, CA: University of
California Press.

Mail & Guardian.(2009). Manto Tshabalala – Msimang dies Retrieved from https://mg.co.
za/article/2009-12-16-manto-tshabalalamsimang-dies

Mayo, P. (1999). *Gramsci, Freire & adult education: Possibilities for transformative
action*. Series: Global perspectives on adult education and training. London: Zed Books.

National Planning Commission (2013). National Development Plan. Retrieved from http://
online.fliphtml5.com/slsf/boiy/#p=1

Nicolson, G. (2015, February 3). South Africa: Where 12 million love in extreme poverty.
Daily Maverick. Retrieved www.dailymaverick.co.za/article/2015-02-03 south-africa-
where-12-million-live-in-extreme-poverty/#.WPJRL1Pyub8

Ojo, O., Louwagie, G., Morojele, N., Rendall-Mkosi, K., London, L., Olorunju, S., and Davids, A. (2010, March 8). Factors associated with female high-risk drinking in a rural and an urban South African site. *South African Medical Journal*, 110(3), pp. 180–182.

Patel, R. (2012). *Stuffed and starved: The hidden battle for the world food system* (2nd ed.). New York: Melville House Publishing.

Patel, R. (2011, October 3). The food movement: Its power and possibilities in what next for the Global Food Movement. *The Nation*, p. 17.

Reconstruction and Development Programme. (1994, September). *RDP white paper*. Discussion document. Retrieved from www.polity.org.za/polity/govdocs/white_papers/rdpwhite.html

SA one of the most unequal societies – Madonsela. (2014, August 17). *News 24. Breaking news first*. Retrieved from www.news24.com/SouthAfrica/News/SA-one-of-the-most-unequal-societiesMadonsela-20140817

Seggie, J. (2012). Alcohol and South Africa's youth. *The South African Medical Journal*, 102(7), pp.587.

Sen, A. (2003). Development as capability expansion. In Fukuda-Parr, S., et al. (Eds.), *Readings in human development*. New Delhi and New York: Oxford University Press.

Sen, A. (2002). *Hunger in the contemporary world*. Discussion paper DEDPS/8, November 1997. The Suntory Center. Suntory and Toyota International Centres for Economics and Related Disciplines. London School of Economics and Political Science. Retrieved from http://eprints.lse.ac.uk/6685/1/Hunger_in_the_Contemporary_World.pdf

Setena, T. (2016, May 11). Unemployment in FS escalating. *News 24*. Retrieved from www.news24.com/SouthAfrica/Local/Express-News/unemployment-in fsescalating-20160510

South African Human Rights Commission. (2014). *The right to food campaign*. Retrieved from www.sahrc.org.za/home/index.php?ipkContentID=112&ipkMenuID=99

Statistics South Africa. (2017). *Free state community survey 2016 results*. Retrieved from www.statssa.gov.za/?p=7993

Statistics South Africa. (2016a, June 2). *General household survey 2015*. Retrieved from www.statssa.gov.za/publications/P0318/P03182015.pdf

Statistics South Africa. (2016b, August 25). *Mid-year population estimates*. Retrieved from www.statssa.gov.za/publications/P0302/P03022016.pdf

WebMD. (2014). *Substance abuse and addiction health center: What are alcohol abuse and alcohol dependence?* Retrieved from www.webmd.com/mental health/addiction/alcohol-abuse-and-dependence-topic-overview

Wilson, F. (1988). In South Africa – the politics of an inquiry for change. *Southern Changes. The Journal of the Southern Regional Council 1978–2003*, 1(10), 4, 6–8. Retrieved from http://southernchanges.digitalscholarship.emory.edu/sc10-1_1204/sc10-1_003/

Wilson, F., and Cornell, V. (Eds.) (2012). *Overcoming poverty and inequality*. Guide to Carnegie 3 conference. September 3–7. University of Capetown. Retrieved from www.saldru.uct.ac.za/projects/current-projects/carnegie-conferences

World Food Program. (2012). *Food security analysis*. Retrieved from http://www1.wfp.org/food-security-analysis

Appendix
Notes and methods

Every good critical inquiry is forged by the irons of good methodology. This book was based on qualitative inquiry with the peoples of the Free State Province, my collaborators and co-creators of this book. In this section, I explain several explanatory notes and definitions of terms used in the book, together with important issues related to the research process,. I will begin with the definitions of terms, then go on to the issues related to the research process.

Definitions of terms

I have incorporated the concise definition of food security and the South African government's definition of food security and sustainability in Chapter 1. I believe it is important to provide here the World Food Program definition of food security, which has adopted the universally accepted definition of this concept; that of the 1996 World Food Summit, as well as the full definition of the Constitution of the Republic of South Africa. Further to this, I explain the conceptualization of the food insecure, and the definition and use of the racial categories in South Africa, as I used them in this study.

World food program definition of food security

The United Nations World Food Program (WFP) delineates food security to be when people "have all-time access to sufficient, safe, nutritious food to maintain a healthy and active life" (WFP: Food Security Analysis, 2012, para.1). This conceptualization of food security is based on the pillars of *food availability*, *food access* and *food utilization* and the WFP delineates these concepts as follows:

> Food availability: Food must be available in sufficient quantities and on a consistent basis. It considers stock and production in a given area and the capacity to bring in food from elsewhere, through trade or aid.

> Food access: People must be able to regularly acquire adequate quantities of food, through purchase, home production, barter, gifts, borrowing or food aid.

Food utilization: Consumed food must have a positive nutritional impact on people. It entails cooking, storage and hygiene practices, individuals' health, water and sanitations, feeding and sharing practices within the household (Food Security Analysis, 2012).

There is a fourth dimension, food stability, which was established with these three at the 1996 World Food Summit. Food stability relates to exposure to food security risk and "the incidence of shocks such as domestic food price volatility, fluctuations in domestic food supply and political instability" (FAO, IFAD and WFP, 2014, The State of Food Insecurity in the World, p. 13). Seen through these conceptual lenses, food insecurity is the situation in which people do not have all-time access to sufficient, safe, nutritious food not subject to the incidence of these shocks to maintain a healthy and active life.

The South African Constitution's inclusive Right to Food

The Constitution of the Republic of South Africa (1996) Section 27 establishes the right to health care, food, water and social security.

1) Everyone has the right to have access to: a) health care services, including reproductive health care; b) sufficient food and water; and c) social security, including, if they are unable to support themselves and their dependents, appropriate social assistance.
2) The state must take reasonable legislative and other measures, within its available resources, to achieve the progressive realization of each of these rights.

In Chapter 1, I gave the South African government's Integrated Food Security Strategy (IFSS) definition of food security. We can see that it follows the same lines as the WFP definition.

Whites, Blacks, Coloreds and Indians

Throughout this work, I use these terms as they are used in South Africa. In South Africa, these are the four racial categories formally established during apartheid and which are still used in daily life today, even though the lines dividing them are sometimes blurry.

Whites

The term *Whites* refers to the people of European descent, South African or otherwise. The South African Whites are generally divided into two categories based on their cultural backgrounds: *Afrikaners*, descendants of European colonizers and settlers (mainly Dutch, French and German) who have Afrikaans cultural norms and speak Afrikaans as their native language, and *English* (or Engels in Afrikaans), who tend to be descendants of the British, have a British cultural background and speak English as their native language.

Blacks

These are the descendants of the peoples of the original nations and tribes of what is today South Africa. The term *Blacks* is used by people of other racial groups to refer to these people, but they refer to themselves mainly as *Africans* as well as *Blacks*. In my study, I use the terms *Blacks* and *Africans* interchangeably. Most Africans speak at least two languages; their native language and English (or Afrikaans if they are older people). Many speak two to five native languages, depending on where they live and what their life experiences have been.

Coloreds

The term *Coloreds* refers to the people of mixed ancestry, including White, Black, Malay, Indian and other immigrants during the centuries of settlement and colonization. These persons speak Afrikaans as their native language but have their own unique Colored cultures, not those of Afrikaners or Blacks. They do not tend to speak Black African languages.

Indians

These are mainly the descendants of the Indians, Malays, Mauritians and peoples of other lands who came as indentured laborers in the nineteenth and early twentieth centuries, as well as traders and other settlers who immigrated to South Africa to try their fortunes. Most of them historically settled in Durban, in what is today KwaZulu-Natal Province. They also have their distinctive South African Indian culture and speak English as their first language.

Important issues related to the research process

To understand the South African society, its history, cultures, peoples and politics, and the contexts within which the stories that are narrated here are interwoven, I used a qualitative methodological approach. My analysis of food insecurity in the province was through a multilayered theoretical framework based on critical theory as related to the understanding of structural social, economic and political inequities and inequalities within a society undergoing political change and racial retribution through narrative inquiry and storytelling as meaning making.

There were several delimitations to my research, which have shaped the focus of this book. My inquiry encompassed five areas of the Free State: the capital city of Bloemfontein with its townships, the semi-urban town of Botshabelo, 50 km outside of Bloemfontein, the rural area of Kestell, the Diyatalawa AgriVillage and the large town of Harrismith. I did participant and non-participant observation in these areas, and from the many people I met and interacted with, I chose small samples of participants for in-depth interviews. This in-depth focus allowed me a window into the lives of these people and their communities, from their own perspectives. As I have explained in the preceding chapters, some of the findings share commonalities with communities in other regions of South Africa, as well as those in other parts of the world, while others are specific to the Free State.

Together with these delimitations, there were also several limitations. The first is that I had gatekeepers to some of the participants, especially in the communities. I met several of my participants mainly through other people and participants, through word of mouth; the snowballing method. These determined whom I met and whom I did not, and under what circumstances. These factors influenced the research, but I used them to my advantage. The second limitation was language. While the majority of people in the Free State speak at least a fair amount of English, and most of my research was carried out in English, there are some older people – Black, Colored and White – who speak very little English but instead speak Sesotho or Setswana, Xhosa, Zulu and/or Afrikaans. During my time in the Free State, I learned some Afrikaans and Sesotho, the two main languages of the province. While I was able to greet older people in their languages and carry on very short conversations, when I spoke with them at length, I needed someone to translate for me. It is possible that the translations may not have always been entirely correct. Whenever possible, I did verification of the translations with other persons, to ensure veracity of the narratives. The third limitation is the fact that I am a foreigner and a woman. These factors influenced my interactions with my participants. I did my best to be conscious of these subjectivities and to determine how they shaped my research, which I endeavored would show through in this book.

Methodological framework

As an important dimension of my methodology, I elucidate my perspective as researcher, that is, my self-identified biases, my experience as researcher and as an outsider in the South African society, and the ways in which I managed these. I also delineate to the best of my ability methodological issues of consideration in addition to any threats that I have perceived to the validity of the research. This is a qualitative study which drew upon ethnographic methods of data gathering, together with documents such as newspapers and periodicals with which I contextualized and triangulated my findings. These methods, which I explain below, are those I considered the most appropriate to direct my inquiry and answer my research questions.

The purpose of this inquiry was to examine how persons who face food insecurity in the Free State Province, South Africa, make meaning of their food circumstances within the sociocultural, political and economic contexts of post-apartheid South Africa, as well as their views of the government's food security policies and programs. Furthermore, I wanted to analyze any forms of agency they may have used to confront their food insecurity and possible educational processes within this agency with regard to the structural issues of inequity and inequality they may face. Based on this purpose, I formulated two main research questions: (i) How do the social, cultural, political and economic contexts of the people who face food insecurity influence their perspectives of their experiences of food insecurity? and (ii) Does their meaning- making lead to agency in their own lives and that of their communities? Underlying these main research questions are several research sub-questions which guided me in carrying out my research and shaping my analysis. I have changed the names of the participants, used pseudonyms, and eliminated characteristics that may identify them.

Critical reflexivity as researcher

My critical reflexivity as researcher played an important role in how I interacted with people on a daily basis, and most particularly with the participants of my study, how I gathered the empirical materials for my research and how I analyzed these materials. The relationships that I established with the participants and how conscious I was of the effects of my interactions were essential in eliciting the data I needed to gather to understand the issues of research. In all cases, I was upfront about explaining why I was in South Africa and what my research was about. Explaining my research time and time again to different people and in different ways to the same people was enriching both for myself as researcher as well as for my research process, because it helped me to continuously re-think and re-conceptualize what it was that I was really studying and realize how the different stages of the process unfolded. Moreover, it helped me to understand how the different dimensions of the issues were conceptualized and revealed themselves through the prisms of the participants' experiences and my growing knowledge and understanding of their lives, and the socioeconomic, political, religious, cultural and geospatial circumstances in which they live.

Establishing rapport with people, explaining the purpose of my study in a non-threatening manner and creating a dialogue with them about what the research means help to set most of them at ease. My approach was always not to create a traditional researcher-interviewee relationship, but rather to involve them in the research, make them part of it, engage them in the process, ask them to critique it and enrich it with me, tell me when what I was doing was not making sense. Quite a few of them became my co-researchers in many ways, as they took ownership of the process and pride in helping me. Engaging them in this manner was immensely enriching for my research process and for me as researcher. I realized with time that it was enriching for some of them too, for it helped them to become more aware of their own potential to confront their socioeconomic situations of vulnerability. It touched me deeply when some of them would come up to me, or call me, to tell me that they had spoken to someone else, made a connection for me, would take me to their communities and so forth. Engaging with them in these ways also made me more aware of my own biases, errors and assertions of conceptualization and many other issues embodied in the fluid spectrum of what conducting qualitative research entails.

Throughout the process, it was also essential for me to not impose my meaning frame upon the persons I was interacting with, as well as with the participants with whom I carried out in-depth conversations as narrative interviewing, but to allow the interview agenda to be open to development and change, depending on the narrator's experiences (Chase, 2005; Hollway and Jefferson, 2000). In this way, I encouraged the narrator to tell his/her story and "take responsibility for 'making the relevance of the telling clear'" (Chase, 1995, p. 2 in Hollway and Jefferson, 2000, p. 31). This also emphasized the meaning that the story was constructed through the interrelationship of researcher–participant.

These experiences while I was carrying out my research reinforced my understanding that the critical subjectivity of the researcher in relation to the construction of the research relationship is an important element in what narratives are created through this relationship. In light of this, the examination of my subjective involvement helped me to shape the way in which I interpreted the interview data (Berg and Lune, 2012). As part of my study, I was also interested in understanding how as a researcher my critical subjectivity influenced my construction of emotional, political and racial/ethnic proximities with the participants, issues and contexts of study.

Being aware of my potential biases, and acknowledging them within the contexts of meanings in which the participants are narrating their stories, was important for me as I established the participant observation and interview relationships with them, and as I analyzed the data. As Bogdan and Biklen (2007) explain,

> the researcher's feelings can be an important indicator of subjects' feelings and, therefore, a source for reflecting. They also can help formulate questions to get at subjects' experiences. In this sense, the observer's emotional reactions are a source for research hunches. If carefully sorted out, selectively presented, and appropriately expressed, they can also be wonderful avenue for building rapport.
>
> (p. 102)

I tried my best to not establish relationships with my participants exclusively as interviewer–interviewee, for to do so would have alienated them. There were three participants with whom I carried out semi-structured interviews and to whom I was introduced on short notice through connection with other persons, so I did not have time to get to know them as well as I did my other participants, who I chose myself. Nonetheless, I did take some time previous to the semi-structured interview to establish some rapport through more quotidian conversation about the day, the weather, life, the children running around, the place where they were working and so on and so forth, as well as engaging in some of their activities. I also continued my interactions with them after the interview was formally over;

not just ending it and saying goodbye. My intention was that they would not feel uncomfortable to be considered "subjects of study". I wanted to establish at least some rapport and if possible, a situational relationship of trust and friendliness with my participants, to the best of my ability and as the situation permitted. I believe I was quite successful in this endeavor, for I learned as I went along, as each engagement with my participants taught me more about what was appropriate to do and what was not. I made many mistakes along the way, but my mistakes helped me to realize how important my critical reflexivity as researcher was to my research process and helped me to strengthen this process.

Another element that contributed to creating the environment of comfort with my participants during my research was that I made every effort to establish the tone I used with them, as well as my body language. I endeavored for both to be as open, welcoming and considerate as possible. In the cases of all the interviews, I strove to be reassuring and supportive.

The importance of language and understanding cultural norms

Speaking the language(s) of the people one is working with and understanding their culture(s) are two of the most important tools a researcher has, together with your genuine interest in and care for the people you are working with. For the first six months of my time in South Africa, I focused on learning about the cultures of the people and learning two of the most predominant languages spoken in the Free State Province: Sesotho and Afrikaans. I believe this time I invested helped me greatly in my work. I speak very little of either of the languages, but I do speak enough to be able to greet people in accordance with their cultural customs and carry on a short conversation. More importantly, learning the cultural norms and expressions of respect in these languages helped me to establish connections with people I met and build rapport with them. Being able to greet the people I met in the culturally appropriate ways, in their own languages made a great difference in how they responded to me. Being able to say to a Sesotho woman and man, *Dumelang Mme le Ntate, Le kae?* (Roughly translated as, *Greetings, Madam and Sir, how are you and your family?*) when I met them, or to an older Afrikaans person, *Goeiemôre Mevrou/Meneer, hoe gaan dit vandag met u? (Good Morning Madam/Sir, how are you today? – the formal you, not informal)* broke the ice immediately, and they would smile. Greeting people respectfully and in accordance with their gender and recognition of their status as elders, for example, was accepted with wonderment and happiness.

Many people warmed up to me when they realized I had made the effort to learn their languages, because it is not something people in South Africa of the different racial groups generally do voluntarily. The majority of Whites, Coloreds and Indians speak no African languages. The Whites and Coloreds speak Afrikaans as their mother tongue, and the Indians speak English. English is widely spoken in South Africa as the primary language of communication among the different racial and ethnic groups. Many older Black Africans speak Afrikaans because they were forced to during apartheid. Many educated Black Africans today who came of age in the 1970s refuse to speak Afrikaans today, however, even though they have learned it at school, because they consider it the language of the oppressor.

Social location as researcher

There were other methodological issues I needed to consider in my study that are in part connected to my critical reflexivity, but need to be explicated separately. One is that I had to acknowledge, critically question, and attempt to frame appropriately, how my social location as researcher (e.g., my race, class, gender, age and personal biography) influenced my research, shaping my analytical perspective Furthermore, I am both a racial and cultural outsider in my research, so I continuously needed to ask myself how these conditions were influencing my research. A third consideration is that I needed to be aware of whether my research project was being manipulated by my own assumptions about partisan politics, poverty, ethnicity and socioeconomic status, among other issues, in the Free State.

Threats to validity

There were some threats to the validity of my study which I had to take into consideration. One was as not being able to do in-depth interviews with Colored men or women. I did do some participant observation with several, but was unable to create meaningful enough rapport to have access to them for in-depth interviews. White women were another racial group I was unable to have access to. I carried out a lot of non-participant observation of poor White women begging on the streets of Bloemfontein, but was unable to have access to any, to establish rapport so as to do participant observation with them or interviews. In the initial stages of my research, I intended to select as wide a range as necessary of participants, but as my research process developed, it took unexpected, albeit very information-rich turns, even though not in the ways I had anticipated.

Another threat to validity is that for some of my participant observation and interviews with older persons living in poverty, I had to depend on translators. In this way, the narratives were filtered by the translators, so I did not always initially necessarily get the whole narrative, as produced by the participant. On these occasions, I asked interrelated questions in different ways.. I also corroborated the content with the person who served as translator as well as through my conversations with other participants. By triangulating my sources, I managed to recreate the contents of the narratives. Through this, I managed to get most of the narrative and was able to do my analysis

One prepares for multiple scenarios as a researcher, but when we do research, we know that the best previsions do not always protect us from the unexpected paths of the research process. What I did as a researcher was to try to be creative in my approach to the research process.

Positionalities and identities

As the researcher, it was fundamental for me to understand my multiple position-alities and identities within my own research. My intersecting positionalities and identities as an outsider, a foreigner, a woman, a person who is not White, but seemingly perceived as either Indian by some or 'foreign' by others, evidently influenced my relationships with the participants of my study, together with all the people I interacted with in the Free State. They also influenced how I continu-ously re-approached my research through my engagement with the participants. My growing awareness of these multiple positionalities led me to negotiating these identities simultaneously (Trinh, 1991 in Nagy Hesse-Biber, 2012), which was in itself an intriguing process.

As an outsider to the social dynamics of the province, I had to observe these dynamics and understand them, to then engage with the people in culturally appropriate ways. I am not South African, so they tended to perceive me not as part of the social structure of the country, looking to evaluate them, or exploit them. Nonetheless, at the beginning of our acquaintance, there was suspicion of my interest in them. With time, this suspicion subsided for many people, but not for all. There were still some poor and vulnerable people with whom I became acquainted over months, who would not open up to me. I understood this, and used it to enrich my reflexivity of my research process. Their recalcitrance made me reframe my thinking, leading me to inquire about my process with questions such as: *Why are these people closed to me? What presence do I represent that makes them prefer not to open up to me? Is it personal or is it historical? Do I rep-resent an agent of exploitation, using them as 'the subject of research'? Does my presence reenact a historical power imbalance for them?* These were questions that enriched my analytical process.

On the other hand, as a non-South African and non-African foreigner, it was in some ways easier for me to gain access to, and establish rapport with some of the participants. In the first instance, mainly because I did not represent the historical power imbalance of being a non-poor, non-Black South African and, in the sec-ond, because I was not subjected to the xenophobia that many poor South Africans feel towards immigrants from other African countries, who they think are stealing their employment opportunities. My engagement with the participants also caused them great curiosity, mainly along the lines of: *Why are you interested in **me**? What experiences can I possibly have that you are interested in knowing about?* In some cases, such as that of the cleaning ladies, it took me several months to gain their trust and for them to open up to me, beyond the exchange of quotidian pleasantries and superficial fibs on their part, saying that they were fine.

As a woman, I also had to be careful how I approached other women and men in culturally and individually appropriate ways, as befitting what is expected of my gender and perceived age. This greatly influenced how I established rapport with the participants. My self-awareness of these intersecting positionalities as researcher grew over time, as the very process of my research led to unexpected avenues, both in practice and in my analysis of the process, strengthening my critical reflexivity as my paths of inquiry spiraled, leading me to continuously rethink the very process and the objectives I had formulated. This reflexivity helped me to reframe the objectives through the midlevel findings of the process.

Attitude and response

There were times during my conversations with poorer people when I would exclaim in wonderment at their achievements or in sadness at their lack of something. Upon reflection, I realized that there were many times when I sounded condescending. One example was with Thabo, when he told me that he had done matric and passed it. My reaction to this was, "You passed matric? Wonderful!" Reflecting upon it, I cringe, for I cannot even begin to imagine how condescending I must have sounded to him. At the time of this particular conversation, I had already known Thabo for a few months, and we had established excellent rapport, so that may be why he did not seem to take offense to my exclamation, but I did notice a flicker in his face when I exclaimed. I tried to be careful in my interactions, but I did find myself sometimes slipping into condescending attitudes. During my interviews in Harrismith with the wastepickers, Boitumelo and Katlego, for example, Dr. Hlalele chided me, and rightfully so, when I exclaimed in utter surprise that the waste pickers earn only R120 every two weeks for their recycling. His words reminded me of how important it is to understand people's lives within their own contexts, their own realities.

It is important to explain that whenever I saw my questions making my participants uncomfortable, I decided not to pursue them. If I had the opportunity to reformulate the question in a different way later, I did, but desisted if I saw it causing discomfort. I noticed the most discomfort among the three participants that faced the most challenges: Katlego, Boitumelo and Mme. Lily. During my writing, there were many moments of struggle with myself about whether to include certain details into my analysis, that would certainly enrich it, but which at the same time could easily lead to identifying the person or institution. This was my struggle with the inner-city NGO. I have deliberately left out important details about its nature and its operations because I do not want it to be identifiable. These are details that would have made my analysis much richer, but I chose to forego this out of respect for the people of this organization, who graciously welcomed me. It would be unethical of me to make them identifiable, for in my analysis, I critique some of their operations. During my time at the organization, based on the agreement that I had established with the Managing Director, I shared some of my initial findings with him, and upon my return to the U.S., I wrote a report on my findings and sent it to him. Over the months, I have kept in touch with the staff at the organization and I was very happy to hear from them that the Managing Director used my report to create favorable changes within the organization. It is important to me that my work actually serves to make a difference in people's lives.

Participants' questions for me

Before I began each interview, I would explain to each participant what my research was about and tell them to feel free to ask me any questions they wanted during our conversation. This was especially important with the participants that I had not known beforehand, those who I was referred to through another person, for with those with whom I had already established rapport over several months felt free to do so. With the participants with whom our acquaintance was more recent, it was important that they also feel free to do so. Then towards the end of each interview, I would ask them again if they had any questions they wanted to ask me, because I thought it was important for them to be able realize that our conversation should be one of reciprocity and not them being the subjects of my analysis. This was an interesting exercise, because it always deepened our conversation.

Some of them – such as the unemployed of Phase 9, Thabiso with his struggling garden in Botshabelo, Mme Lily, the HIV-positive grandmother, and Eugenia, the unemployed mother and wife in Kestell – asked me if there was anything I could do for them, to help them in their situation. David, on his part, asked me what I was going to do with my research and suggested that I write an article in the newspapers about the homeless people. I answered everyone by explaining that there was nothing material or immediate that I could do for them, but that my intention was to share my work with the policy makers that I knew in the Free State and hope that my findings would contribute to understanding some of the issues that are of importance to the poor and vulnerable of the province. It was the most difficult part of our interaction, but it was important for me to be truthful. All of their questions made me reflect on my research as I was doing it and helped me to improve how I was shaping it.

It was Katlego, the young woman waste picker in Harrismith, however, who made me really think deeply about my research as I was coming to the end of it, which has greatly helped me in my analysis. She asked me, point blank: *Why are you here?* Katlego was my last interview participant, so her question was not able to help me improve my inquiry process through any other interviews, but it did help me to improve the last stage of my inquiry through informal conversations and observation. Moreover, it helped me to shape my analysis more meaningfully, for at different moments throughout the analytical process, I asked myself, *Why was I there? What am I hoping to achieve with my research?* And my concise answer is that with my research, I am hoping to cast a light on some of the pressing issues that people enmeshed in structural poverty, with its ensuing socioeconomic inequity and inequality, experience in the Free State province, and in societies around the world. Moreover, I hope that my work makes a strong case that they must be included in the formulation of policies that are directed towards them.

References

Berg, B., and Lune, H. (2012). *Qualitative research methods for the social sciences* (8th ed.). Boston, MA: Prentice Hall.

Bogdan, R. and Biklen, S. (2007). *Qualitative research for education. An introduction to theories and methods. 5th ed.* Boston, MA: Pearson Allyn & Bacon.

Chase, S. (2005). Narrative inquiry: Multiple lenses, approaches, voices. In Denzin and Lincoln (2005). *The Sage handbook of qualitative research* (3rd ed.). Thousand Oaks, CA: Sage Publications.

Denzin, N., and Lincoln, Y. (Eds.). (2011). *The sage handbook of qualitative research* (4th ed.). Thousand Oaks, CA: Sage Publications.

Food and Agriculture Organization of the United Nations (FAO), International Fund for Agricultural Development (IFAD), & World Food Programme (WFO). (2014). The state of food insecurity in the world 2014. Strengthening the enabling environment for food security and nutrition. Retrieved from http://www.fao.org/3/a-i4030e.pdf

Hesse-Biber, S. N. (Ed.). (2012). *The handbook of feminist research* (2nd ed.). Thousand Oaks, CA: Sage Publications.

Hollway, W., and Jefferson, T. (2001). *Doing qualitative research differently: Free association, narrative and the interview method.* London: Sage Publications, Ltd.

Mayo, P. (1999). *Gramsci, Freire & adult education: Possibilities for transformative action.* Series: Global perspectives on adult education and training. London: Zed Books.

Merriam, S. B., Caffarella, R. S., and Baumgartner, L. M. (2007). *Learning in adulthood: A comprehensive guide* (3rd ed.). San Francisco, CA: Jossey-Bass.

World Food Program. (2012). Food Security Analysis. Retrieved from http://www1.wfp.org/food-security-analysis

Index

For Product Safety Concerns and Information please contact our EU
representative GPSR@taylorandfrancis.com
Taylor & Francis Verlag GmbH, Kaufingerstraße 24, 80331 München, Germany

www.ingramcontent.com/pod-product-compliance
Ingram Content Group UK Ltd.
Pitfield, Milton Keynes, MK11 3LW, UK
UKHW021612240425
457818UK00018B/515